WHITMAN CO

JEFFERSON AND MADISON

THE MERRILL JENSEN LECTURES

IN CONSTITUTIONAL STUDIES

Sponsored by

The Center for the Study of
the American Constitution

The State Historical Society
of Wisconsin

JEFFERSON
AND MADISON

*Three Conversations from
the Founding*

LANCE BANNING

MADISON HOUSE

Madison 1995

Banning, Lance
Jefferson and Madison
Three Conversations from the Founding

LIBRARY OF CONGRESS CATALOGING IN PUBLICATION DATA

Banning, Lance, 1942–
        Jefferson and Madison : three conversations from the Founding /
Lance Banning.
        p.   cm. — (The Merrill Jensen lectures in constitutional
studies)
        Includes bibliographical references and index.
        ISBN 0-945612-42-7
        1. United States—Politics and government—1789–1815.
2. United States—Constitutional history.   3. Jefferson, Thomas,
1743–1826—Correspondence.   4. Madison, James, 1751–1836—
Correspondence.
I. Title.   II. Series.
E310.B33   1994
973.4'092'2—DC20   94-39090
                                                                CIP

Typeset in Janson
Designed by William Kasdorf

Printed in the United States of America on acid free paper
by Edwards Brothers, Inc.

Published by Madison House Publishers, Inc.
P.O. Box 3100, Madison, Wisconsin 53704

FIRST EDITION

Contents

To Clint again,
and Larry

FOREWORD

ALTHOUGH NEVER LOSING SIGHT OF THEIR Virginia heritage and never totally divorcing their actions from their Southern planter upbringing, Jefferson and Madison more than most prominent politicians of their day rose above their sectional loyalties in their constitutional and philosophical thought. Jefferson and Madison are not usually thought of exclusively as Virginians; the latter is pictured as the first great American constitutional statesman—the father of the Constitution and the Bill of Rights; the former as a Renaissance man and a citizen of the world.

Lance Banning has come to understand Thomas Jefferson and James Madison as have few others. In numerous articles, in *The Jeffersonian Persuasion*, and in *Sacred Fire of Liberty*, Banning has plumbed the philosophical depths of these two thoughtful men. In the three essays presented in this volume, Banning guides us along as the two Virginians converse by letter about issues of immense importance to their generation as well as ours—the nature of government and how best to preserve liberty with a declaration of essential rights; society's responsibility to the present and future generations in matters of private property, public debt, and legislation and constitution-making; and the need for public spiritedness among political leaders.

Although these conversations took place in private correspondence, often written at their leisure in the evening (after he had "retired to my fireside," said Jefferson), they were not purely theoretical. Both men adapted their thoughts to their public actions and hoped that future generations might be informed by their conversations. As part of that first generation of independent Americans, Jefferson and Madison realized that they occupied a special place in history. They were setting precedents for a new people—a new nation. Reason, they hoped, would now be our guide "instead of English precedent, the habit of which fetters us with all the political heresies" of that nation. Banning acknowledges, however, that neither Jefferson nor Madison, nor any of their generation for that matter, managed to abide consistently by their ideals. Few individuals live up to their highest aspirations. But the two Virginians set goals for themselves and their countrymen that we continually can strive to achieve.

In exploring these three conversations, Banning has demonstrated Jefferson's and Madison's understanding of human nature and government as well as their consistency of thought over long years. He has made clear what was unclear before in a beautifully written and persuasive work of history.

Madison, October 1994   JOHN P. KAMINSKI

PREFACE

WHEN JOHN KAMINSKI ASKED ME TO PRESENT the Jensen Lectures, I suggested as a working title something like "Three Lessons from the Founding." Retaining that would not have been a good idea. Mistaking my intentions, some of those whom I was most concerned to reach might have rebelled at reading lessons. Historians who saw that title might have wondered whether I had turned my coat, recanted fundamentals of the code, and crossed into the ranks of those who would exploit the past in order to provide sophistical support for a particular political agenda. While I was willing to annoy the critics who might argue with the concept of a "Founding," I did not intend to violate the code of the profession, and the "lessons" I imagined were a good deal more like tales or conversations.

Of all of the varieties of scholars, historians are probably the most resistant to the notion that the past can be approached in order to discover rules that citizens or statesmen (if any such survive) can handily apply to a contemporary situation. I am no exception. Indeed, with most historians, I think the clearest lesson of the craft is that the past was truly different from the present, that tomorrow will be truly different from today, and that we often draw the wrong conclusions from deceptive similarities between a past and present problem.[1]

Does history, then, have any relevance at all? And can historians, without a violation of the standards of their craft, reach out beyond the narrow circle of their fellow academics to suggest what kind of relevance it has? These essays are an effort to respond to these important questions, which are often asked by friends who like a story but are not content with history "for its own sake," with studies aimed exclusively at other academics, or with stories told in order to assume a righteous moral posture. The exercise, I trust, is not the sort of study that historians condemn: the plundering of records to support positions taken for contemporary reasons. In fact, if pressured on this point, I would insist that in so far as I agree at all with the ideas that I am trying to explain, I do so as a *consequence* of being influenced by the individuals I study—men who may be worth approaching with the standard rules of evidence and with professional respect for the distinctive circumstances under which they spoke.[2] My job as a historian is not to advocate or preach, but to present the past, as faithfully as I can manage, as those who lived it understood it. Apart from telling stories, the object is to "translate" old ideas into a language more accessible to moderns. If that can be accomplished, we can then decide if there is anything to keep.

To me, of course, there does seem much to learn by studying the founding and the founders—terms I do not hesitate to use. Historians do not expect the dead to solve the problems of the living. No one can discover the original intentions of the founders by exploring two of several hundred men who had a hand in those events. Even if we could, we might still doubt that the intentions of the founders are the

x

same intentions we should have today. Nevertheless, for all the differences between their time and ours, we still employ ideas and live with institutions that the founding generation shaped. We still define ourselves, in part, by reference to the values of their Revolution. And even when we righteously (or should I say, self-righteously?) condemn the founders' failures—their failure, for example, to abolish slavery or otherwise to live according to their highest aspirations—we might do well to realize that many of the founding generation, fallible and mortal though they were, did think about the fundamentals with a clarity and depth that few today have matched. Sometimes this was true when they confronted issues not dissimilar to those that trouble us today: the usefulness and limitations of a bill of rights; a swollen public debt; disparities of wealth in a republic; the necessity of public spirit; or the nature of a sound relationship among the citizens of a republic and between those citizens and democratic statesmen. When this was so, it may be worth our while to listen in on their discussions and to notice how they thought. Not infrequently, this can encourage us to see familiar problems from a different angle and in terms that seem as fresh, when they are resurrected, as they were when they were first employed.

These essays, then, are steps onto a ground that a historian would normally concede to theorists and lawyers. They are best approached as three attempts to lay before the reader three of many conversations that occurred between two founders on some matters of continuing concern. They are not addressed primarily to scholars, though I hope, of course, that scholars find some points that may be worth their while. They are written mostly for Americans who may know less about this era, but are willing to suspect that dialogues between these founders, or between these two and others of their time, may speak to us as well.

For this experiment, I lean primarily on Jefferson and

Madison, the founders I know best. I focus mostly on the years immediately surrounding the adoption of the Constitution. Jefferson and Madison, of course, are not the only founders from whom we might learn, and these are not the only conversations we might probe. Partly for this reason, roughly half the volume will consist of some of the materials on which the essays have been based—and from which other explorations might begin. Nevertheless, with these Virginians, we enjoy the great advantage of a long and intimate political collaboration which was entering upon its most productive years and which bequeathed the richest and most influential correspondence of this sort in all our national annals. Neither of the men requires an introduction. We can simply listen in.

o   o   o

I am grateful to John Kaminski and the Center for the Study of the American Constitution for the opportunity to give the Merrill Jensen Lectures; to Virginia Bernhardt, Peter Onuf, and the Thomas Jefferson Memorial Foundation for a chance to try the first one out at the Universities of Virginia and of St. Thomas; to members of the audience on all of these occasions; and to all the friends with whom I have explored and argued over the creation of the federal republic at symposia and conferences throughout the last ten years. Ralph Lerner, whose talents as an essayist I have admired for years, took time from studies of his own to read the lectures and suggest a number of improvements. John Kaminski and Richard Leffler caught most (I hope) of the remaining gaffs. Lynn Hiler battled the computer. The work is dedicated to my brother and my son, but had some other patrons and inspirers. The University of Kentucky provided a sabbatical to speed it to completion, and acknowledgement is due to Pierre Goodrich, those who sit around his table, and those who tend his fire. They provoked it, listened (mostly patiently) to many of the thoughts, and shared some stimulating times.

NOTES

1. Historians are not exceptions when they venture on this ground. None of my professional acquaintances anticipated the abrupt collapse of the Soviet Empire. Many, drawing on the "lessons" of the war in Vietnam, predicted an American disaster in the confrontation with Iraq, failing to allow for differences between a jungle and a desert.

2. On this matter, my position—or my understanding of myself—is much the same as J. H. Hexter's. See the classic essay "The Historian and His Day," in *Reappraisals in History: New Views on History and Society in Early Modern Europe* (Evanston, Ill., 1961), 1–13.

ONE

Parchment Barriers and Fundamental Rights

IN A TEXTBOOK, ON A TIMELINE, 1789 might well be printed in bold type. In France, that year saw the beginning of the most profound upheaval in the history of Western Europe. In the new United States, it witnessed the inauguration of the federal republic. In August, in both nations, legislators wrote a bill of rights; and in both cases, Thomas Jefferson was actively involved. In neither case was Jefferson the draftsman of the charter. Throughout his life (and doubtless to his lasting disappointment), fate deprived the brilliant penman of a seat in the assemblies where organic laws were being shaped. Nevertheless, through friends among the liberal aristocracy, he made at least a minor contribution to the Declaration of the Rights of Man and the Citizen. And already, through his correspondence, he had taken an important part in urging quick amendment of the infant federal Constitution, helping to secure the constitutional additions commonly referred to, then and since, as the American Bill of Rights.

In 1789, Jefferson was U.S. minister to France, a post in which he had succeeded Benjamin Franklin in 1784. As a

philosopher himself, he had been socializing for the past five
years with many of the most important *philosophes* in France,
for all of whom he was a never-failing spring of information
on American affairs. As a respected revolutionary statesman,
he was naturally consulted by these friends as Lafayette and
other "Patriots" among the nobles talked of joining with the
Third Estate and writing a revolutionary constitution.
Jefferson's advice to his aristocratic friends was mostly fairly
cautious. The Virginian's boldness as a theorist was tempered
in the early stages of the French Revolution, as it was
throughout his life, by a profound concern for what was practical within the context. Accordingly, while he himself was
deeply dedicated to a strictly democratic system, he eschewed
extreme solutions to the crisis, doubting that the French were
ready for a reconstruction that would move beyond a constitutional monarchy to a government derived entirely from
elections. By September, when he sailed for the United
States, events were rapidly outrunning his initial caution,
and even liberal aristocrats were coming under popular suspicion. Thus, his thoughts proved too conservative to have
much influence on the National Assembly; and although he
long remained a champion of revolutionary efforts, it would
not be many years before his early skepticism seemed to be
confirmed.

Jefferson's specific contributions to the French discussions are difficult to trace. Early in July, before the fall of
the Bastille, Lafayette consulted him about a bill of rights
before presenting his own proposals to the National Assembly.[1] Jefferson made several suggestions, but the most important ones—a broader definition of religious liberty and
an exclusion of the rights of property from those that were
to be declared inalienable and natural—were not incorporated in the final legislation. Jefferson was not directing
Lafayette or other revolutionary actors. Still, the principal
American example for the great French charter was undoubt-

edly the Virginia Declaration of Rights, the first of several bills of rights adopted as the British colonies were drafting revolutionary constitutions.[2] In countless unrecorded conversations, Jefferson had doubtless drawn attention to Virginia's declaration and had kept his friends informed about the numerous American experiments that had transfixed the French imagination. In the Declaration of Independence, he had eloquently summarized the general understandings underlying all these eighteenth-century charters. Circulation of his *Notes on the State of Virginia* and, of course, of his Virginia Statute for Establishing Religious Freedom (which still may have no equal as an unforgettable defense of freedom of the human conscience) were not the smallest of his unrecorded contributions.[3]

The absence of a written record quickly frustrates efforts to recover Jefferson's specific role in the discussions leading to the French Declaration of the Rights of Man. In the American case, however, the surviving records tell a full and captivating story. On May 4, 1789, four days after Washington's inauguration and a single day before the convocation of the Estates General in France, Congressman James Madison was on his feet in the first House of Representatives to announce that he would shortly introduce a series of amendments to the newly ratified Constitution. Without James Madison, who was the most important framer of the new federal charter (as well as the assemblyman who had secured enactment in Virginia of Jefferson's Bill for Establishing Religious Freedom), there would have been no federal Bill of Rights—not, at least, in 1789. Scholars universally agree that "the father of the Constitution" was even more unquestionably the father of the first amendments, which were passed by a reluctant Congress only as a consequence of his determination, his hard work, and the unmatchable esteem with which his colleagues honored him at this creative moment. But Madison himself had once been

3

hesitant about a federal bill of rights, and Jefferson had played a role in causing him to change his mind. The dialogue between these two close friends is worth our close attention. A revealing segment of their forty years of partnership in the pursuit of freedom, it also holds some lasting lessons in the uses of a bill of rights, in statesmanship, and in the reasons why a bill of rights is absolutely insufficient, taken by itself, to guard the liberties it is intended to secure.

Before proceeding to this dialogue, however, we should reconstruct the background. Posted overseas as minister to France, Jefferson had not been able to attend the Constitutional Convention. If he had, his presence in Philadelphia in the summer of 1787 might not have been an unmixed blessing. On the other hand, perhaps the author of the Declaration might have saved the great convention from its worst mistake. On September 12, as the convention rushed toward a conclusion, George Mason, author of Virginia's revolutionary charters, insisted that the meeting ought to add a bill of rights to the emerging constitution. By working from the several declarations of the states, he pointed out, the members could prepare a federal bill in very little time, and its addition might permit him to endorse the finished plan. With no significant debate—Roger Sherman simply noted that the declarations of the states were not to be repealed by the convention's plan "and being in force are sufficient"— every delegation present voted no to Mason's plea. In the Virginia delegation, Madison, George Washington, and Judge John Blair outvoted Mason and Governor Edmund Randolph, both of whom refused to sign the finished Constitution.[4] Thus it came about that, starting with the initial sentence of George Mason's published condemnation of the Constitution, the absence of a bill of rights became the central feature of a potent opposition to the popular approval of the plan—an opposition, we are in the habit of forgetting, that included nearly half of those who chose the state conventions which eventually approved the framer's Constitution.

Jefferson himself was seriously ambivalent about the Constitution, though he moved increasingly to its support. His first, quick look left him amazed at the convention's radical departures from tradition. The really necessary changes, he suggested to John Adams, could have been effected by a few amendments to the Articles of Confederation.[5] He was very much concerned that fears provoked by Shays's Rebellion had led the great convention to set up a hawk to keep the henyard in order, and he was not a friend of an overly energetic system.[6]

Madison soon disabused his friend of the idea that some amendments to the old Confederation might have solved the country's problems.[7] And, indeed, beginning from the time that he received the younger man's extended explanation of the plan, the minister abandoned his initial thought that lesser changes might have been sufficient and moved increasingly toward open admiration of most of its essential features.[8] By the early part of 1788, Jefferson was writing that the document contained "a great mass of good . . . in a very desirable form," but also "a bitter pill or two."[9]

Those bitter pills, however, were extremely difficult for Jefferson to swallow. He objected first—and strongly—to the absence of a limitation on the chief executive's capacity to stand for reelection. He was fearful that, in practice, a perpetual reeligibility to this imposing office would entail a president for life—and maybe, over time, a monarch. Most of all, however, like George Mason, Jefferson denounced the absence of a bill of rights. On the morning after getting Madison's detailed report, he answered with a lengthy letter praising most of the convention's work, but vigorously objecting to omissions he disliked. "A bill of rights," he wrote, "is what the people are entitled to against every government on earth, general or particular, and what no just government should refuse or rest on inference."[10] By February, 1788, Jefferson was giving up the hope that anything was likely to be done about the president's capacity to stand indefinitely for reelection. Still, his dedication to a bill of rights remained so fierce that he was telling Madison and others that he thought that nine states should adopt the Constitution, securing all of its great benefits, but that the other four should not approve until a bill of rights was added. This proposal proved a serious embarrassment to Madison when Patrick Henry used it in Virginia's narrowly divided state convention.[11] It was one of many reasons why the Constitution was defeated in neighboring North Carolina.

Now, from our perspective, Jefferson and other critics seem so obviously right that readers may be stunned to learn that anyone opposed the first amendments. The Bill of Rights, in many minds, is much the most essential portion of the Constitution. What do we mean, more times than not, when we say that a measure is unconstitutional? Usually, that it violates one of the first ten amendments. What needs explaining, then, is why the Constitutional Convention should have voted overwhelming *against* the preparation of a bill of rights and why a thinker of the caliber of Madison—by general agreement probably the finest democratic theorist that the United States has ever seen—should have continued to resist its addition.

There were three main reasons, none of which had anything to do with a hostility to civil liberties per se. The first and possibly the most important—certainly to Madison himself—was purely tactical in nature. As Madison would put it after he had won approval from Virginia's state convention, the friends of the reform were under the necessity, as long as the adoption of the Constitution was in doubt, to stubbornly oppose *all* efforts that would make a state's approval contingent on one or another alteration or addition.[12] Madison did not believe the Constitution perfect; in his first re-

6

port to Jefferson he had declared that he was willing to support amendments (or even a second general convention) "as soon as time shall have somewhat corrected the feverish state of the public mind and trial shall have pointed its attention to the true defects of the system." Yet Madison and other framers did believe that, for the present, the convention's plan was certainly the best that had a chance to be adopted—and possibly the final hope for liberty on earth. They were convinced that a successful effort to insist that it be changed before it was accepted would in practice mean that there would be no constitutional reform at all. If some states should demand a bill of rights, then others might demand a range of other changes that would have no chance of gaining general approval. Nine states, at minimum, would have to ratify a single plan to put the document into effect. Thus, the farthest that the Federalists could go was to adopt the strategy devised by compromisers in the Massachusetts state convention, which had ratified the Constitution while *recommending* several changes to the first new Congress. Jefferson himself eventually conceded that the Massachusetts plan was better than his own suggestion that the last four states should not adopt until a bill of rights appeared.[13] Meanwhile, Madison had been compelled to offer recommendatory changes to secure approval in Virginia. And, for Madison, a promise was a promise.

Strategy, however, was not the only reason for the framers' hesitation to support a bill of rights—and plainly not the reason for the Constitutional Convention's original refusal. Two other thoughts were also much at work. As Madison expressed it in his state convention—before he was obliged to make his promise—a declaration of essential rights was both unnecessary and potentially pernicious.[14] It was unnecessary, he explained, because the Constitution delegated only limited authority to the new central government, whose lawful powers did not extend into the areas that were conventionally protected by a bill of rights. And adding one could prove a danger, he believed, because an effort to enumerate essential rights could not be safe unless it was complete. Any list of rights might inadvertently omit a vital claim, and its omission could become the ground for an insistence that the government *could* act on matters that were never meant to be included in its province.

Let me expand. At Philadelphia, the eagerness to finish the convention's work was not the only reason why a bill of rights was speedily and overwhelmingly rejected. When Sherman said that it would not be necessary to prepare a bill, he was addressing men who had been working for four months to frame the Constitution. No one understood more clearly than these delegates themselves that the convention had been working from the start to shape a limited regime: a central government that was to be responsible primarily—indeed, almost exclusively—for matters that the several states were individually incapable of handling. Even modern scholars commonly forget, because the situation is so different today, that at its origins, this was to be a government of delegated and enumerated powers—a government, that is, profoundly different from the governments of Europe or even of the several states, which were assumed to have a plenary authority to act, in any area at all, unless the people or the natural rights of man imposed a prohibition. On this understanding, to insist upon a federal bill of rights was simply to misapprehend the fundamental nature of the government they were creating. In fact, it was to make an error that was anything but friendly to the natural rights that the proponents of a bill were anxious to protect. The reason isn't difficult to see. If this new government were understood to have *no* powers other than the ones the Constitution granted, then it had *no* lawful right to enter into any other province. It was forbidden by its very nature to encroach on nearly all of that preserve where human rights are practiced and expressed.

And this preserve was therefore safer, on this understanding, than could ever be the case as a result of any mortal effort to define it. For who could ever make a comprehensive list of all the liberties that were entitled to protection? Do we have a right to wear the color red? To grow a beard? To go to bed when we desire and get up when we please? The list is practically endless.[15]

The members of the Constitutional Convention did not spell this out, so far as we can tell, in their immediate response to Mason's plea. They did begin to do so, though, as soon as they encountered opposition. James Wilson warned against the dangers of a bill of rights in his speech at the Pennsylvania statehouse on October 6, 1787.[16] Alexander Hamilton discussed the subject in *Federalist* 84. And it is clear that Madison was deeply influenced by the same considerations (and by both of these important texts). In his surviving papers from the period before Virginia's state convention, there is nothing of significance about a bill of rights. At this time, he was determined to defeat *all* previous amendments. But after the convention had adjourned, he carefully explained to Jefferson the nature of his stand.[17]

Madison had never, he confessed, regarded the omission of a bill of rights as a "material defect" of the Constitution, nor was he eager to supply one now "for any other reason than that it is anxiously desired by others." The rights in question, he maintained, were guarded to a great degree "by the manner in which the federal powers are granted." Any effort to protect them more explicitly would run the risk of an omission or of framing things in terms that might imply a grant of federal powers that was never "meant to be included in the enumeration." More than that, he added, there was every reason to be fearful that "a positive declaration of some of the most essential rights could not [in practice] be obtained in the requisite latitude." Freedom of religious conscience seemed an obvious example, and one he knew would

9

weigh quite heavily upon his friend. "I am sure," he wrote, that this essential right would be defined more narrowly if it were currently submitted to a public definition than either he or Jefferson was willing to accept.

The "father of the Constitution" probed the subject to a depth that even Hamilton and Wilson had not plumbed. Experience, he argued, showed that bills of rights were always ineffective on precisely those occasions when their influence was the most to be desired. "Repeated violations of these parchment barriers have been committed by overbearing majorities in every state," he wrote. "In Virginia, I have seen the bill of rights violated in every instance where it has been opposed to a popular current." "Wherever there is an interest and power to do wrong, wrong will generally be done, and not less readily by" a ruling majority than by a prince. An obvious example, he reminded Jefferson, was Patrick Henry's effort in Virginia to impose a tax in order to support the Christian churches. This had very nearly passed despite Virginia's declaration of essential rights and would still pass, despite the Statute for Religious Freedom, if a popular majority was of a single sect. The best protection for the dearest human rights was not a parchment declaration, Madison believed. It was the institution of a large republic with a governmental structure that would make it harder for an overbearing, interested majority to rule without restraints.

Jefferson was not convinced, as Madison anticipated when he wrote this letter. The minister to France had seen James Wilson's speech and had rebutted it in his December missive.[18] He understood, in other words, that the convention's plan proposed a limited regime, and he was conscious of the argument about the danger from omissions. Still, he pointed out, the great convention had itself seen fit to write explicit guarantees of certain rights into the body of the Constitution—a prohibition of religious tests for office, of ex post facto laws, and such.[19] Jefferson demanded similar protection for the freedom of the press, freedom of religion, and other fundamental rights, insisting that the dearest liberties should not be left to rest on "inference" alone. Accordingly, when he received the news that nine states had approved the Constitution, he was at his desk again to say that he rejoiced in the decision, but he still believed that voices north to south were calling for a bill of rights. If Madison was fearful of an inadvertent error, Jefferson advised, the difficulty could be solved by making prohibitions absolute in cases where there seemed a difficulty in agreeing on legitimate exceptions—monopolies or standing armies for example.[20]

Jefferson did not elaborate this argument as fully as he might have, but Madison could readily supply the missing steps as he had heard them from the Constitution's other critics. Granting that the central government was limited to its enumerated powers, they observed, the Constitution did contain a clause declaring it the supreme law of the land. In case of conflict, it would clearly override state bills of rights. And in addition to its delegated powers, Congress also had the power to enact such other laws as might be "necessary and proper" to carry its enumerated powers into action. In judging what was necessary to enforce its delegated powers, Congress might decide that freedom of the press or other fundamental rights would have to be constrained.[21]

Madison did not agree with Jefferson on all these points. He reasoned, for example, that "absolute restrictions" ought to be "avoided" in cases that were "doubtful" or in cases where emergencies would override the plainest charter prohibitions. If Spain or Britain, for example, should send an army to the neighborhood, a prohibition of a peacetime force would speedily be overruled. "No written prohibitions on earth," Madison wrote, would prevent a measure if necessity and overwhelming public pressure should demand it; and "repeated violations" of such absolute restrictions would destroy the value of a bill of rights in "ordinary" cases. Madison had always thought it dangerous to write into a constitution clauses that necessity would overturn, for clauses of this sort would lead to necessary usurpations, "every precedent for which is a germ of unnecessary and multiplied repetitions."[22] By this time, however, Madison had made his promise to his state convention and was making it again to his constituents in the first congressional elections.[23] He did so, I believe, for reasons that are not to be accounted for by politics alone.

There is a standard view of what transpired in 1789. Madison, this stresses, was a very able, very worried politician. Under pressure from the Henryite majority in his home state, forced into a stressful contest for a seat in the first Congress, and frightened by a movement for a second federal convention, he succeeded brilliantly in counteracting all these threats. Combing through the numerous amendments recommended by the state conventions, he extracted those that he considered harmless, talked the Federalists into approving them, fractured the opponents of the Constitution, and restored his damaged standing in Virginia.[24]

Most of this is true. Most of it, in fact, was candidly admitted by the sponsor of the first amendments in his speeches to the House. The problem with the standard story is that it is told too often *only* in these terms—served in such a heavy sauce of modern disillusionment with politicians that most of the authentic flavor has been lost. Too often, nearly all the emphasis is placed on what needs emphasizing least—on Madison's determination to exclude amendments that would change the structure or reduce the powers of the new regime, or on the congressman's supposed concern about his own political position. This emphasis on politics alone does not just underestimate a most extraordinary man. It hides some of the deepest lessons from the founding.

In the early months of 1789, there was indeed significant support for the meeting of a second constitutional convention, especially among those Antifederalists who wanted major changes in the basic powers of the new regime. Madison and Jefferson both deprecated this idea. In November, for example, Jefferson had written that *The Federalist* had "rectified" some of his early thinking on the Constitution. He still desired a bill of rights, remarking that its friends were "too respectable not to be entitled to some sacrifice of opinion in the majority—especially when a great proportion of them would be contented with a bill of rights." Still, he added, if the first new Congress would itself initiate the changes, "I should not fear any dangerous innovation in the plan."[25] Madison was similarly open and explicit—both in Congress and in private letters—that he favored only those amendments that would offer an additional security for fundamental rights, that he believed that these would "quiet the fears" of many, that he hoped "to separate the well meaning from the designing opponents" of the Constitution and, in that way, to make it more secure.[26] There was nothing underhanded in these tactics, nor do I believe that Madison was much concerned about his reputation in Virginia.[27]

To some of his congressional opponents, Madison's amendments did indeed seem mere "whip-syllabub": "frothy and full of wind, formed only to please the palate," a tub thrown out by sailors to amuse the whale and gain safe passage for the ship.[28] These proposals, they complained, were not the substantive amendments many Antifederalists demanded. Madison himself admitted that they mostly offered some additional securities for liberties that Congress was without the power to infringe. Moreover, on his other side, a number of his fellow Federalists in Congress certainly believed that Madison was asking them to sacrifice their own opinions to the views of the opponents of the Constitution. These higher-flying Federalists objected bitterly to changes they considered both unnecessary and improper, changes that could agitate the public and perhaps throw everything into confusion. But despite his early reservations, this was not how Madison himself was thinking of the project, and not what he believed that he was asking other Federalists to do. Of all the founding fathers, none was less vainglorious than this diminutive Virginian. Madison had shown that he was capable of thinking that the members of the Constitutional Convention, reasoning together through four months, had finished with a plan that was superior in most respects to the proposals he had drafted in his closet: the ideas which had become the basis for the resolutions (the Virginia Plan) with which the great convention had begun.[29] Similarly, Madison was capable of learning from the critics of the Constitution, many of them friends to whom he listened with sincere respect. Like Jefferson, moreover, Madison was a committed revolutionary statesman, the sort of politician who believed that every action should be taken with an eye toward the creation of a sound republic, not simply with a view toward getting past an urgent current problem. All of this, and not exigencies alone, contributed importantly to his decisions.

While Madison *was* skeptical, at first, about the value of a federal bill of rights, he did not draft it merely as a sharp political maneuver. Rather, to begin with, he had come by now to recognize the force of Antifederalist objections. Thus, some months before, in the October letter which explained to Jefferson the reasons for his reservations, he had also said that while he found the arguments against a bill of rights persuasive, he did not consider them conclusive. If amendments could be properly prepared, the dangers from omissions or from implications might be skirted. The result would not just ease the anxious minds of men whose judgments he respected (though, of course, this was a sound republican objective in itself). A bill of rights would have at least two further uses. In the first place, "the political truths declared in that solemn manner [would] acquire by degrees the character of fundamental maxims of free government." As they became "incorporated with the national sentiment," he wrote, these truths would "counteract the impulses of interest and passion," even among majorities themselves. In the second place, while he believed that rights would usually be threatened by an interested majority in a republic, he saw that there might still be times when dangers might originate with governing officials. At such times, a bill of rights would be "a good ground for an appeal to the sense of the community. Perhaps, too, there may be a certain degree of danger that a succession of artful and ambitious rulers may by gradual and well-timed advances finally erect an independent government on the subversion of liberty. Should this danger exist at all, it is prudent to guard against it, especially when the precaution can do no injury."

On June 8, when he presented his amendments to the House, Madison incorporated all these arguments, together with the most persuasive Antifederalist appeals for "additional guards for liberty," including the protection that a bill of rights would offer from abuses of the federal power to decide what might be "necessary and proper" to carry the enumerated powers into practice. He added yet another argument that Jefferson had given him in a letter of March 15: the legal check on governmental usurpations that a bill of rights would put into the hands of federal judges.[30] Once these changes were incorporated in the fundamental law, he said, "independent tribunals of justice will consider themselves in a peculiar manner the guardians of those rights; they will be an impenetrable bulwark against every assumption of power in the legislative or executive" branches. Finally, but not the less importantly, the draftsman of the first amendments urged the other representatives to "act the part of wise and liberal men," to live up to the character of leaders of a great republic, to "evince" the spirit of "deference and concession" that so many Antifederalists had shown in quietly submitting to the Constitution. "A great number of our constituents are . . . dissatisfied," he said, among whom were many who were to be respected for their talents, their patriotism, and their valor. Respecting their concerns, the champions of constitutional reform should show by their initiative in framing a bill of rights that they were as devoted to liberty and a republican government as any of their critics.[31] Most of those who had opposed the Constitution, Madison insisted, did so because they thought their liberties unsafe, "*nor ought we to consider them safe* while a great number of our fellow citizens think these securities necessary." Not only was it well to seek reunion with the two non-ratifying states, it was important in itself "to extinguish from the bosom of every member of the community any apprehension that there are those among his countrymen who wish to deprive them of the liberty for which they valiantly fought and honorably bled." "If we can make the Constitution better in the opinion of those who are opposed to it, without weakening its frame or abridging its usefulness . . . , we act the part of wise and liberal men."[32]

Madison would not have framed the Bill of Rights if he had not decided that the arguments in favor of the measure were, on balance, stronger than the arguments against it. His determination to disarm the critics of the Constitution was by no means the exclusive reason for his change of mind. Indeed, for Madison, even the expedient considerations were to be conceived of in a way that is impossible to capture in a cynical, reductionist assessment. The leader of the first new Congress was unquestionably an able politician, but he was also a committed revolutionary statesman. As a revolutionary statesman, he was genuinely dedicated to a special concept of the way in which decisions should be made in a republic. He believed that a republic ultimately rests on mutual respect among its citizens and on a recognition on the part of all that they are members of a free community of mutually-regarding equals: participants in a political society that asks them to be conscious that they are, at once, the rulers and the ruled.[33] Legislators were by no means an exception. Not only did their duty tell them not to disregard the wishes and concerns of many valued brethren, it instructed them not to break the promise they had made in order to secure reform in states like Massachusetts and Virginia. Their position as the leaders and creators of a model revolutionary state compelled them to exemplify the mutual respect and the awareness of the whole community that were essential in the citizens of a republic.

If Madison had had his way entirely, the Bill of Rights would have been different in significant respects from the amendments that were finally approved. The changes would have been incorporated into the body of the Constitution, not tacked onto its end.[34] More suggestively, the Constitution would have opened with a declaration

> That all power is originally vested in, and consequently derived from the people.
>
> That government is instituted, and ought to be exercised for the benefit of the people; which consists in the enjoyment of life and liberty, with the right of acquiring and using property, and generally of pursuing and obtaining happiness and safety.
>
> That the people have an indubitable, unalienable, and indefeasible right to reform or change their government, whenever it be found adverse or inadequate to the purposes of its institution.

Adoption of these clauses would have meant, of course, that it could never have been plausibly denied that the fundamental principles of the Declaration of Independence (or of the Virginia Declaration of Rights, from which the language was taken) are part of the American Constitution, along with the specific liberties protected by the first amendments. But Madison himself admitted in his June 8 speech that it might not be "absolutely necessary" to insert the "absolute truth" of "the perfect equality of mankind" at the head of the Constitution; and many of the Federalists in Congress plainly sought to limit the amendments to the fewest and the briefest that opponents would accept. Therefore, a select committee which reported on July 28 substituted a single sentence in place of Madison's initial declaration, and even that was dropped on August 18 when it did not receive approval from two-thirds of the House.[35] Similarly, a clause explicitly enunciating the implicit constitutional principle of separation of the three great branches of government was deleted by the Senate.[36]

Again, if Congress and the states had thoroughly indulged its sponsor, the Bill of Rights would have included from its origins a clause that was not put into effect until the twentieth century—and then by way of the judiciary's understanding of the First and Fourteenth Amendments—to wit: "No *state* shall violate the equal rights of conscience, or the freedom of the press, or the trial by jury in criminal cases." This proposal to extend these guarantees to cover state as well as federal measures, which Madison regarded as "the most valuable . . . on the whole list,"[37] passed the House of Representatives in 1789 but was deleted by the Senate. The amendments proposed that year and ratified in 1791 did not provide additional securities against state or local legislation.

Which brings us back, for a conclusion, to the lessons we might find in Madison's and Jefferson's exchanges. In the first place, we might note, Madison was clearly right when he observed that it might not be possible to win approval of a bill of rights that would protect some liberties in all the amplitude that he and Jefferson preferred. He was unable to secure the liberties of conscience and the press against the possibility that they could be infringed by local legislation. He was unable, for that matter, even to secure as broad and firm a guarantee of freedom of religion at the federal level as he would have liked. Madison's original proposal would have read:

> The civil rights of none shall be abridged on account of religious belief or worship, nor shall any national religion be established, nor shall the full and equal rights of conscience be in any manner, or on any pretext infringed.

The final language of the First Amendment was considerably less sweeping and has laid the ground for countless modern arguments about the prohibition's meaning and extent: "Congress shall make no law respecting an establishment of religion, or prohibiting the free exercise thereof."

All of Madison's initial reservations, we might argue, were correct to some degree. Conscious of the danger from omissions—indeed, as has been seen, he worried that a Bill of Rights could do more harm than good unless this danger could be skirted—Madison was careful to include proposals that became the Ninth and Tenth Amendments:

> The enumeration in the Constitution of certain rights shall not be construed to deny or disparage others retained by the people.

and

> The powers not delegated to the United States by the Constitution, nor prohibited by it to the States, are reserved to the States respectively, or to the people.

As usual, Madison's own language would have made these guarantees still more explicit.[38] And yet, whatever language had been used, there was, indeed, a danger that a list of cer-

19

tain rights would lead to arguments that rights not listed lack the same protection. A recent essay spells this danger out in full, but all of us are probably aware, at minimum, of recent arguments that privacy is not a right protected by the Constitution.[39] And some of us may have reflected on the tortuous judicial reasoning that finds it necessary, in our positivistic age, to seek protection for some liberties by roundabout constructions of the various provisions (or penumbra) of the Bill of Rights and the Fourteenth Amendment rather than by arguments that unenumerated rights are guarded by the Ninth Amendment—reasoning which is the very obverse of the sort that Madison expected judges to apply.[40]

Nevertheless, as Jefferson had put it, half a loaf has surely proven better than no bread at all. In the end, Madison's colleagues in the First Federal Congress did indulge the sponsor of the first amendments very far indeed. With the exceptions of the article concerning state infringements of essential rights and one that would have placed a monetary floor on appeals to the federal courts, not a single substantive proposal was defeated. For all of the stylistic alterations, the twelve amendments offered to the states were very much the ones that Madison had drafted.[41] To Madison himself, moreover, as I hope that I have shown, the reasons not to frame a bill of rights seemed sound, but not decisive. The countervailing arguments, when everything was said, were even stronger than the arguments against it.

Credit Madison's capacity to learn, and credit also the capacity of Jefferson and other critics of the unamended Constitution to instruct its most important framer. For, indeed—to modify the metaphor that Jefferson suggested— history seems to show that Madison's amendments might be better likened to a yeast that has expanded over time until our loaf is fuller now than it has ever been before. The Bill of Rights *has* worked—in much the way and largely for the reasons that the two Virginians hoped. Before the Civil War, the federal courts did not become the special guardians of civil liberties against infringements by the other federal branches.[42] Later—and especially since World War II—they have. Moreover, if the courts did not assume this function in the years before the Civil War, that may have been, in part, because the Bill of Rights was there to warn against infringements in the first place. It is even likely that the federal bill restrained the states—not legally, but rather, as the two Virginians hoped, because the principles and guarantees that it proclaimed in such a solemn manner (as did many of the constitutions of the states) did indeed acquire the character of fundamental maxims in the minds of many of the people.

And perhaps this is the final lesson that these two Virginia founders would have wanted us to learn. "Paper barriers" or "parchment declarations," Madison insisted, would become substantial only in so far as they were manned by citizens who were informed enough, and vigilant enough, to stand behind these ramparts. Madison believed, as most of us remember, that the written Constitution, with its multiple restraints against abuses, was itself a more effective safeguard for essential rights than the amendments he proposed. (Most of these, he still believed, amounted to redundant guarantees against the exercise of powers never granted.) But it was Madison as well—although it could have been his friend—who said that even after paying all the tribute that was due to checks and balances and other constitutional devices, it should always be remembered that these mechanisms "are neither the sole nor the chief palladium of constitutional liberty. The people, who are the authors of this blessing, must also be its guardians."[43] If citizens were unprepared for freedom, unaware of liberty's demands, or so immersed in private occupations that they lost respect for the community in which they were included, no form of government, said Madison, "can render us secure." It was a lesson driven home within a decade by the fate of liberty in France. It is a lesson that has had to be restudied—and has never been quite learned—from 1800 to the present.

NOTES

1. Lafayette to Jefferson, July 6, 1789; Jefferson to Lafayette, July 6, 1789; Lafayette to Jefferson, July 9, 1789; and Lafayette's draft of a declaration, in *The Papers of Thomas Jefferson*, ed. Julian P. Boyd et al. (Princeton, 1950—), 15:249, 250, 255, 230–33 (hereafter *PTJ*). See, further, Louis Gottschalk and Margaret Maddox, *Lafayette in the French Revolution: Through the October Days* (Chicago, 1969), 90–98.

2. See Jefferson to Madison, January 12, 1789, *PTJ*, 14:437. The Virginia Declaration of Rights is reprinted as document 1 below.

3. Documents 2 and 3.

4. Proceedings of September 12, 1789, in *The Records of the Federal Convention of 1787*, ed. Max Farrand, 4 vols. (rev. ed., New Haven, Conn., 1937), 2:588.

5. Jefferson to Adams, November 13, 1787, *PTJ*, 12:350–51.

6. See documents 5 and 8.

7. See documents 6 and 7.

8. Jefferson to Madison, February 6, 1788; to Washington, November 4, 1788; to Francis Hopkinson, March 3, 1789; *PTJ*, 12:569–70, 14:328, 650–51.

9. Jefferson to Edward Carrington, December 12, 1787, *PTJ*, 12:446.

10. Jefferson to Madison, December 20, 1787, in *The Papers of James Madison*, ed. William T. Hutchinson et al. (Chicago and Charlottesville, Va., 1962–), 10:336–38 (hereafter *PJM*). Included below as document 8.

11. Julian Boyd's editorial note, *PTJ*, 13:354–55, is a tidy account of the exchange between Henry and Madison over Jefferson's letter to Alexander Donald of February 7, 1788.

12. Madison to George Eve, January 2, 1789, *PJM*, 11:404–5. Document 11.

13. Jefferson to Francis Hopkinson, March 13, 1789, *PTJ*, 14:651.

14. Speech of June 24, 1788, *PJM*, 11:172–77.

15. I have paraphrased the complaint of Theodore Sedgwick, in the course of the congressional debate on the right of the people to assemble, that it was "trifling" and redundant to include protections for every "self-evident, unalienable right which the people possess." See *Creating the Bill of Rights: The Documentary History from the First Federal Congress*, ed. Helen E. Veit et al. (Baltimore, 1991), 159.

16. Available in *The Documentary History of the Ratification of the Constitution*, ed. Merrill Jensen et al. (Madison, Wisc., 1976–), 13:337–44 (hereafter *DHRC*). See also Wilson's widely published speeches at the Pennsylvania ratifying convention in November and December 1787, *ibid.*, 2:382–83, 387–91, 469–71. But Madison himself may have been the first to make this point in the aftermath of the convention. When Richard Henry Lee objected in the Confederation Congress to the absence of a bill of rights, Madison replied: "A bill of rights [is] unnecessary because the powers are enumerated and only extend to certain cases." See "Melancton Smith's Notes," *ibid.*, 1:332–33, 335–36.

17. Madison to Jefferson, October 17, 1788, *PJM*, 11:297–300. Document 10.

18. Document 8.

19. Irving Brant counted 24 elements of a bill of rights in the body of the Constitution, thirty more in the first ten amendments.

20. Jefferson to Madison, July 31, 1788, *PJM*, 11:212–13. Document 9.

21. Among the best Antifederalist arguments for a bill of rights were "Agrippa," numbers 15 and 16; "The Federal Farmer," numbers 4 and 16; and "Brutus," number 2.

22. Document 10, together with *The Federalist* 41 and 44.

23. Madison to George Eve, January 2, 1989, *PJM* 11:404–5. Document 11.

24. See the suggestions for further reading.

25. Jefferson to Madison, November 18, 1788, *PJM*, 11:353–54.

26. Madison to Jefferson, December 8, 1788, *PJM*, 11:382–83; speech of June 8, 1789, *ibid.*, 12:198.

27. Madison had come within five votes of being chosen for the Senate by a state assembly dominated by his foes. Then, on February 2, 1789, in a congressional district deliberately rigged against him, he defeated James Monroe, a formidable opponent, by a margin of 1308 to 972, winning 57% of the popular vote. Moreover, had Monroe defeated him in this election, Madison would unquestionably have been appointed to high executive office in Washington's administration. Why should he have been alarmed about his popularity at home?

28. Speech of Aedanus Burke, August 15, 1789, in *Creating the Bill of Rights*, 175. Whip-syllabub was a contemporary light dessert. The reference to the tub to the whale, which seems ubiquitous in the contemporary records, derived from Jonathan Swift's "A Tale of a Tub."

29. A full demonstration is attempted in Banning, *The Sacred Fire of Liberty: James Madison and the Founding of the Federal Republic, 1780–1792* (Ithaca, N.Y., 1995).

30. Jefferson to Madison, March 15, 1789, *PJM*, 12:13. Document 12. Most of Jefferson's letters reached Madison only after the latter had made his decisions on other grounds. Arriving at the end of May, this is the only one that clearly exercised a demonstrable specific influence.

31. Speech of June 8, 1789, *PJM*, 12:197–209, quotations at 207, 198–200.

32. My italics. The final quotation is at *ibid.*, 209.

33. For more on this concept, see my essay, "Some Second Thoughts on Virtue and the Course of Revolutionary Thinking," in *Conceptual Change and the American Constitution*, ed. Terence Ball and J. G. A. Pocock (Lawrence, Kans., 1988), 194–212.

34. Madison believed that interweaving the amendments into the body of the text would make the Constitution more accessible to ordinary understandings (and possibly that this would make the changes as authoritative as the rest). But Roger Sherman and others argued that the Constitution as originally approved had

been the highest sovereign action of the people and should not be alloyed with amendments that would be the less authoritative act of Congress and the states (*Creating the Bill of Rights*, 105, 108–9, 117–18, 125–26, 271).

35. *Ibid.*, 29, 198. No debate was reported on the decision of August 18.

36. "The powers delegated by this Constitution [are] appropriated to the departments to which they are respectively distributed, so that the legislative department shall never exercise the powers vested in the executive or judicial, nor the executive exercise the powers vested in the legislative or judicial, nor the judicial exercise the powers vested in the legislative or executive departments" (*ibid.*, 14).

37. *Ibid.*, 188–89; *PJM*, 12:344.

38. For what became the Ninth Amendment: "The exceptions here or elsewhere in the Constitution made in favor of particular rights shall not be so construed as to diminish the just importance of other rights retained by the people; or as to enlarge the powers delegated by the Constitution; but either as actual limitations of such powers, or as inserted merely for greater caution."

39. Hadley Arkes, "On the Dangers of a Bill of Rights: A Restatement of the Federalist Argument," in Sarah Baumgartner Thurow, ed., *To Secure the Blessings of Liberty*, vol. 1: *First Principles of the Constitution* (Lanham, Md., 1988), 120–45. See, further, Ralph A. Rossum, "*The Federalist's* Understanding of the Constitution as a Bill of Rights," in Charles R. Kesler, ed., *Saving the Revolution: The Federalist Papers and the American Founding* (New York, 1987), 219–33.

40. For the growing literature on the "forgotten" Ninth Amendment, see Gaspare J. Saladino, "The Bill of Rights: A Bibliographic Essay," in *The Bill of Rights and the States: The Colonial and Revolutionary Origins of American Liberties*, ed. Patrick T. Conley and John P. Kaminski (Madison, Wisc., 1992), 507-10 or *The Rights Retained by the People: The History and Meaning of the Ninth Amendment*, ed. Randy E. Barnett (Fairfax, Va., 1989).

41. Two of the twelve amendments approved by the First Congress—one intended to assure enlargement of the House of Representatives and one providing that the salaries of congressmen

could not be raised without an intervening federal election—were not ratified by the requisite number of states in 1791. The latter, of course, has finally been added after more than 200 years, following an infamous example of the sort of congressional conduct that Madison hoped to avoid.

42. Indeed, during this period, the Supreme Court overturned only two federal measures, neither of them on grounds that they violated the first amendments: a portion of the Judiciary Act of 1789, and infamously, in *Dred Scot v. Sandford*, the Missouri Compromise of 1820.

43. "Government of the United States," published originally in the *National Gazette*, February 4, 1792, and reprinted in *PJM*, 14:217–19.

TWO

---

*"The Earth Belongs to the Living":
Property and Public Debt
in a Republic*

SHORTLY AFTER THEIR DISCUSSION OF THE Bill of Rights, Jefferson took up his pen again to ask his friend to turn another subject over in his mind, applying to it all the "perspecuity and cogent logic so peculiarly yours."[1] The minister to France was in his last few days in Paris, recuperating from an incapacitating bout with his recurring migraines and expecting to depart on leave of absence for America as soon as he could make arrangements for the passage. Eleven days before, on August 26, 1789, the National Assembly had approved the Declaration of the Rights of Man, and it was trying now to frame a constitution. But bread was scarce, there were reports of rioting and murders in the country, and Parisians worried that the king might follow seven princes of the blood in fleeing into exile, which could touch off civil war. As before, momentous happenings in France, conjoining with the launching of the federal government in the United States, prompted Jefferson to write, although he did not know by what conveyance he would get the letter to his friend.[2]

"The question whether one generation of men has a right to bind another seems never to have been started either on this or our side of the water," Jefferson began. It had been forced upon his mind in course of the reflections in which everyone in France was currently immersed, and those reflections had suggested that the answer should affect "the fundamental principles of every government" on earth.

"That no such obligation can be so transmitted" seemed to Jefferson "very capable of proof." He started from a principle that he supposed "self-evident" and therefore not in need of further demonstration: "*that the earth belongs in usufruct to the living*': that the dead have neither powers nor rights over it. The portion occupied by any individual ceases to be his when himself ceases to be, and reverts to the society" in which he lives. If that society has made no laws concerning the descent of lands, the property will naturally be "taken by the first occupants," usually the wife and children of the deceased. If the society does have established rules, the laws may give the property to them, to one or more of them, to the decedent's other legatees, or to his creditors in payment of his debts. "But the child, the legatee, or the creditor takes it, not by any natural right, but by a law of the society of which they are members and to which they are subject." Inheritance is not a natural right. Neither can an individual, "by *natural right*, oblige the lands he occupied, or the persons who succeed him in that occupation, to the payment of debts contracted by him. For if he could, he might, during his own life, [mortgage his lands to the whole of their value], eat up the usufruct of the lands for several generations to come, and then the lands would belong to the dead and not to the living, which would be the reverse of our principle."[3]

Thus far, as Merrill Peterson has pointed out, Jefferson was building logically, though pointedly, on well-established eighteenth-century principles of natural right and on the

Lockean conception that the earth is given mankind as a common stock; individuals appropriate specific parcels only when they intermix their labor with the land and are entitled to protection in their individual possession only while they live.[4] But "what is true of every member of the society individually," Jefferson continued, "is true of them all collectively": "the earth belongs always to the living generation." Each successive generation has it "fully and in their own right," to "manage it and what proceeds from it" as they may choose. Each acquires it "clear of the debts and encumbrances" of the preceding generation, who had no right to bind posterity by their decisions. "Between society and society, or generation and generation, there is no municipal obligation, no umpire but the law of nature. We seem not to have perceived that, by the law of nature, one generation is to another as one independent nation to another. . . . The earth belongs to the living and not to the dead."

Even to this point, a claim of philosophical originality for Jefferson might be too much.[5] But this is not the case for his conclusions. Drawing on Buffon's discussion of mortality, he calculated that in any generation, half of those who have attained adulthood will be dead in nineteen years, a new majority will have replaced them. Nineteen years was thus "the term beyond which neither the representatives of a nation, nor even the whole nation itself assembled" could validly extend its laws. Public debts contracted for a longer term were not legitimately binding; payment was a matter of expediency and honor, not of right. Indeed, it followed from the same considerations "that no society can make a perpetual constitution, or even a perpetual law." The living generation are the masters of their persons and estates, "which make the sum of the objects of government," the laws and constitutions of their predecessors having naturally expired "with those who gave them being." If old enactments are enforced beyond the term of nineteen years, "it is an act of force and not of right"; and realistic reasoners cannot maintain that the succeeding generation's power to repeal old laws is an equivalent to the capacity to act afresh. Rather than assuming that succeeding generations tacitly assent to laws and constitutions they do not repeal, legislators faithful to the rights of man should limit their enactments to this natural term.[6]

The applications of this concept, Jefferson observed, were sweeping, most especially in France. There, the principle "that the earth belongs to the living" could enter into the decision whether an assembly of the nation could legitimately alter the descent of lands, abolish feudal charges, change the regulations granting lands in perpetuity to the Church or other institutions, revoke perpetual monopolies of commerce, or—indeed—attack hereditary offices, hereditary orders, and hereditary appellations and distinctions. Jefferson believed it could—and by the time he wrote this letter, doubtless that it would and should.[7] For years, he had been thunderstruck by the enormous gulf in France between the vastly rich and millions of the miserably poor. In 1785, he had described to Madison a trip to Fontainebleau and an encounter with a wretched working mother who was often unemployed and desperate to feed her children. "I asked myself," he wrote, why there should be so many beggars seeking work in a country where there was also "a very considerable portion of uncultivated lands":

> Whenever there is, in any country, uncultivated lands and unemployed poor, it is clear that the laws of property have been so far extended as to violate natural right. The earth is given as a common stock for man to labor and live on. If, for the encouragement of industry, we allow it to be appropriated, we must take care that other employment be furnished to those excluded from the appropriation. If we do not, the fundamental right to labor the earth returns to the unemployed.[8]

Even at this early point in his experience of France, the U.S. minister had drawn some radical conclusions from his willingness to think of something like a natural right to a subsistence.[9] Enlightened legislators, he observed, "cannot invent too many devices for subdividing property, only taking care to let their subdivisions go hand in hand with the natural affections of the human mind." In America, he thought, the abolition of the laws of primogeniture and entail, combined, perhaps, with taxes rising geometrically in line with the ability to pay, might prevent the inequalities and miseries of Europe, though even there it did not seem to him to be "too soon to provide by every possible means that as few as possible shall be without a little portion of land."[10] In France, however, he had even then maintained that "every man who cannot find employment, but can find uncultivated land, [should] be at liberty to cultivate it, paying a moderate rent." And now, in 1789, with revolution in the air, he noted that his principle would render "reimbursement" for attacks upon the inequalities embedded in the laws "a question of generosity and not of right." In all the cases he had mentioned, he insisted, "the legislature of the day" had had the right to "authorize such appropriations and establishments for their own time, but no longer; and the present holders [of these privileges and titles], even where they or their ancestors have purchased, are in the case of *bona fide* purchasers of what the seller had no right to convey."[11]

Madison was markedly more cautious, so much so that commentators commonly refer to his "critique" or "refutation" of the theory.[12] When, at length, he had the letter in his hands, the leader of the infant House of Representatives discovered many practical objections.[13] "However applicable in theory," he observed, the doctrine would be "liable in practice to some very powerful objections"—at least so far as Jefferson intended to apply it to a constitution. "Would not a government" that would be subject to revision every nineteen years "become too mutable to retain those prejudices in its favor which antiquity inspires, and which are perhaps a salutary aid to the most rational government in the most enlightened age?" Summarizing portions of *The Federalist*, in which he had objected at great length to Jefferson's idea that constitutional disputes between the branches of a government could be repeatedly decided by conventions of the people,[14] Madison observed that automatic, periodical revisions of a constitution would produce "pernicious factions" and, in many cases, a complete collapse of civil order. Even in the case of ordinary statutes, he remarked, if every law were written so that it would automatically expire unless there was "a positive and authentic intervention of the society itself, . . .

> all the rights depending on positive laws, that is, most of the rights of property would become absolutely defunct; and the most violent struggles be generated between those interested in reviving and those interested in new-modelling the former State. . . . The uncertainty incident to such a state of things would on one side discourage the steady exertions of industry produced by permanent laws, and on the other, give a disproportionate advantage to the more, over the less, sagacious and enterprising part of the society.[15]

Madison had theoretical as well as practical objections to the principle at issue. "If the earth be the gift of nature to the living," he observed, the living's title could extend "to the earth in its natural state only. The *improvements* made by the dead form a charge against the living who take the benefit of them." This charge could only be repaid by executing the desires of those who were responsible for the improvements. Similarly, public debts might be incurred "for purposes which interest the unborn" as much or more than the living: "such are debts for repelling a conquest, the evils of which descend through many generations"; such, "perhaps," might be the current debt of the United States, incurred to win its independence but perhaps too great to be discharged in nineteen years. "There seems then," Madison concluded, "to be a foundation in the nature of things, in the relation which one generation bears to another, for the *descent* of obligations from one to another. Equity requires it. Mutual good is promoted by it. All that is indispensable in adjusting the account between the dead and the living is to see that the debits against the latter do not exceed the advances made by the former."

In the end, as Madison pursued his friend's suggestion, he could find "relief" from his objections only in the old idea "that a tacit assent may be given to established constitutions and laws, and that this assent may be inferred" where there is no positive action to the contrary. While he did not deny that there were dangers in this old convention, he did believe that it was less impractical to remedy those dangers, "by wise plans of government," than to find a remedy for those that seemed "inseparable" from Jefferson's suggestion. In fact, as he applied the logic so peculiarly his, he doubted that the concept of implied consent could be forsworn entirely "without subverting the foundation of civil society." "On what principle does the voice of the majority bind the minority?" he asked. The rule of the majority was not a "law of nature" but a "compact" grounded in convenience. More than a majority could be demanded by a constitution, as the U.S. Constitution, for example, called for the consent of three-fourths of the states to pass a constitutional amendment. Strict consistency with compact theory, he observed, really "presupposes the assent of every member [of society] to the establishment of the rule [of the majority] itself."

If this assent cannot be given tacitly, or be implied where no positive evidence forbids, persons born in society would

33

not on attaining ripe age be bound by acts of the majority; and either a *unanimous* repetition of every law would
be necessary on the accession of new members or an express assent must be obtained from these [new members]
to the rule by which the voice of the majority is made the
voice of the whole.

New majorities, said Madison's incisive logic, do not appear
at intervals of nineteen years, but every time a voter reaches
his adulthood. And every time this happens, we assume that
an adult who chooses to remain in the society in which he
has been reared implicitly acknowledges his membership in
that society, his willingness to live by the majority's decisions, and the validity of the established constitution.[16]

Small wonder that the body of the finest recent scholarship has treated this exchange as most instructive for its revelation of the philosophical and temperamental differences
between the two Virginians. Throughout their long collaboration, Adrienne Koch remarked, Jefferson was the impetuous projecter: innovative, speculative, bold in bringing forth
the new ideas that made it possible for Madison "to sparkle
with borrowed warmth." Madison was less impetuous, more
cautious, and more profoundly penetrating as a thinker and
a politician, reining in his bolder friend and giving Jefferson
the means "to remain a philosopher in politics—a philosopher, that is, charged with real power." Nowhere in their
fifty years of friendship, Koch believed, was there a better
instance of the "reciprocity" that made these piedmont
neighbors so effective as a team. Madison politely recognized the force of Jefferson's idea and then proceeded "to
attack . . . virtually every specific proposal the letter contained."[17]

Later commentators have developed these distinctions
with surpassing skill. Madison's "cool and critical reply,"
writes Richard Matthews, "attests to the acute variances in

their political theories." Where Jefferson proposed to institute a revolutionary mechanism of "perpetual transition,"
Madison, who saw no other reason for the forming of a civil
order "than a sort of Hobbesian prudence," confined himself to "quibbles" over practice. The exchange was a revealing "outgrowth of their divergent concepts of man and
society and about the fulfillment of both."[18]

If Matthews goes too far in saying that the friends were
"miles apart" in their opinions on the matter—and later on,
that Madison was closer on the whole to Alexander Hamilton
than to his neighbor in his concepts of "property, man, government and society"[19]—this is seldom true of Drew McCoy.
McCoy's insightful exploration of the friendship recognizes
commonalities that kept the two together through half a
century of active public life.[20] Nevertheless, McCoy agrees
that these impressive letters powerfully illuminate "the very
different philosophical shadings of their respective republican faiths"; "Madison's sensitivity to the dangers of passionate disorder shaped a fundamentally conservative vision of
popular government" which contrasted sharply with
Jefferson's deductions from the natural rights of living generations.[21] As McCoy maintains, the younger man was hardly
quibbling when he pointed out that an obligatory reconsid-
eration of all existing laws would "foster popular disaffec-
tion and public unrest in any popular regime that adhered
to it." Jefferson ignored "the sternest challenge in the sci-
ence of republicanism: how to protect the integrity of free
institutions from the threat of their most dangerous enemy,
the disorder that arose from passionate contention among
the people."[22] Madison's republican commitment "was in-
fused with a philosophical conservatism, largely absent from
Jefferson's formal thought, in which the dead and the living
. . . were inextricably and on the whole happily bound together," with an almost Burkean awareness of the ties that
bind the present with the future and the past.[23]

The differences between the two Virginians are undeniably instructive and important; and as all these analysts contend, those differences did not derive exclusively from different temperamental inclinations (present though these were). Rather, from his years in Europe, Jefferson may well have gained a deeper, more immediate, more vivid sense of the profound inequities embedded in prescription, of the tyranny exerted on the present by the past, and of the "wretchedness" entailed on countless ordinary people by the property and other rights that had been settled on a few by ancient practice and arrangements. Lacking a direct experience of Europe, Madison could only imagine the massive misery that Jefferson had seen.[24]

Experience, of course, had also worked the other way around. While Jefferson was travelling and working in the old regime, walking with the wretched woman on the outskirts of Fontainebleau, and witnessing, or even sharing, something of the violent rage that had already vented in the taking of the Bastille, Madison was living in a North American society that had already gained most of the goals that European intellectuals were seeking. Throughout the 1780s, he had struggled with an ineffective federal system and with fourteen local governments (I count Vermont) that seemed to act repeatedly with no regard for "justice" or the long-term public good. Madison possessed the keener understanding of the vices of established democratic systems.

But there are other lessons to be learned from these impressive letters, both about the texture of the two Virginians' partnership for freedom and about the fundamental principles that both of them attempted, with at best a mixed success, to work into the infant federal system and to press into the public consciousness of their contemporaries and successors.

To grasp these other lessons, we might start by recognizing that the younger man did not, in truth, reject his colleague's doctrine root and branch. He said, instead, that he did not consider it "in *all* respects compatible with the course of human affairs," that limiting the term of "national acts" to the existence of the living generation "is *in some instances* not required by theory, and in others cannot be accommodated to practice."[25] On balance, to be sure, the instances to which he drew attention hardly constituted small exceptions. On the other hand, it is by no means accurate for commentators to suggest that Madison swept off his hat and bowed politely to his friend's idea before proceeding to destroy it, calling it a "great one," then rejecting nearly all its implications. The relationship between these statemen did not work that way. In fact, it would be hard to name a single instance in the long relationship in which the younger partner failed to find great merit in his friend's proposals and ideas. Certainly, in every case that has been pointed to repeatedly to illustrate their disagreements, he treated Jefferson's suggestions as entitled to unusual respect and even to at least a limited acceptance. Analysts should not be struck so forcefully by Madison's insistence on exceptions as not to recognize his general acceptance of the rules.

The right of living generations to revise a constitution, the people's sovereign right to act as the authority of last resort in cases where the different branches of their governments collided over the construction of the constitution, or—withal—the people's indefeasible authority to overturn their fundamental law entirely when their happiness required, were clearly not exceptions to the rule. Commentators on *The Federalist* or on the junior partner's criticisms of his friend's proposals for revising the Virginia constitution have been slow to notice that, in both these cases, Madison *began* with Jefferson's ideas—a fact suggesting that he surely saw them as the best afloat—modified or qualified the older man's suggestions, but did not reject the central principles in toto.[26] He did the same with Jefferson's assertion that the dead have no authority to make arrangements for the living. *True*, he says, in thinking through its applications, though practicality and theory both suggest that we cannot dispense entirely with the doctrine of implied consent.

Madison did demonstrate a sensitivity to a society's persistence through the generations which is largely lacking in the theoretical opinions of his friend. But let us not forget that Madison's most memorable achievements started with a bold assertion of the people's revolutionary right to overturn an established constitution, that he drew attention pridefully to the provision for amendments to the new one, and that he moved in the proceedings on the Bill of Rights for the insertion in the present Constitution of a declaration of the people's right to alter or abolish even that.[27] From Charles A. Beard until the present, scholarship has made too much of Madison's determination to protect the propertied minority from popular abuses. He *was* concerned with that, but taken as a whole, his life was anything except a stubborn and conservative defense of the established order—except so far as that established order was itself republican and dedicated to the proposition that the people have the right, and the capacity, to rule.

And let us also turn the point around. If Madison, like Jefferson, was wholly dedicated to the first great democratic revolution (and a champion, as well, of revolutionary change in France), Jefferson himself was not as altogether lacking in a sensitivity to intergenerational connections as is sometimes said or hinted. In the early stages of the Revolution overseas, as is well known, his practical advice was relatively cautious, grounded as it was on skepticism that the French had been prepared by their historical experience to move beyond a limited monarchy like Britain's to a fully popular regime. But even as a theorist—and even in the letter we are currently reviewing—Jefferson could demonstrate a more profound awareness of the links between the generations than some of his detractors would suggest.[28]

The letter on the rights of living generations was inspired, as Jefferson remarked and analysts have often emphasized, by what was happening or what seemed possible in France. The letter was addressed, however, to the legislative leader of the newly reconstructed government of the United States. It was not an unadulterated exercise in abstract theory. It also had specific policy objectives, and these objectives throw a different light on Jefferson's concerns as well as on his friend's reception of the doctrine.

Commentaries on the famous letters have traditionally focused on the sentences suggesting regular revision of the laws and on the passages discussing implications of the concept for the old regime in France. From this perspective, Jefferson was obviously justifying to himself (and to the philosophically inclined of every age and country) what was soon to prove the most complete and shattering upheaval in the history of Western Europe. In France, he plainly thought, the laws of nature authorized the total reconstruction of the social and political arrangements saddled on the living by the dead. Living Frenchmen were entitled to destroy hereditary privilege and titles, confiscate estates, reclaim the lands that had belonged for generations to the Church, revoke the charters of established corporations, and, in short, to make a wholly new arrangement of their common stock—all of this without obligatory compensation to the current claimants. The natural rights of living generations trump prescription and permit the overthrow of even the most ancient ordinary statutes.

But this was not the lesson Jefferson was asking Madison to teach, and these were not the applications he expected or desired in the United States. Although the letter does contain a most important paragraph applying the idea to France, the central topic of the missive is the proper management of national debts, a subject Jefferson was well aware would be the principal preoccupation of the coming, second session of the new federal Congress. His most specific or immediate objective was to get his friend to bring the principle to bear in these discussions (and in Congress' initial laws concerning patents, copyrights, and such).[29] Considered in this context, it is clear that Jefferson as well as Madison was thinking more of duties than of rights. As he envisioned it in operation on the western side of the Atlantic, Jefferson's insistence on the rights of living generations had as much to do with the *responsibilities* entailed upon the living by the rights of their *descendants* as with any claim the present might assert against the past.[30]

"Your station in the councils of our country," Jefferson advised, "gives you an opportunity of . . . forcing [the idea] into discussion." There, admittedly, it might at first be "rallied" as a flight of speculative fancy. Nevertheless, a statement of this principle "would furnish matter for a fine preamble to our first law for appropriating the public revenue; and it will exclude at the threshold of our government the contagious and ruinous errors of this quarter of the globe, which have armed despots with means, not sanctioned by nature, for binding in chains their fellow men." America, he pointed out, had given other nations one example of an efficacious means of chaining up "the dog of war, by transferring the power of letting him loose from the executive to the legislature, from those who are to spend to those who are to pay." A declaration that the nation's borrowing would not exceed the current generation's ability to repay might prove a "second obstacle" to wars. And, in America, a declaration of this sort would be entirely feasible as well theoretically correct, "since we do not owe a shilling which may not be paid with ease, principal and interest, within the time of our own lives." Moreover, an acceptance of the maxim in the early laws concerning revenues and debts could lay the groundwork for establishing the principle that patents, copyrights, and other claims to an exclusive exploitation should be limited to nineteen years as well.

What was Madison's response? He did, as has been said,

object that debts incurred to benefit descendants might legitimately extend beyond the lifetime of the current generation. He did confess that he had "little hope" of seeing the enactment of the principle at issue, "the spirit of philosophical legislation" having never reached some portions of the Union or even coming into fashion in the Congress. He also said, however, that his friend's idea suggested "many interesting reflections to legislators, particularly when contracting and providing for public debts." None of his objections, he explained, were "meant . . . to impeach either the utility of the principle in some particular cases or the general importance of it in the eye of the philosophical legislator. On the contrary, it would give me singular pleasure to see it first announced in the proceedings of the U. States, and always kept in their view as a salutary curb on the living generation from imposing unjust or unnecessary burdens on their successors."[31]

Madison's reply to Jefferson's discussion of the rights of living generations was written just before the House of Representatives initiated its discussion of the funding of the revolutionary debt—exactly seven days, in fact, before the younger partner intervened in those deliberations with a shocking plan to unilaterally rewrite the government's existing contracts with the holders of its notes. For this—although the standard studies of the episode are silent on the point—is just what Madison's proposal to discriminate between original and secondary holders would have done. Disgusted by the speculative orgy fueled by Hamilton's report, understanding that the secretary's plan implied enormous windfall profits for the monied few who had acquired certificates of debt for fractions of their face value (mostly from the former revolutionary soldiers who had sold the government's uncertain promises for cash), and drawing back in horror from the prospect that the nation would "erect the monuments of her gratitude, not to those who saved her liberties, but to those who had enriched themselves in her funds," Madison insisted that the case was so extraordinary that it had to be decided "on the great and fundamental principles of justice," not on ordinary principles of law.[32] As an alternative to Hamilton's insistence that the debt be funded at its full face value, to the present holders of the notes, Madison suggested paying secondary holders the highest value that certificates had reached on private money markets, subtracting that amount from the certificates' face value, and returning the remainder to the citizens to whom the notes had been originally issued.[33]

Madison's opponents, who were legion on this issue, saw his resolution as a violent breech of governmental contract, certain to destroy the country's credibility with future lenders. They understood immediately—and threw it in his face— that his proposal would involve as gross a governmental interference with existing private bargains as any of the stay laws, moratoria on taxes, or paper money schemes that he had earlier condemned. Indeed, I think it no exaggeration to suggest that Madison's discrimination plan was probably the era's clearest instance of a scheme that would have taken property from some and given it to others on considerations that were plainly redistributive in their intent.

Madison, of course, might well have said that putting things this way is not entirely fair. For him, discrimination was a case of simple justice. The Confederation's inability to keep its promises in 1783 (and for some years thereafter) had compelled disbanding revolutionary soldiers, who were paid with promissory notes, to sell their final-settlement certificates for fractions of their face value. Victims of the government's original default, they would be victimized again by Hamilton's insistence that the federal government must now fulfill the letter of its promise: to pay a certain sum, with interest, to the bearers of its notes. Madison recoiled from the injustice. Ordinary citizens, including former soldiers, were never to receive the value they had given at the moment of the nation's greatest need. On top of that, these ordinary citizens were now to pay the taxes that would fill the pockets of the men who had been quick to take advantage of their situation. This, he thought, was dreadful policy as well as an egregious violation of the moral principles on which republics ought to act.

To Madison, the sheer injustice of the funding plan was rendered all the more outrageous by its other implications. With Jefferson and many other revolutionaries, Madison believed that sound republics have to rest upon a relative equality of wealth, that people's governments are incompatible with huge disparities between the many and a few. Property, in this conception—landed property was the ideal—was the foundation for the personal autonomy that made it possible for citizens to vote or fight according to their own desires, not according to the wishes of their landlords or employers, whose economic power could become too great for the political equality that was the central feature of republics. Madison's resistance to the Treasury's proposals flowed from these considerations too, from the beginning and, increasingly, as Hamilton unveiled his larger economic program in his series of reports.[34]

Nothing in Madison's papers, to my knowledge, proves that he approved—or disapproved—of Jefferson's provision in his drafts of constitutions for Virginia for a grant of fifty acres of public land to any citizen who lacked it. But there is much in Madison's career to show that he was deeply sympathetic to the spirit of the measure—and to others that would operate to level great extremes of wealth (providing always, to be sure, that government respected both the positive and natural rights of property in cases where the government's default was not the source of the original injustice). From the early 1780s through the younger man's retirement, Madison and Jefferson worked constantly to open western lands and to connect the older states to new ones in the Mississippi Valley. Expansion over space of the republic of the Jeffersonian ideal—a nation resting squarely on a sturdy base of independent farmer-owners—was a well-defined alternative to Hamilton's design for rapid and intensive economic growth, which the Virginians feared would replicate the miseries and inequalities of Europe.[35] Partible inheritance, taxation in proportion to ability to pay, avoidance of monopolies of commerce, and resistance to the grant of property in perpetuity to corporations (even churches)—all were Madisonian as well as Jeffersonian ideas.[36] And nearly all of them displayed at least as much concern for the conditions under which posterity would live as for the welfare of the current generation.

Finally, of course, the most immediate proposal of the famous letter on the rights of living generations—that America should lead the world in stating and in making it a fundamental practice that the living would confine their borrowing to sums that they themselves could pay—became a central policy for Jeffersonian Republicans from their beginnings through the Age of Jackson, when they became the Democratic Party. Madison's initial opposition to the funding bill was based in part on its inequities, in part on the impolicy of widening the gap between the many and the few, but in another part, as well, on his resistance to provisions meant to limit the amount of principal redeemable in any year, provisions he regarded quite correctly as intended to prolong or even to perpetuate the national debt.[37]

Jefferson articulated one of his and Madison's concerns in one of several late-life letters recapitulating the ideas of 1789:

> We must not let our rulers load us with perpetual debt. We must make our election between *economy and liberty* or *profusion and servitude*. If we run into such debts as that we must

be taxed in our meat and in our drink, in our necessaries and our comforts, in our labors and our amusements, for our callings and our creeds, as the people of England are, our people, like them, must come to labor sixteen hours in the twenty-four, give the earnings of fifteen of these to the government for their debts and daily expenses; and the sixteenth being insufficient to afford us bread, we must live, as they now do, on oatmeal and potatoes; have no time to think, no means of calling the mismanagers to account; but be glad to obtain subsistence by hiring ourselves to rivet their chains on the necks of our fellow-sufferers. Our landholders, too, like theirs, retaining indeed the title and stewardship of estates called theirs, but held really in trust for the treasury, must . . . be contented with penury, obscurity, exile, and the glory of the nation. . . . . Private fortunes are destroyed by public as well as by private extravagance. And this is the tendency of all human governments. A departure from principle in one instance becomes a precedent for a second; that second for a third; and so on, till the bulk of the society is reduced to be mere automatons of misery, and to have no sensibilities left but for sinning and suffering. Then begins, indeed, the *bellum omnium in omnia* [the war of all against all], which some philosophers observing to be so general in this world, have mistaken it for the natural, instead of the abusive, state of man. And the fore-horse of this frightful team is public debt. Taxation follows that, and in its train wretchedness and oppression.[38]

Madison expressed another worry (not as colorfully, of course, but in a manner that confirmed his large agreement with the precept) in an essay written early in the party struggle over Hamilton's designs. Building on his friend's determination to erect another obstacle to wars, the legislative leader took the maxim yet another step:

War should not only be declared by the authority of the people, whose toils and treasures are to support its burdens, instead of the government which is to reap its fruits, but each generation should be made to bear the burden of its own wars, instead of carrying them on at the expense of other generations. . . . Each generation should not only bear its own burdens, but . . . the taxes . . . should include a due proportion of such as by their direct operation keep the people awake . . . to misapplications of their money.[39]

The Jeffersonian Republicans despised a public debt, for every year that it existed, they believed, was one more year in which the taxes of productive artisans and farmers would fill the purses of the non-productive rich. They never recommended its repudiation, to be sure, but they were willing to subordinate much else to its retirement with as much dispatch as preexisting governmental contracts would permit. Jefferson proclaimed the purpose in his first inaugural address, and his administration followed it with such consistency that Henry Adams charged them with assuming that the national debt posed greater dangers to the country than the risk of foreign aggression.[40]

Obviously, we have learned some lessons from these founders better than some others. We insist upon our rights, but live upon our children, eating up the usufruct that properly belongs to future generations. In 1992 alone, we added $340 billion to the national debt, saddling future generations with an annual tax of roughly $24 billion—in perpetuity, of course, if recent history is any guide—merely to make the interest payments on the money borrowed during this single year: about the same amount we spend each year for food stamps ($25 billion). Annual interest payments on a national debt of more than $4 trillion are now $200 billion: more than two and a half times the annual cost of Medicare ($76 billion); significantly more than the combined annual cost of all means-tested federal programs ($162 billion); more than any other items of the federal budget except Social Security and national defense.[41] During the 1980s, we retreated from the imposition of progressive taxes. To save a few from dislocations (or to save the relatively modest taxes necessary if we were to see these dislocations as a public charge and burden), we hesitated to require the preservation of the land on which descendants are to live. Most Americans, for now, can manage to avoid the blight and poverty of devastated inner cities, with their swelling underclasses and appalling violence, although these consequences of the current malapportionment of wealth would surely have been seen by Jefferson or Madison as probably the greatest danger to the very viability of the republic.[42] But there are signs, our optimistic selves may say, of an increasing consciousness of our responsibilities as well as of our rights.[43] There are undoubtedly important precedents from our beginnings as a nation for a politics that might be conscious of them both.

NOTES

1. Jefferson to Madison, September 6, 1789, *PJM*, 12:382–87, quotation at 386. Also in *PTJ*, 15:392–97. Document 15.

2. Jefferson had received permission for a leave of absence, from which he would never return. As things turned out, he carried the letter, dated August 26, with him to America, talked about its contents with Madison when they were together at Monticello in December, but did not actually mail it until January 9, 1790.

3. "Usufruct" was a Roman legal concept referring to a right to make such use of a thing as does not damage the substance of the thing itself, to enjoy the fruits and profits of an estate for a period of years or for life. Developing his principle in a late-life letter to John Wayles Eppes, in which he still referred to it as "no less a [natural] law" than those formally acknowledged in American declarations of rights, Jefferson again compared the situation of a current holder of land to that of a tenant for life (June 24, 1813, in *Thomas Jefferson: Writings* ["Library of America," 1984],

1280–1282; document 17). For another late-life development of the principle, see Jefferson to Samuel Kercheval, July 12, 1816, *ibid.*, 1400–1402, quoted in the text below and printed as document 30.

4. Merrill Peterson, *Thomas Jefferson and the New Nation: A Biography* (New York, 1970), 383; John Locke, *Two Treatises of Government*, ed. Peter Laslett (2nd ed.; Cambridge, 1980), chap. 5: "Of Property." (The latter should be read all the way through to p. 302, Locke's paragraph 51: "In governments [in contrast to in nature] the laws regulate the right of property, and the possession of land is determined by positive constitutions.") Jefferson's acceptance of this concept of land ownership went back at least as far as his *Summary View of the Rights of British America* of 1774: "All the lands within the limits which any particular society has circumscribed around itself are assumed by that society, and subject to their allotment only. This may be done by themselves assembled collectively, or by their legislature to whom they may have delegated sovereign authority; and if they are alloted in neither of these ways, each individual of the society may appropriate to himself such lands as he finds vacant, and occupancy will give him title" (*PTJ*, I, 133). For more on the natural law thinkers on property, see, as a beginning, C. B. Macpherson, *The Political Theory of Possessive Individualism* (Oxford, 1962); Richard Tuck, *Natural Rights Theories: Their Origin and Development* (Cambridge, 1979), James Tully, *A Discourse on Property: John Locke and His Adversaries* (Cambridge, 1979); Thomas A. Horne, *Property Rights and Poverty: Political Argument in Britain, 1605–1834* (Chapel Hill, N.C., 1990); Michael P. Zuckert, *Natural Rights and the New Republicanism* (Princeton, 1994); and Jerome Huyler, *Locke in America* (Lawrence, Kans., 1994), chaps. 4–5.

5. Peterson quotes Adam Smith as having asserted "that every successive generation of men have . . . an equal right to the earth, and to all that it possesses" (*Thomas Jefferson*, 383). Adrienne Koch, *Jefferson and Madison: The Great Collaboration* (New York, 1964), 81–88, argues persuasively that it is more likely that Thomas Paine drew on conversations with Jefferson or on a draft of Jefferson's letter to Madison for "strikingly similar" language in *The Rights of Man* than that Jefferson got the point from 1789

conversations with Paine. I would also agree with Koch that an early September note from Jefferson's English physician, Dr. Richard Gem—available in *PTJ*, 15:391–92 and assumed by Peterson (383) and Julian Boyd to have stimulated the letter to Madison—reads more like a limited rebuttal of thoughts that Jefferson had already communicated to Gem. (The fullest discussion of Gem and his possible influence is in Boyd's editorial note, *PTJ*, 15:384–87.) Certainly, both Gem and Paine were intermittently included in the circle of liberal French aristocrats who were engaged with Jefferson in the "course of reflection" prompted by the Revolution, and we cannot be sure who first advanced the propositions Gem discussed: "That one generation of men in civil society have no right to make acts to bind another," that "the earth and all things whatever can only be conceived to belong to the living; the dead and those who are unborn can have no rights of property." But these would seem such logical extrapolations from the matrix of Enlightened theory that any member of this circle might have gone this far. No one else, however, seems to have anticipated what would follow.

6. See document 15 for Jefferson's fuller denial that the power to repeal a law, when joined with the concept of tacit consent, is equivalent to a power to act afresh. The best discussion of Jefferson's originality in this letter is Herbert Sloan, "'The Earth Belongs in Usufruct to the Living,'" in *Jeffersonian Legacies*, ed. Peter S. Onuf (Charlottesville, Va., 1993), 281–315, which appeared after my lecture was delivered. "Characteristically," Sloan remarks, Jefferson "took matters literally and pressed on where others stopped." The concept that the earth belongs to the living generation was commonplace, but "the principle that the earth belongs *in usufruct* to the living generation *of nineteen years* was something new" (299, with my italics emphasizing Sloan's main point.)

7. On August 11, the National Assembly had in fact abolished most feudal privileges in France.

8. Jefferson to Madison, October 28, 1785, *PTJ*, 8:681–82; *PJM*, 8:385–87. Document 13.

9. The reference to a right to a subsistence—or, to put it more precisely, a right to earn a subsistence—is borrowed from Koch,

79, who misindentified the recipient of the letter of 1785 but was the first of many to relate it to the observations of 1789.

10. Jefferson, of course, was the prime mover of Virginia's revolutionary abolition of the ancient laws of primogeniture and entail, which had fallen out of use but were intended to preserve the great estates by passing them intact to eldest sons of individuals who died intestate. In his 1776 draft of a constitution for Virginia (*Thomas Jefferson: Writings*, 343) he has also provided for a grant of 50 acres (and with it the right to vote) to anyone who lacked that much, although he does not seem to have been thinking at that time of a natural right to a subsistence.

11. Here I do not wish to represent Jefferson as more radical than he was. This was the same man who wrote: "To take from one, because it is thought his own industry *or that of his fathers* had acquired too much, in order to spare to others who, *or whose fathers*, have not exercised equal industry and skill, is to violate arbitrarily the free principle of association, the guarantee to everyone a free exercise of his industry and the fruits acquired by it" (Jefferson to Joseph Milligan, August 16, 1813—my italics). Even in the letter of 1785—document 13—after reflecting on "that unequal division of property which occasions the numberless instances of wretchedness . . . in this country and . . . all over Europe," Jefferson specifically observed that he was "conscious that an equal division of lands is impracticable," focusing his disapproval on disparities so huge that great proprietors were placed "above attention to the increase of their revenues" and able to keep vast tracts completely idle, "mainly for the sake of game." The practical and "politic" solutions, he suggested, were laws requiring "the descent of property of every kind . . . to all the children . . . in equal degree," together with exemption from taxation for the very poor and "geometrical progression" of the taxes on the rich. Legislation of this sort would work against excessive concentrations of property and still accord with the "natural affections of the human mind," without endangering the just protection of the fruits of different levels of industry and skill. Nevertheless, Jefferson implied that the right to earn a subsistence had priority over positive laws and the wishes of the rich. The unemployed could evidently cultivate the unimproved lands of the rich whether

the owners liked it or not, "paying a moderate rent."

12. Koch, *The Great Collaboration*, 72; Peterson, *Thomas Jefferson*, 384. The editors of *PJM* entitle their headnote "Madison's Rebuttal to 'the Earth Belongs to the Living' Concept." Additional examples are discussed below.

13. Madison to Jefferson, February 4, 1790, *PJM*, 13:18–21. Document 16.

14. See his *Federalist* 49, discussed more fully below.

15. The final passage here also echoes a neglected point from *The Federalist* 44. We have too seldom recognized that Madison's complaint against the "mutability" of legislation, which he often made in close conjunction with complaints about majority "injustice," was grounded no less firmly on his sense that "sudden changes and legislative interferences in cases affecting personal rights become jobs in the hands of enterprising and influential speculators and snares to the more industrious and less informed part of the community." Madison was as much concerned as Jefferson to shield the ordinary laborer or farmer from advantage-taking by the few.

16. For Locke on tacit consent—and some of Jefferson's reasons for challenging this doctrine—see the Second Treatise, paragraphs 118–22.

17. Koch, *The Great Collaboration*, 63, 70, 209.

18. Richard K. Matthews, *The Radical Politics of Thomas Jefferson: A Revisionist View* (Lawrence, Kans., 1984), 23–24, and chap. 2 more broadly.

19. *Ibid.*, 24, 98.

20. Drew R. McCoy, *The Last of the Fathers: James Madison and the Republican Legacy* (New York, 1989), 44–73. The letters on the rights of living generations are discussed at 53–60.

21. *Ibid.*, 44–45, 53.

22. *Ibid.*, 57.

23. *Ibid.*, 58–60.

24. Madison's imagination, however, was strong; and it is possible that he compared the plight of Europe's masses to conditions in the slave society around him. At the Constitutional Convention, he remarked that he had seen "the mere distinction of color made in the most enlightened period of time, a ground of

the most oppressive dominion ever exercised by man over man" (speech of June 6, *Records of the Federal Convention*, 1:135).

25. Document 16. The first set of italics are Madison's, the second set is mine.

26. *The Federalist* 49, reprinted as document 18, was certainly not a gratuitous attack on Jefferson's suggestion that conventions of the people should decide in cases where the branches of the government disagreed on the construction of the Constitution. This was an idea that Madison had himself explicitly endorsed in his recommendations for a constitution for Kentucky (Madison to Caleb Wallace, *PJM*, 8:350–57); and in the forty-ninth *Federalist*. Before developing his objections to a *frequent* recurrence to the people, Madison allows that "a constitutional road to the decision of the people ought to be marked out and kept open for certain great and extraordinary occasions." Similarly, his recommendations for a constitution for Kentucky *began* with Jefferson's proposed revisions of the constitution of Virginia and disagreed with Jefferson mostly over details.

27. During the 1780s Madison referred to the Articles of Confederation quite often as the "constitution" and concerned himself repeatedly with what was "constitutional" within their framework. See Banning, "James Madison and the Nationalists, 1780–1783," *William and Mary Quarterly*, 3rd ser., 40 (1983): 227–55. For his assertion of the revolutionary right to overturn the Articles, see *The Federalist* 43 and 45.

28. Ralph Lerner remarked at this point that we might also remember Jefferson's caution as a member of the committee to revise Virginia's laws. He opposed Edmund Pendleton's suggestion that the committee write a whole new code.

29. Julian Boyd was uncharacteristically obtuse in his editorial note on the letter, which argued that the great body of the text was "irrelevant to the existing situation in America," that Jefferson's applications of the doctrine to that situation were essentially an afterthought, "anti-climactic and almost trivial" (*PTJ*, 388–89). Contrast Sloan, who insists that the issue foremost in Jefferson's mind was what was to be done in America, not in France (284), and who traces the germination of the concept partly to Jefferson's struggle with the load of debt he had assumed along with his father-in-law's estate.

30. With other commentators, Sloan generally emphasizes the differences between the two Virginians (300), but he also sees the "Burkean" dimension of Jefferson's suggestion (299). The earth belongs to the living only *in usufruct*, only in trust. "The freedom each generation enjoys is circumscribed by the duty to respect the rights of its successors" (281–81).

31. Although the burden of their commentaries emphasizes Madison's objections to the concept, most commentators do acknowledge his favorable reaction to this point. Koch, *The Great Collaboration*, 73–74, is probably the most emphatic: "In the main, [Madison] himself accepted Jefferson's objective[s]: to make constitutions sensitive to the majority will of each successive generation"; and also to require the present generation "to respect the natural rights—the basic needs—of coming generations." See also Peterson, *Thomas Jefferson*, 384.

32. Speech of February 18, 1790, *PJM*, 13:48–49.

33. Madison's opposition to Hamilton's funding and assumption plans is discussed in more detail in chap. 10 of Banning, *The Sacred Fire of Liberty*.

34. On these points see Drew R. McCoy, *The Elusive Republic: Political Economy in Jeffersonian America* (Chapel Hill, N.C., 1980), and my own forthcoming essay, "Political Economy and the Creation of the Constitution," in David Konig, ed., *Devising Liberty*, vol. 5 of *A History of Modern Freedom* (Stanford, Calif., 1995).

35. The sources just cited provide fuller references on these points. But some of the best known examples include query xix of Jefferson's *Notes on the State of Virginia* and Madison's 1792 essays "Republican Distribution of Citizens" and "Fashion," included as documents 19–21.

36. See the note on "Monopolies, Perpetuities, and Corporations" in James Madison, "Detached Memoranda," ed. Elizabeth Fleet, *William and Mary Quarterly*, 3rd ser., 3 (1946), 556–58. Jefferson, of course—see chapter one—would have included an absolute prohibition of monopolies in the Bill of Rights.

37. For Madison's repeated denunciations of prolonging or "perpetuating" the national debt, see his speeches of Febuary 11 and March 10–12, 1790, together with Madison to Henry Lee, April 13, 1790, in *PJM* 13:34–39, 99–100, 148. To protect credi-

tors against early calls of their notes, Hamilton's original plan would have limited redemption of the debt to one percent per year. The annual profits from the postal service, estimated at $100,000, would have been deposited into a sinking fund and used from time to time to purchase the securities on private markets.

38. Jefferson to Samuel Kercheval, July 12, 1816, in *Thomas Jefferson: Writings*, 1400–1401. Document 30.

39. "Universal Peace," which appeared originally in the *National Gazette* of January 31, 1792 is reprinted in *PJM*, 14:107–8 and included below as document 22. Here, of course, Madison was thinking of wars based on "reasons of state," not wars to protect descendents as well as the current generation from the consequences of being conquered.

40. Henry Adams, *History of the United States During the Administrations of Thomas Jefferson and James Madison*, 9 vols. (New York, 1889–1890), 1:251. See, further, Lance Banning, *The Jeffersonian Persuasion* (Ithaca, N.Y., 1978), 277–79.

41. Statistics, rounded to the nearest billion, are from the January 1994 report of the Congressional Budget Office on "The Economic and Budget Outlook: Fiscal Years 1995–1999," principally tables 2–1, 2–6, 2–9, and E–2. The deficit figure includes the $50 billion borrowed from the Social Security Trust Fund. Annual interest payments on the debt are projected at $298 billion rather than $200 billion in 1994 if we include the interest being paid to this and other trust funds. This $298 billion might be compared to a total of only $229 billion for all non-defense discretionary spending. Annual interest payments on the debt, with interest rates at multi-year lows, are currently equal to 57% of the revenues from all personal income tax receipts. The national debt now amounts to more than $16,000 for every American man, woman, and child. The 1992 deficit alone amounted to $1,300 for every American.

42. CBS News reported on September 3, 1992, that there were 250 violent deaths per month in Los Angeles in July and August of that year. The Census Bureau figures that, in 1991, 35.7 million Americans (14.2%) were living in poverty, which they define as cash income of less than $14,000 for a family of four. Thirty

million were judged to be inadequately nourished. One in four Americans benefits from food stamps.

43. Federal taxes have become slightly more progressive since 1990 and are now about as progressive as in 1977. The effective federal tax rate in 1994 is estimated at 5.1% for the least wealthy 20% of the population, 27.7% for the most wealthy 20%. The spending cuts and tax increases of the Omnibus Budget Reconciliation Act of 1993 promise that the budget deficit will shrink from $255 billion in 1993 (excluding the $50 billion borrowed from Social Security) to $170 billion in 1995 before rising again to about $200 billion in 1999. These are still, of course, stupendous figures. We will add a trillion dollars of debt between 1990 and the end of 1994, almost none of it to benefit succeeding generations. Even if the budget act of 1993 is scrupulously respected (and we use fairly optimistic projections for interest rates), we still will add about a trillion dollars of new debt between 1992 and 1996.

THREE

Public Spirit

I hold it that a little rebellion now and then is a good thing, and as necessary in the political world as storms in the physical.[1]

The tree of liberty must be refreshed from time to time with the blood of patriots and tyrants. It is its natural manure.[2]

RADICALS ADORE THOMAS JEFFERSON, and some conservatives despise him, for his often-quoted praise of popular rebellions. Few in either camp have fully understood him, just as few in any camp at all have fully understood some famous passages in which James Madison is often said (with undertones of either praise or blame) to have abandoned revolutionary dreams of a regime erected on the people's virtue in favor of a realistic scheme of government that might secure essential rights and long-term public goods even in a world where individuals are bent almost exclusively on the pursuit of selfish interests:

57

Ambition must be made to counteract ambition. The interest of the man must be connected with the constitutional rights of the place. It may be a reflection on human nature that such devices should be necessary to control the abuses of government. But what is government itself but the greatest of all reflections on human nature? If men were angels, no government would be necessary. If angels were to govern men, neither external nor internal controls on government would be necessary. In framing a government which is to be administered by men over men, the great difficulty lies in this: You must first enable the government to control the governed; and in the next place, oblige it to control itself. A dependence on the people is no doubt the primary control on the government; but experience has taught mankind the necessity of auxiliary precautions.[3]

Juxtaposed so starkly, passages like these might seem to speak primarily to underlying differences between the two Virginians; and, in fact, some students of the long relationship believe that it was under greater strain when these remarks were written than at any other time.[4] However that may be, a fuller understanding of these famous comments must begin by fitting them into their contexts. When that is done, they may not seem as unrelated to each other, or to other passages from both men's writings, as might at first appear. The link, I will suggest, can be discovered in an underlying concept of the civic life that guided Madison as well as Jefferson throughout their partnership for freedom.

This concept, to be sure, is one that neither of these statesman ever wrote about with philosophical precision—one, perhaps, that both of them assumed was generally familiar in their time, however often citizens and politicians needed a reminder. It is a concept that historians and theorists have argued over at great length, but still have not explored as thoroughly or systematically as they will have to do if they are ever to resolve some current controversies over the political inheritance and culture of the new republic.[5] It is a concept, too, that citizens might bring to bear in analyzing modern problems, some of which could surely be ascribed to modern ignorance, forgetfulness, or even sheer contempt for what the two Virginians had in mind.

A label for this bundle of ideas is problematic. Madison referred to it on one occasion as "a spirit of diffusive patriotism,"[6] although the modern usage of this term is far too narrow to convey his meaning. To call it "civic virtue" would be better, but this might court a jaundiced hearing from the scholars who believe that we have heard enough of "virtue," "civic humanism," and the like. Talk of civic virtue was, in any case, a bit old-fashioned by the early 1790s, though Madison and others did continue to employ that terminology from time to time and, certainly, were still attempting to articulate ideas about the character of citizenship in a republic—among the populace, among their leaders, and between those leaders and the people—which did, indeed, derive from neo-classical traditions. For want of more imagination, then, and in an effort to avoid these problems, let me call it simply *public spirit*; and let me offer some preliminary thoughts about the content of this concept in the minds of these two founders, bare beginning though these thoughts may be toward the intensive exploration which is ultimately needed.

Jefferson's remarks on popular rebellions (1787) offer a beginning. In western Massachusetts, farmers had been struggling since the peace with heavy debts, hard times, and insufficient specie. Their hardships were compounded when the eastern-dominated legislature levied higher, specie taxes in an ill-advised determination to retire the revolutionary debt. Popular conventions in the western counties asked the legislature for relief. When it refused, petitioning gave way to open insurrection. Fearing seizures or foreclosures on their property, crowds of farmers forced the courts to close in several western counties and, under local leaders such as Daniel Shays, a revolutionary captain in the Continental Army, began to organize for further action. During the winter of 1786–1787, as the states appointed delegates to the Constitutional Convention, Massachusetts forces under William Shepard and Benjamin Lincoln marched into the western counties, shattered the resistance, and defeated the rebellion.[7]

Jefferson did not, in truth, approve of this particular rebellion. The very letters praising insurrections also spoke of "anarchy" in Massachusetts and described the Shaysites' acts as "absolutely unjustifiable."[8] Both letters, nonetheless, moved on immediately to state the author's hope that the insurgency would not provoke "severities" from the New England governments or lead Americans "too hastily" to think that anarchy was spreading everywhere in the United States, proving that the human character "was insusceptible of any other government but that of force."[9] Jefferson was more concerned that popular disturbances would generate a dangerous reaction than he was with the insurgency itself. Admitting that a certain "turbulence" was an endemic "evil" of a popular regime, he nevertheless insisted, first that these "irregularities" were "nothing" in comparison to the "oppressions" of a European system—"a government of wolves over sheep"—and second that the evil was itself productive of some good. "It prevents the degeneracy of government, and nourishes a general attention to the public affairs." "An observation of this truth should render republican governors so mild in their punishment of rebellions as not to discourage them too much. It is a medicine necessary for the sound health of government."[10]

Jefferson's initial reading of the Constitution tended to confirm his fear of a conservative reaction sparked by Shays's Rebellion. The hirelings of the British ministry, he wrote, had hammered out their "lies" about American conditions until Americans themselves were starting to believe them. The Constitutional Convention had been overly alarmed by the rebellion, "and in the spur of the moment, they are setting up a kite to keep the henyard in order." But where, except in Massachusetts, he asked John Adams's son-in-law, had anarchy ever existed in the new United States? And "God forbid we should ever be 20 years without such a [relatively harmless] rebellion."

> The people cannot be all, and always, well informed. The part which is wrong will be discontented in proportion to the importance of the facts they misconceive. If they remain quiet under such misconceptions, it is a lethargy, the forerunner of death to the public liberty. We have had 13 states independent 11 years. There has been one rebellion. That comes to one rebellion in a century and a half for each state. What country before ever existed a century and half without a rebellion? And what country can preserve its liberties if their rulers are not warned from time to time that their people preserve the spirit of resistance? Let them take arms. The remedy is to set them right as to facts, pardon and pacify them. What signify a few lives lost in a century or two? The tree of liberty must be refreshed from time to time with the blood of patriots and tyrants. It is its natural manure.

To Jefferson, the people's vigilance and spirit of resistance were the very lifeblood of republics.[11]

James Madison, recipient of some of these remarks, was more disturbed by Shays's Rebellion. Early on, he took respected correspondents at their word when they reported frantically distorted "news" from Massachusetts. Repeating language from a frightening report from Henry Lee, he told his father that the rebels were "as numerous" as the supporters of the Massachusetts government "and more decided in their measures. . . . They profess to aim only at a reform of their constitution and of certain abuses in the public administration, but an abolition of debts public and private and a new division of property are strongly suspected to be in contemplation."[12] Soon thereafter, Washington informed him that intelligence from Henry Knox reported that the rebels' "creed is that the property of the United States has been protected from confiscation of Britain by the joint exertions of *all* and therefore ought to be the *common property* of all." Knox suggested, Washington continued, that the Massachusetts rebels could be joined by discontented farmers from Connecticut, Rhode Island, and New Hampshire "so as to constitute a body of twelve or fifteen thousand desperate and unprincipled men, . . . chiefly of the young and active part of the country."[13] Other correspondents warned that Shays's forces might be leagued with the Vermonters and that British agents were encouraging the insurrection.[14] Madison was primed to credit that as well.[15]

The gross exaggerations circulating in the fall of 1786 had been corrected by the time that Madison and others gathered for the Constitutional Convention. In the meantime, nevertheless, the young reformer called this armed revolt within the commonwealth whose constitution many thought of as the best in the United States, "distressing beyond measure to the zealous friends of the Revolution."[16] Hardly less distressing were the widespread rumors of a rapid growth of deeply counterrevolutionary sentiments among New England's leading men and, just as the convention opened, authentic news of Shaysite sentiments and acts in Madison's own Virginia.[17] The constitutional provisions guaranteeing every state a republican form of government and permitting federal intervention to suppress "domestic violence" were direct results of Shays's Rebellion, as was Madison's acknowledgement that force and right, power and the will of the majority, could not be automatically assumed to be "synonimous" in a republic.[18]

But this is not to say that Madison himself was interested in setting up a hawk to keep the hens in order. Neither does it signal an agreement with the view that Madison intended to create a system that could guarantee the public good without requiring any virtue in the people, a system resting simply on the counterbalancing of interests, powers, and ambitions. As I have argued elsewhere, Madison's alarm about majority injustices and popular commotions was undoubtedly a major influence on the shaping of the Constitution. Nevertheless, predominant interpretations overemphasize these fears and gravely underestimate the very great extent to which the most important framer of the Constitution blamed the popular abuses on the weaknesses of the Confederation, set about to build a Union capable of treating underlying, economic sources of the troubles, and fixed his mind throughout on saving the republican experiments already underway in Massachusetts and Virginia.[19]

For Madison, the really frightening conclusions to be drawn from the American experience since Independence were not that men were selfish, not that they would take advantage of each other when they could, not even that the people might rebel against oppression. That much had seemed entirely obvious to English-speaking politicians long before the Revolution, which helps explain why framers of the first state constitutions had divided governmental powers and incorporated numerous protections for the people's fundamental rights. For Madison, the crisis came when he could not deny that even in republics, under poorly balanced constitutions, the majority itself could be a "faction," willing and imposing policies that seemed persistently at odds with private rights or long-term public needs—and when an armed minority resisted the majority in Massachusetts. In

Shays's Rebellion and in many other things, the foremost framer did indeed detect abundant signs of insufficient public virtue. Too many people seemed to be contemptuous of other people's rights, neglectful of the public business, or unwilling to submit themselves to the community's decisions. But the solution, Madison insisted, did not lie in doubting the necessity of virtue or denying that the body of the people still possessed sufficient virtue to maintain the revolutionary order. "Is there no virtue among us?" he would ask Virginia's state convention. "If there be not, we are in a wretched situation. No theoretical checks, no form of government, can render us secure. To suppose that any form of government will secure liberty or happiness without any virtue in the people, is a chimerical idea."[20]

For Madison, the sound solution to the crisis of the middle 1780s—the only remedy consistent with the revolutionary faith—was the creation of a large, compound republic, the establishment of governmental mechanisms calculated to impose additional restraints on passion, and national policies which could correct the economic difficulties that were at the source of moral and political malaise. "Most of our political evils," Madison had said, "can be traced up to our commercial ones, as most of our moral may to our political."[21] A flood of foreign luxuries, together with restricted foreign markets for domestic goods, was threatening the economic preconditions of a virtuous participation in the public life, making citizens incapable of looking further than their hardships and their wants.[22] But if these constitutional and economic weaknesses could be repaired, the people's underlying virtue could be reasserted; and Madison believed, as Jefferson believed, that in the last analysis, the people's virtue was the only ground on which the revolutionary enterprise could stand.

The people's virtue, to be sure, did not denote for Madison the Spartan quality of self-renouncing, superhuman dedication to an abstract public good that Montesquieu had said was known to moderns "only by tradition."[23] But it is probable that only a minority of revolutionary leaders ever wanted or expected such heroic, self-effacing, totally disinterested participation in political affairs. What most republicans demanded, what Madison described as indispensable in passages like these, and what he would encourage as consistently as Jefferson throughout the rest of their careers was pretty much what eighteenth-century critics of the British system of administration and finance had called for in the writings that impelled the early Revolution: jealous, vigilant commitment to the public life; a recognition on the part of all that a republican belongs to a community of self-governing equals; uncoerced submission to majority decisions; and continuing participation in a politics that trusted only limited responsibilities to national officials and demanded, even then, that these officials be continuously watched for any signs of an appearance of an interest separate from the interests of the body of the people. What Madison described as indispensable in a republic was not so very different from the spirit of resistance celebrated in his friend's remarks on popular rebellions—as, indeed, the younger man was very soon to prove.[24]

Here, I know, I may be flirting with extremes and should repeat that even Jefferson was not the unrestrained enthusiast for bloody, armed resistance who emerges when his comments on the tree of liberty are quoted out of context. Nevertheless, within three years of the initiation of the reconstructed government, the two Virginians did embark on a determined effort to arouse the people and encourage vigilant, continuous, intense involvement in the nation's public life, which both of them had come to see as seriously threatened by a governmental plot to undermine the Constitution and the Revolution.[25]

The people did become engaged. Indeed, by 1794, the

western parts of Pennsylvania were literally in arms against the excise tax on whiskey, levied to finance the federal assumption of the states' revolutionary debts.[26] Madison had voted for this tax, and neither he nor Jefferson condoned minority defiance of the law, which came to be more violent and extensive than had been the case in western Massachusetts eight years before. Thus, although the two Virginians watched uneasily as 13,000 federalized militia, with Alexander Hamilton along to represent the War Department, marched across the mountains and dispersed the Whiskey Rebels—this time, happily, without a fight—they both condemned the Pennsylvanians' conduct.[27] Then, however, in his annual message to Congress, Washington denounced the "self-created societies"—the Democratic-Republican clubs—whose agitation and denunciations he believed responsible for stirring up the trouble.[28] Calling this "the greatest error" of the president's political career—in private, he condemned a governmental censure of the popular societies as an "attack on the most sacred principles of our Constitution and of republicanism"—Madison responded much as Jefferson had done to news of Shays's Rebellion.[29]

Serving, as he always did, on the committee to prepare the House of Representatives' reply to Washington's address, Madison preferred to pass silently over the president's denunciation of the popular associations. His draft of a reply expressed the legislators' grief "that any part of our fellow citizens should have shown themselves capable of an insurrection"—the deep regret of good republicans that enemies of liberty might turn this "flagrant" violation of the "public order" into "a calumny against it"—then hurried on to note the members' gratification that the "great body" of the people had demonstrated to the world their firm attachment to the "luminous and vital principle . . . that the will of the majority shall prevail."[30] Federalists, however, were determined to employ the president's prestige to devastate the growing opposition to their measures. ("The game," said Madison, "was to connect the democratic societies with the odium of the insurrection—to connect the Republicans in Congress with those societies—[and] to put the President ostensibly at the head of the other party, in opposition to both.")[31] Therefore, even at the cost of public disagreement with the great commander, Madison resisted efforts to insert an echo of the president's remarks into the House reply. The actions, publications, and opinions of the popular societies, he said, were "innocent in the eye of the law" and "could not be the object of censure to a legislative body." When the people formed the Constitution, they had retained the rights that they did not expressly delegate to others. "Opinions are not the objects of legislation. . . . If we advert to the nature of republican government, we shall find that the censorial power is in the people over the government, and not in the government over the people."[32]

The House defeated Federalist attempts to echo the president's condemnation of the "self-created" clubs and rescued Washington from an implied rebuke by substituting a reference to the "individuals or combinations of men" who might have misrepresented government measures. Even this, of course, was more than Madison approved, but he had made his point that it was "indefensible in reason" and "dangerous in practice" to accept the principles that "arbitrary denunciations may punish what the law permits and what the legislature has no right, by law, to prohibit," that "the government may stifle all censures whatever on its misdoings; for if it be itself the judge, it will never allow any censures to be just, and if it can suppress censures flowing from one lawful source, it may [also suppress] those flowing from any other—from the press and from individuals as well as from societies, etc."[33] "If the people of America are so far degenerated already as not to see, or to see with indifference, that the Citadel of their liberties is menaced by such a precedent," he wrote to Jefferson, "they require abler advocates than they now have to save them from the consequences."[34]

In fact, of course, the people's liberties have rarely had a more effective champion than this Virginian. Madison was undeniably determined that the well-considered reason of the people, not their temporary passions, would direct the public course, that the majority would be restrained from violating private rights or sacrificing public needs to more immediate considerations. No American has ever given deeper thought to governmental mechanisms likely to secure these ends. But it is also true that no American has ever said more clearly that mechanical contrivances are not enough:

> In bestowing the eulogies due to the partitions and internal checks of power, it ought not the less to be remembered that they are neither the sole nor the chief paladium of constitutional liberty. The people, who are the authors of this blessing, must also be its guardians. Their eyes must be ever ready to mark, their voice to pronounce, and their arm to repel or repair aggressions on the authority of their constitutions.[35]

To Madison, as surely as to Jefferson, it never seemed sufficient to conceive of a republic merely as a government deriving from elections and providing multiple securities for people's private rights. This was essential, to be sure, and yet "the genius of republican liberty" required "not only that all power should be derived from the people, but that those entrusted with it should be kept in dependence on the people by a short duration of their appointments" and many other things.[36] If Madison expected, on the one hand, that the large election districts of the federal republic would encourage the selection of representatives who would be less inclined to sacrifice the rights of the minority or long-term public needs to the majority's immediate demands, he also understood that federal officials would be less familiar with the people's needs and better shielded from their wrath and clamors than the members of the state assemblies. Therefore, he insisted, the Constitution had entrusted federal officials only with those great and national matters, few and carefully defined, on which they *could* be trusted to reflect the people's needs and will, leaving local matters to the states.[37] Madison's defense of the completed Constitution had assumed from the beginning both that federal representatives would actually remain responsive to the people—that constitutional reform would not destroy the republican "communion of interests and sympathy of sentiments" between the rulers and the ruled—and that the people would defend the constitutional restrictions and divisions of responsibilities that they had built into their charter.[38]

In 1787, Jefferson had said that if he had to choose between "a government without newspapers or newspapers without a government," he would "not hesitate a moment to prefer the latter." This comment, too, was prompted by the insurrection in the western parts of Massachusetts—more precisely, by "the interposition of the people themselves on the side of government" to put the insurrection down. "The good sense of the people," Jefferson maintained,

> will always be found to be the best army. They may be led astray for a moment, but will soon correct themselves. The people are the only censors of their governors; and even their errors will tend to keep these to the true principles of their institution. . . . The way to prevent these irregular interpositions of the people is to give them full information of their affairs through the channel of the public papers, and to contrive that those papers should penetrate the whole mass of the people. The basis of our governments being the opinion of the people, the very first object should be to keep that right. . . . Cherish therefore

69

the spirit of our people, and keep alive their attention. Do not be too severe upon their errors, but reclaim them by enlightening them. If once they become inattentive to the public affairs, you and I and Congress and assemblies, judges and governors, shall all become wolves. It seems to be the law of our general nature, in spite of individual exceptions; and experience declares that man is the only animal which devours his own kind, for I can apply no milder term to the governments of Europe and to the general prey of the rich on the poor.[39]

Madison concurred. And so, as the Virginians came to see in Hamilton's financial schemes a program that could center governmental power in officials least responsive to the voters and "administer" the new republic toward a system certain to oppress the most productive portion of the people, their first response was to promote the founding of the *National Gazette*, a semi-weekly paper meant to educate the people and alert them to the danger. To that paper, during 1791 and 1792, Madison contributed some nineteen essays, many of them emphasizing that informed, continuous participation by the people was the ultimate security for every free regime, that citizens would have to be enlightened and united so "that after establishing a government, they should watch over it, as well as obey it."[40] Popular associations like the democratic clubs were other means to this essential end, and Madison was quick to take offense at efforts to condemn them. Finally, of course, when the divisions of the 1790s culminated in an even more outrageous effort to suppress increasing criticism of Federalist designs, Madison was so alarmed that he was willing to cooperate with Jefferson in a notorious attempt to use the legislatures of Virginia and Kentucky to condemn a federal law.

With the Sedition Act of 1798, Congress rendered it a criminal offense to "write, print, utter, or publish . . . any false, scandalous, and malicious writing or writings against the government of the United States, or either house of the Congress of the United States, or the President of the United States with an intent to defame [them] . . . or to bring them . . . into contempt or disrepute." Under the Sedition Act or under the common law of seditious libel, both of which were ruthlessly enforced by a partisan judiciary and a vigilant, high-Federalist Secretary of State, every important Republican newspaper in the country was attacked, and some were driven out of business. Matthew Lyon of Vermont, a Republican congressman, was imprisoned for a publication incident to his reelection campaign, as were two Republican pamphleteers. Men were prosecuted under the Sedition Law for offenses as diverse and as trivial as circulating a petition for its repeal, erecting a liberty pole, or expressing a drunken wish that a cannon ball had struck the president in his behind.[41]

Confronted with this "reign of witches," as Jefferson described it, the two Virginians each prepared a secret draft of legislative resolutions. Madison, who had decided not to stand for reelection to Congress in 1796, gave his set to John Taylor of Caroline, Virginia's agricultural thinker and another influential party pamphleteer. Vice President Jefferson slipped his draft to John Breckinridge of Kentucky. On November 16, 1798, Kentucky's legislature resolved that the repressive laws of 1798 were "unauthoritative, void, and of no force." On December 24, 1798, Virginia voted a similar condemnation and called upon the other states to join the protest, branding the Sedition Law a danger to "that right of freely examining public characters and measures, and of free communication among the people thereon, which has ever been justly deemed the only effectual guardian of every other right."[42]

The other states refused to join Virginia and Kentucky on a path that led, much later, to nullification and secession. Several states, in fact, defended the constitutionality of the

Alien and Sedition Laws and condemned Virginia's and Kentucky's intermeddling in the federal sphere. In answer to their criticisms, Madison prepared the Virginia Report of 1800, which ranks among the most important early expositions of the meaning of the constitutional liberties of freedom of speech, freedom of the press, and freedom of association. Insisting that the common law of crimes had never been adopted by the Union as a whole, Madison insisted also that the English definition of the freedom of the press—prohibiting the outright censorship of writings, but making authors, publishers, and printers liable for the seditious tendencies of publications—could never be "admitted to be the American idea of it." In America, he argued, "the people, not the government," were sovereign; the very nature of a constitutional republic demanded that the press should be exempt "not only from the previous inspection of licensers, but from the subsequent penalty of laws." Without an unrestricted flow of "information and communication," the people's right to choose their governors, and through that right, their power to protect all other rights— "the essence of a free and responsible government"—would soon be utterly destroyed. The First Amendment meant exactly what it said: that Congress could pass *no* law "abridging the freedom of speech, or of the press, or the right of the people peaceably to assemble, and to petition the Government for a redress of grievances."[43] Madison would surely have been pleased that this is one of those essential maxims that our modern courts enforce, one of those enduring principles of liberal republics that seems, indeed, to have become so thoroughly "incorporated with the national sentiment" that it may even serve, from time to time, to "counteract the impulses of interest and passion" among the citizenry themselves.[44]

Neither Madison nor Jefferson, however, would be altogether pleased about the other ways in which the nation's sentiments have turned. For popular awareness and involvement, together with a genuine, continuous responsiveness of rulers to the ruled, were not the sum of public spirit as they understood it. Citizens and their elected leaders also had to understand the kind of polity in which republicans are called upon to live. Vigilance against the separate interests and ambitions of elected rulers was one of the essential attributes of such a state. So was a continuing and vigorous assertion by the people of their own desires and needs.[45] But in republics, it was not enough for citizens to be involved, or even for those citizens and their elected agents to assert their own specific interests while displaying due respect for the inherent liberties of others. It was necessary, too, for citizens and politicians to be conscious of the interests and opinions of those others: to remain aware that sound republican decisions are the product of community deliberations to which everyone contributes his particular conception of the good, yet does so in a forum in which all particular conceptions and desires will be corrected and restrained by the specific wishes, equal powers, and autonomous conceptions of his fellows. Sound republican decisions were regarded as accommodative in their nature; and after these decisions had been made, the makers were expected to submit themselves to the community's decisions, to obey the law without continual coercion.[46]

Public spirit, thus conceived, is easily distinguished from the modern, pluralistic understanding that the public good— if there is really such a thing as public good at all—is simply the residuum of bargaining among contending interests, with tough luck for the losers. As Madison observed, it is entirely possible for policies "to be accommodated to the particular interests of every county or district, when considered by itself, and not so when considered in relation to each other and to the whole state." The general interest can be sacrificed or lost if all the representatives attend exclusively "to the interests or prejudices of their respective constituents."[47]

Public spirit, thus conceived, should also be distinguished from the classical idea, which Montesquieu had summarized and then condemned, that citizens (or their elected representatives) foreswearing *all* particular considerations, should pursue the public good without regard to any lesser interest. In eighteenth-century English and American opinion, citizens were not expected to *surrender* their specific interests when they set about to make political decisions. Rather, independent citizens would make political decisions on the basis of their own autonomous perceptions, choosing what was good for them *as well as* for the public, pursuing their specific interests while remaining conscious of the interests of their peers and of participating in a collectivity of equals. Sound republican decisions would be reached in such a way that every citizen would be continuously conscious both of ruling and of being ruled, of advocating his specific interests in a public sphere in which all selfish needs and every fallible opinion would be subject to correction or restraint. James Harrington, whose *Commonwealth of Oceana* was a major source for eighteenth-century anglophonic thought, captured the ideal by asking how two serving girls might fairly split a cake. One of them should cut it; the other should select between the pieces. Equity results from a procedure in which each asserts her interest, but does so in the knowledge that the other's interest and the other's power have to be considered. The common good emerges from a mutually respectful act of two autonomous, inherently self-interested people.[48]

Public spirit, then, might even be distinguished from "disinterestedness" as that idea has been defined in the recent writings of Gordon S. Wood.[49] The officers of a republic (Wood does not apply this concept to the voters) were indeed expected to forego their personal and private interests and ambitions—to foreswear the use of public office to enrich themselves at their constituents' expense—but they were not expected (not by Jefferson or Madison at least) to abnegate a vigorous pursuit of the specific interests of their districts.[50] Even in the legislature of a large republic, the pursuit of local interests would become destructive only in so far as representatives refused to recognize that their particular constituencies were not the only ones to be considered.

Jefferson and Madison were not political philosophers, but active, thoughtful politicians. Neither of them paused to write extensively about the subject I am raising. Neither they nor any other member of their generation managed to abide consistently by the ideal. Humans seldom manage to fulfill their highest aspirations. Nevertheless, the content of the concept, as the two Virginians understood it, can be glimpsed, if not completely reconstructed, from their limited attempts to put it into words, to urge it on their colleagues, and to teach it by example. On more than one occasion, they enjoyed at least a limited success; and there is evidence that what they taught was widely understood, if all too seldom acted on, by others of their generation. People may be weak, but they are sometimes better for their aspirations.

Illustrations may be helpful, and, among them, none is more instructive than the one discussed in chapter one: Madison's decision to support a bill of rights, followed by his effort to explain to his reluctant colleagues why the public good demanded this concession to their Antifederalist opponents. As we saw, the framer did not sponsor his amendments merely to defeat demands for more substantial alterations of the Constitution. He did not confine himself to arguing that the addition of a bill of rights was both expedient and right. To him, it was a matter also of fulfilling an implicit contract, of establishing the democratic *bona fides* of supporters of the charter, and of grounding the experiment upon a vivid demonstration of the public spirit necessary to sustain it. Let us not, he argued, be so absolutely confident that we are safe without a bill of rights when many of our valued countrymen believe that we are not. Let us demonstrate the spirit of "deference and concession" that the Antifederalists themselves had shown in quietly submitting to the national decision. Let us "act the part of wise and liberal men," adjusting our opinions to the national will and winning the support of all except the plotting and ambitious.

From the moment when the first new Congress gathered in New York, Madison had set about deliberately to illustrate and urge the attitude that he considered proper for the legislators of a great republic. In his answer for the House to Washington's inaugural address, he had the representatives assure the president that they concurred with him in the determination to "cherish a conscious responsibility for the destiny of republican liberty," which could only be secured by a "system of legislation . . . directed by the spirit of a diffusive patriotism."[51] The first priority for Congress was to raise the steady revenues on which its other measures would depend, and on the first full day of business, Madison proposed a set of resolutions looking toward an impost. Then, throughout the long debate that followed, he attempted both by word and personal example to infuse this patriotic spirit into the proceedings and the law, urging "mutual concession" and consideration of "the general interests of the Union" as well as the particular desires of members' states and regions.[52] As he explained, he would accept a tax on salt, which would weigh heaviest upon the poor, the backcountry, and the South, provided that the system as a whole distributed the burden fairly and in some proportion to ability to pay.[53] In order to secure such equity, he urged an eight-cent levy on molasses, which would make New England pay its fair proportion of the duties. New England's opposition to this duty sorely tried his famous disposition.

"Why these apprehensions for one part of the Union more than the other?" he asked. "Are the northern people made of finer clay? . . . Are they the chosen few? Are all others to be oppressed . . . and they to take their course easy and unrestrained?"

In the House of Representatives, Madison's plea for "justice and impartiality" defeated the New England effort.[54] Unhappily, the northerners were more successful in the Senate.[55] The Impost Act did not achieve the equity that Madison had sought, and disappointment over the advantage-taking by New England, which was quickly reinforced by the maneuvers of his northern colleagues in continuing debates about a permanent location for the federal government, prepared the ground for Madison's determined opposition to the funding plan and for the bitter clash with other Federalists that marked the origins of parties. "No government, he said, not even the most despotic, could, beyond a certain point, violate that idea of justice and equal right which prevailed in the mind of the community. In republican governments, justice and equality form the basis of the system. . . . In a federal republic, . . . it is even more necessary that a sacred regard should be paid to these considerations."[56]

For Jefferson as well as Madison, the readiness of the northerners in Congress to pursue a sectional advantage, which was just what southern Antifederalists had feared, was part of the essential background for the early opposition to Hamiltonian finance. That program, they perceived, entailed a major shift of wealth from South to North, from West to East, and from the body of the people to a few rich men whose fortunes would expand dramatically as a result of federal largesse. In 1789, as Jefferson was finishing his tour in France and making his decision to accept appointment as the first secretary of state, his younger friend became increasingly alarmed about the eastern tilt of federal measures and its probable effects on the remainder of the country. He

had advocated equity between the sections, conscious dem-
onstrations of congressional awareness of the popular and
federal foundations of the new regime, and a consistent
effort to secure the people's loyalty by making private
standards of morality a touchstone for the public. The
northerners, it seemed, had been contemptuous of southern
feelings, western interests, and the Antifederalists' demands.
The sectional and class inequities of Hamilton's designs appeared to strengthen this distressing trend and, in conjunction with the moral and political considerations discussed in
chapter two, propelled the two Virginians into opposition.
This they carried to the public when it melded in their minds
with Federalist attempts to force the reconstructed system,
by a broad construction of the Constitution, into shapes profoundly different from the one they thought the people had
intended.

A full discussion of the early party quarrel is beyond the
scope of what can be attempted in this place. It is important,
nonetheless, to understand how central to that quarrel was
the incompatibility of Federalist objectives and opinions with
the two Virginians' concepts of the character of leadership
in a republic and the nature of a sound relationship between
such leaders and the body of the people. Attentiveness to
popular desires and strict construction of the Constitution
were never merely tactics for the two Virginians. If broad
constructions of the Constitution were accepted by the government and public, "every power that can be deduced from
them will be deduced and exercised sooner or later by those
who may have an interest in doing so," Madison warned.

> The character of human nature gives this salutary warn-
> ing to every sober and reflecting mind. And the history of
> government in all its forms and in every period ratifies
> the danger. A people, therefore, who are so happy as to
> possess the inestimable blessing of a free and defined con-
> stitution cannot be too watchful against the introduction

nor too critical in tracing the consequences of new principles and new constructions that may remove the land-
marks of power.[57]

"If this licentiousness in constructive perversions of the
Constitution [should] continue," Madison complained to
Jefferson in 1800, "we shall soon have to look into our code
of laws and not the charter of the people for the form as well
as the powers of our government."[58] As early as his condemnation of the national bank, in language reminiscent of his
speeches on the Bill of Rights, Madison insisted that the
Constitution was the people's law, which was to be revered
and not remolded by their servants. In his speeches on the
bank, he also called again on congressmen around him to be
conscious that their honor was at stake. It was dishonorable
to break a solemn promise: to secure the Constitution by
insisting that its "sweeping clauses" could not lead to federal abuses, and then proceed as though these clauses authorized the Congress to do anything it pleased; to turn the
brilliant victory of 1788 into an underhanded trick. Doing
so, moreover, could profoundly threaten its survival, for the
Union rested on essential equity among its different sections
and on popular conviction that the government was genuinely grounded in continuing consent.

Federalist resistance to an active form of popular consent was always an important count in Madisonian and
Jeffersonian indictments of their foes.[59] As they conceived
it, one of the emerging parties was composed of those who
were

> more partial to the opulent than to the other classes of
> society; and having debauched themselves into a persua-
> sion that mankind are incapable of governing themselves,
> it follows with them, of course, that government can be
> carried on only by the pageantry of rank, the influence of
> money and emoluments, and the terror of military force.

The Jeffersonians, by contrast, believed that men were "capable of governing themselves," and therefore would consistently oppose every measure "that is not strictly conformable to the principles and conducive to the preservation of republican government."[60] An anti-republican might believe that "the people are stupid, suspicious, [and] licentious"; that when they have established a good government and elected their representatives, "they should think of nothing but obedience, leaving the care of their liberties to their wiser rulers." The Republican, however, would conclude "that the people ought to be enlightened, to be awakened, to be united, that after establishing a government they should watch over it, as well as obey it." The best keepers of the people's liberty were the people themselves—and officers who were continually responsive to the needs and will of the political nation as a whole.[61]

Looking back from his retirement, Madison responded to the charge that, once they came to power, the Republicans had accepted most of the distinctive policies of their opponents, while the Federalists, in turn, had come to share the democratic sentiments that the Republicans had long expressed. Though it was true, he said, that changing times had reconciled the Jeffersonians to policies that had been "premature" and dangerous when they were first advanced, the people who detected an amalgamation of the views of the conflicting parties overlooked "the overbearing and vindictive spirit, the apocryphal doctrines, and rash projects which stamped on Federalism its distinctive character, and which are so much in contrast with the unassuming and unavenging spirit which has marked the Republican Ascendancy." Apart from their distrust of the political capacity of ordinary people, what Madison could least forgive in his opponents of the 1790s were the persecuting spirit typified by the Sedition Law, together with the willingness of Federalists to ground their rule on special favors for distinctive classes and specific sections of the Union.[62]

Positive examples of the sort of public spirit Madison had hoped for at the outset of the new regime—the attitude that he had tried to inculcate in members of the first new Congress and, by way of their example, in the nation as a whole—could easily be multiplied beyond the space afforded by an essay. Three of these, however, may be helpful: two that deeply influenced Madison and Jefferson themselves; and one that may suggest how deeply thinking of this sort affected lesser figures of their time.

For Madison and Jefferson alike, the first great principle of a republic was that the majority must rule. For both, however, this essential axiom had always to be qualified by two reminders: first, that the majority be reasonable and just, respecting the inherent rights of others; second, that on certain fundamental issues or on truly critical occasions, bare majorities are insufficient.[63] In modern legislative bodies, legislative leaders commonly assume that their objective is to forge a bare majority and keep this fragile coalition together long enough for a decision. The barest one will do, and it may be assembled for the moment by employing any means not legally forbidden, including the effective purchasing of votes by special favors for the districts of the pliable or the reluctant. However critical the subject, they assume, decisions, once achieved, can always be enforced by the coercive power of the state. The founding generation started from a different set of suppositions (though, at times, they were reduced to operating in the modern way). In the first place, they could not presume that any of their fragile, infant governments possessed sufficient muscle to enforce unpopular decrees against significant resistance. In the second, they assumed that something like consensus ought to be the object—or, at least, that leaders should attempt to garner such an overwhelming popular support for their decisions as would guarantee their ultimate success. The substance of decisions and the way in which decisions were achieved were equally important for this purpose.

During his own retirement, Jefferson prepared some autobiographical reflections. He included reminiscences and notes from service in the Second Continental Congress, allotting a revealing portion of his space to efforts by the radicals in Congress to avoid outpacing the reluctant and even to conciliate a single, well-respected man. Shortly after he was seated in the body (on June 21, 1775), Jefferson was added to a small committee charged with drafting a declaration of the causes and necessity of taking arms against the British. He prepared a draft. John Dickinson, an influential leader since the early days of the resistance, thought the language would foreclose the possibility of reconciliation with the mother country. Dickinson, as Jefferson recalled, "was so honest a man, and so able a one, that he was greatly indulged even by those who could not feel his scruples." The committee simply passed the job to him, and notwithstanding general "disgust" with the "humility" of Dickinson's own language, "Congress gave a signal proof of their indulgence to Mr. Dickinson, and of their great desire not to go too fast for any respectable portion of our body," by approving his revision and then permitting Dickinson himself to draft its second petition to the king. "Mr. Dickinson's delight . . . was the only circumstance which reconciled them to it."[64]

Similarly, Jefferson incorporated in the "Autobiography" his notes of the congressional proceedings, one year later, on Virginia's motion for American independence. As before, Dickinson and several others pleaded for delay until the people of the middle colonies were clearly ripe for the decision. Unable to persuade them, but unable also to delay until there was a "perfect unanimity" in Congress, the radicals agreed to wait three weeks to let opinion in the middle colonies mature. Congress then voted nine states to two for independence. At this juncture, Edward Rutledge of South Carolina, representing one of the two dissenters, asked for a delay until the morrow, suggesting that his colony would join the others for the sake of unanimity even though its delegates opposed the resolution. The final vote was thus postponed until the second of July. Another delegate from Delaware arrived, permitting it to vote. Pennsylvania and South Carolina both reversed their opposition. The resolution carried 12–0, and only Dickinson declined to sign the Declaration.[65]

For Madison, the archetypal instance of a similar display of public spirit was the Constitutional Convention. At that meeting, as he never tired of pointing out, no delegate or state obtained exactly what they wanted, though all of them contended fiercely for their wishes. In light of all of the contending views and interests represented at the meeting, complicated by the novel task that members were attempting, it was utterly amazing, Madison believed, that unanimity had nonetheless developed. It was impossible, he wrote, for a religious man "not to perceive in it a finger of that Almighty hand which has been so frequently and signally extended to our relief in the critical stages of the Revolution."[66] As the meeting closed, however, Benjamin Franklin, whom Madison and Jefferson revered, appealed to every member who retained objections to the plan, as he himself retained objections, to "doubt a little of his own infallibility" and sign the finished Constitution.[67] Every delegation represented at the moment, and all the delegates but three, "were either satisfactorily accommodated by the final act or were induced to accede to it by a conviction of the necessity of sacrificing private opinions and partial interests to the public good."[68] Later in his life, as animosities between the North and South reached dangerous extremes, the willingness of members of the great convention to accommodate each other's needs and to be conscious of the greater good to which their own desires would have to be adjusted was a model Madison recurred to time and time again as an exemplar of the spirit necessary to preserve the Union they had sealed.[69]

The spirit that produced the Constitution was hardly less essential to its ratification. The central act in this extended drama was the Massachusetts state convention, where a large majority initially opposed the unamended plan, but where a number of the delegates of every rank and station offered a remarkable display of the accommodative spirit Jefferson and Madison admired. The most important actors in this play were Governor John Hancock and his aging revolutionary ally, Samuel Adams, whom Hancock had avoided ever since the Adams cousins backed George Washington for the position as commander of the Continental Army. Neither of these Massachusetts heroes was at ease with all of the provisions of Constitution, but both of them believed that an invigorated union was essential to protect the nation's revolutionary gains; and both of them were fundamentally committed to the revolutionary notion that republics call for a fraternal spirit and a style of politics that seeks as much consensus as can possibly be reached. Perhaps from the beginning of the state convention, but certainly as it became apparent that the Federalists' insistence on an unconditional approval of the plan could only end in its rejection, the two old revolutionaries drew together to preserve the unity of the Confederation and the harmony of Massachusetts.

Suffering from gout and probably desiring to remain aloof from the proceedings, Hancock had been absent from the meeting since the opening of its deliberations (January 9, 1788). Adams, who had been observed in several private meetings with the governor and his lieutenants, had participated only lightly and equivocally in the debates. Then, on January 31, as the convention neared the time for a decision, Hancock took his place as president of the convention. As debates proceeded, General William Heath, a moderate supporter of the Constitution (and a long-time friend of Hancock's), suggested that the difficulties of a number of opponents might be eased if the convention ratified the Constitution but instructed Massachusetts members of the reconstructed Congress to support its quick amendment. Though "conscious of the impropriety" of speaking as the chairman of the meeting, Hancock quickly introduced a measure to remove some gentlemen's objections and to overcome the great "dissimilarity of sentiments" revealed by the debates: to ratify the document while *recommending* several amendments. Following a noon recess, Hancock read his propositions and called immediately on Adams, who announced that the proposals would resolve his own objections. The moderate supporters of the Constitution, with whom the measure must have been concerted, quickly jumped aboard. Former governor James Bowdoin "expressed his hearty approbation of the propositions . . . , as they would have a tendency to relieve the fears, and quiet the apprehensions" of the "worthy gentlemen who had expressed their doubts." With Adams carefully explaining how the governor's amendments would alleviate the most important fears and many members arguing that the example of the state would certainly be followed by its sisters, member after member fell in line with this solution. The convention voted 187 to 168 to ratify the Constitution on these terms, with several members of the large minority declaring their attention to abide by the majority's decision.[70]

Even with a Hancock and an Adams throwing their enormous weight behind the Constitution, the victory in Massachusetts was a close one. In this state, the social and political elite was so one-sidedly in favor of the Constitution that their uniform support (and even their rhetorical superiority in the convention) seem to have provoked unconquerable

suspicions. Amos Singletary, one of many of the more obscure opponents of the Constitution, put the difficulty in a
sentence often quoted in accounts of the division:

> These lawyers, and men of learning, and moneyed men,
> that talk so finely, and gloss over matters so smoothly, to
> make us poor illiterate people swallow down the pill, ex-
> pect to get into Congress themselves; they expect to be
> the managers of this Constitution, and get all the power
> and all the money into their own hands, and then they
> will swallow up all us little folks, like the great *Leviathan*,
> Mr. President; yes, just as the whale swallowed up *Jonah*.[71]

Not so often quoted is the answer of a member who was
every bit as ordinary as was Amos—indeed, the record does
not even indicate which "Mr. Smith" this was, Josiah or
John K.:

> My honorable old daddy there [pointing to Mr. Singletary]
> won't think that I expect to be a Congress-man, and swal-
> low up the liberties of the people. I never had any post,
> nor do I want one. But I don't think the worse of the Con-
> stitution because lawyers, and men of learning, and mon-
> eyed men, are fond of it. They that are honest men
> themselves are not apt to suspect other people. . . . These
> lawyers, these moneyed men, these men of learning, are
> all embarked in the same cause with us, and we must all
> swim or sink together.[72]

As in Virginia and New York, the Constitution was approved
in Massachusetts because a number of the back-bench delegates refused to run the risk that the Confederation might
collapse if they declined to trust the men who promised subsequent amendments. And much like Madison, a number of
the latter were determined to respect the worries of dissenters, to bend as far as prudence would allow, and thus to re-

unite the nation in support of a reform in which the great majority could cheerfully concur. Both parties were presuming, Samuel Adams said, "that we shall exercise candor towards each other."[73] "Blessed are the peacemakers," said the Reverend Samuel Stillman, an unqualified supporter of the Constitution who was willing, nonetheless, to accept amendments that would "tend to conciliation."[74] Let "every member" be inspired with such a "disposition," Stillman said: "Then shall we lay aside every opposite interest, and unite, as a band of brothers."[75] And "let the question be decided as it may," John Hancock finished, there should be "no triumph on the one side or chagrin on the other. Should there be a great division, every good man, every man who loves his country, will be so far from exhibiting extraordinary marks of joy, that he will sincerely lament the want of unanimity, and strenuously endeavor to cultivate a spirit of conciliation, both in Convention and at home."[76]

Jefferson and Madison were not naive. They knew that even on the most essential issues—and even in their own extraordinary time—the spirit of ideal republican decisions was a rare commodity indeed. Day to day and on less critical divisions, both in Congress and the legislatures of the states, logs were rolled and pork was packaged much as is the case today. At peaks of fierce political collisions, such as those which separated the Republicans from their opponents of the 1790s, mutual distrust between the parties and rhetorical abuse of rivals was easily a match for anything a listener might hear on talk shows of the present.[77] Still, it is surprising to discover just how far into the population the ideal of sound republican decisions penetrated in their day. The pastors and the farmers at the Massachusetts state convention were by no means singular in their assimilation of this concept. Even the association of mechanics in Providence, Rhode Island, appealing for protective legislation, repeatedly requested an attention to their needs *so far* as an encouragement of native manufactures seemed "consistent with a proper regard to the revenue."[78]

For Thomas Jefferson and his successor in the nation's highest office, the words of Jefferson's inaugural address were not extracted solely by the dictates of the moment. During the ferocious contest of the last ten years, "the animation of discussions," Jefferson admitted, had sometimes "worn an aspect" that might startle "strangers unused to think[ing] freely and to speak and to write what they think." And yet, this contest having been decided by the people, "all" would nonetheless, "of course, arrange themselves under the will of the law, and unite in common efforts for the common good." "Let us all," the president appealed,

> unite with one heart and one mind. Let us restore to so-
> cial intercourse that harmony and affection without which
> liberty and even life itself are but dreary things. And let
> us reflect that, having banished from our land that reli-
> gious intolerance under which mankind so long bled and
> suffered, we have yet gained little if we countenance a
> political intolerance as despotic, as wicked, and capable
> of as bitter and bloody persecutions.

"Every difference of opinion," Jefferson insisted, "is not a difference of principle. We have called by different names brethren of the same principle. We are all Republicans, we are all Federalists. If there be any among us who would wish to dissolve this Union or to change its republican form, let them stand undisturbed as monuments of the safety with which error of opinion may be tolerated where reason is left free to combat it."[79]

As presidents, both Jefferson and Madison—the latter, probably, with more consistency and more success—at-tempted to conduct themselves according to this spirit. As mortals, either man could come up short. In hindsight, sev-eral of their policies may seem egregiously mistaken.[80] But, surely, Jefferson was not without some grounds for saying in his final letter to his friend:

> If ever the earth has beheld a system of administration conducted with a single and steadfast eye to the general interest and happiness of those committed to it, one which, protected by truth, can never know reproach, it is that to which our lives have been devoted.[81]

And, surely, neither of these founders, if transported to today's republic, could suppress a deep alarm about the fabric of our politics today.

"Liberty, equality, fraternity" was not a slogan of the founders' Revolution. Fraternity, withal, was certainly an indispensable component of the sort of polity that they envisioned. Transported to our time, the great Virginians might discern a multitude of reasons for concern. Liberty, which they defined as popular self-governance as well as the protection of the people's private rights, might seem to them endangered by the multitudes who do not vote and who profoundly doubt that governments at any level truly represent the wishes of the people, by politicians who refuse to look beyond the next election or beyond the clamors of their own particular constituencies, by the increasing practice of surrendering political decisions to the courts, and by our futile hope that carefully articulated legal codes and regular procedures can deliver total justice. Equality, said both of the Virginians, is the vital principle of all republican legislation. Increasingly, by contrast, we demand entitlements, "empowerment," or "rights" as members of distinctive social groups and not as equal citizens of a republic, oblivious to the inherent difficulty of requiring brotherhood and an equality of mutual respect from rival groups whom we perceive as anything but brothers. But nearly every aspect of our own malaise might seem to Madison or Jefferson to be related to the fragile or decaying sense of genuine community in the contemporary great republic. We simply do not like, or trust, or listen to each other in the way they thought essential.

As eighteenth-century thinkers, to be sure, the two Virginians were unable to imagine that political equality would one day mean equality for women, though the legacy they left was clearly a beginning for this movement. In theory, both of them did think that the inherent rights of man *should* mean equality for blacks. In practice, nevertheless, neither could commit himself wholeheartedly to the emancipation of the slaves, in largest part because they both believed that as a consequence of slavery and of color, neither blacks nor whites could ever hold for one another the fraternal feelings necessary for a viable republic. We can hope that they were wrong. Both, I think, would be delighted if we manage to rebut them and decline to treat them as exemplars in every aspect of their conduct. Still, there may be cause to fear that Madison was right when he suggested that the best-developed codes, the most elaborate and regular procedures, and the finest constitutional contrivances that human ingenuity could offer would never, by themselves, suffice to render us secure. Measures *can* be tailored to the special needs of nearly every interest while the greater good of the community is lost. Patriotic leaders might do well to recognize this truth. Rather than competing to discredit our political opponents, we might listen, sometimes, to their voices; we might even, on occasion, try persuading those of different mind instead of hooking them by sharp political maneuvers. And patriotic citizens might well reflect, with the Virginia founders, not only that "our duties are the Guardians of our Rights,"[82] not only that self-governance demands a vigilant, continuing participation in political affairs, but also that the spirit of republics is a spirit of collective consciousness that we are all embarked together, as individuals and equals, on a common quest for happiness and justice. Forgetting that may well endanger all the other lessons the Virginians tried to teach.

NOTES

1. Jefferson to Madison, January 30, 1787, *PJM*, 9:248; document 23. See, further, same to same, December 20, 1787; document 8.

2. Jefferson to William Stephens Smith, November 13, 1787, *PTJ*, 12:356. Document 5.

3. *The Federalist*, 51.

4. Koch, *The Great Collaboration*, 52–55, and McCoy, *The Last of the Fathers*, 45–53 and below, both remark that it was nearly a year before Madison informed Jefferson of his authorship of *The Federalist*. In combination with Madison's "rejection" of Jefferson's proposals in *The Federalist* 49 and in the letter on the rights of living generations, this seems to both a sign of strain. I am less inclined to make so much of a silence that can be explained in other ways, the more so when Jefferson plainly approved of *The Federalist* and believed that Madison had written most of the collection.

5. Especially the long and frequently misguided argument about the relative importance or relationship of "liberal" and "republican" traditions. For an introduction to the bulky literature on this, see Robert Shalhope, "Republicanism and Early American Historiography," *William and Mary Quarterly*, 3rd ser., 39 (1982), 334–56; *The Republican Synthesis Revisited: Essays in Honor of George Athan Billias*, ed. Milton M. Klein *et al.* (Worcester, Mass., 1992), and Daniel T. Rodgers, "Republicanism: The Career of a Concept," *Journal of American History* 79 (1992), 11–38.

6. Reply of the House of Representatives to Washington's inaugural address, *PJM*, 12:133.

7. The fullest, most recent account is David P. Szatmary, *Shays' Rebellion: The Making of an Agrarian Insurrection* (Amherst, Mass., 1980). Also still useful is Robert J. Taylor, *Western Massachusetts in the Revolution* (Providence, R.I., 1954). A good brief account of

the aftermath is Richard D. Brown, "Shays's Rebellion and the Ratification of the Federal Constitution in Massachusetts," in Richard Beeman, Stephen Botein, and Edward C. Carter II, eds., *Beyond Confederation: Origins of the Constitution and American National Identity* (Chapel Hill, N.C., 1987), 113–27.

8. Jefferson to William Stephens Smith, November 13, 1787, *PTJ*, 12:356; Jefferson to Madison, January 30, 1787, *PJM*, 9:247; documents 5 and 23 below.

9. Quotations from the letter to Madison, *PJM*, 9:247.

10. *Ibid.*, 247–48.

11. Jefferson to Smith, *PTJ*, 12:356.

12. Madison to James Madison, Sr., November 1, 1786, *PJM*, 8:154. Lee's letter, which JM opened while attending the autumn session of the Virginia General Assembly, referred to "authentic information" in the hands of Congress and estimated that the five "seditious counties" in western Massachusetts contained 40,000 of the state's 75,000 men between 16 and 60. Brown, 115 n. 5, believes that Shays's forces probably never numbered more than 2,500.

13. Washington to Madison, November 5, 1786, *PJM*, 8:161.

14. William Grayson to Madison, November 22, 1786, *ibid.*, 174.

15. Madison to George Muter, January 7, 1787, *ibid.*, 231.

16. *Ibid.*

17. For Madison's fear of anti–republican sentiments in New England see, for example, Madison to Washington, Febuary 21, 1787, and his notes on congressional debates of the same date, *ibid.*, 286, 291–92. For reports of "inflammatory summonses" and Shaysite sentiments in Virginia, see Madison's letters from Governor Edmund Randolph of March 1, March 7, and March 15 and from John Dawson (an ally in the Virginia Assembly) on April 15, *ibid.*, 301, 303, 312–13, 381. On June 12, after the Constitutional Convention had begun, Dawson wrote that arsonists had burned the courthouse in King William County, and Randolph was receiving regular reports of jailbreaks, threats against the courts, and other anti-tax and anti-debt commotions in Virginia.

18. "Vices of the Political System of the U. States," *ibid.*, 350–51: "A minority may in an appeal to force be an overmatch for the

majority. .... If the minority happen to include all such as possess
the skill and habits of military life, and such as possess the great
pecuniary resources, one third only may conquer the remaining
two thirds."

19. Preliminary reinterpretations of Madison's positions have
been offered in "James Madison and the Nationalists, 1780–1783";
"The Hamiltonian Madison: A Reinterpretation"; "The Practi-
cable Sphere of a Republic"; and "1787 and 1776: James Madison,
Patrick Henry, the Constitution, and the Revolution." These are
brought together in Banning, *The Sacred Fire of Liberty: James
Madison and the Founding of the Federal Republic* (forthcoming;
Cornell University Press, 1995).

20. *DHRC*, 10:1417.

21. Madison to Jefferson, March 18, 1786, *PJM*, 8:502.

22. For more on this connection, see the sources cited in note
19; Drew R. McCoy, *The Elusive Republic: Political Economy in
Jeffersonian America* (Chapel Hill, 1980), chap. 3; and Lance Banning, "Political Economy and the Creation of the Federal Republic," in David F. Konig, ed., *Devising Liberty*, vol. 5 of *A History of
Modern Freedom* (Stanford University Press, 1995).

23. Book 3, chap. 5 of *The Spirit of the Laws*, p. 23 of the edition translated by Thomas Nugent with an introduction by Franz
Neumann, "Haffner Library of Classics" (New York, 1966; originally published in 1949).

24. For a fuller, more systematic discussion of prevailing er-
rors in recent studies of the revolutionary and eighteenth-century
concept, see Banning, "Some Second Thoughts on Virtue and the
Course of Revolutionary Thinking," in Terence Ball and J. G. A.
Pocock, eds., *Conceptual Change and the Constitution* (Lawrence,
Kans., 1988), 194–212.

25. *The Jeffersonian Persuasion*, chaps. 4–6.

26. Thomas P. Slaughter, *The Whiskey Rebellion: Frontier Epi-
logue to the American Revolution* (New York, 1986).

27. Jefferson, who had retired from his position as secretary
of state, plainly saw the government's recourse to massive military
force as premature and wondered how "such an armament against
people at their ploughs" would be explained and received (to Madison, October 30, 1794, *PJM*, 15:366). As he later wrote to James

Monroe, "an insurrection was announced and proclaimed and armed against, but could never be found" (May 26,1795, *WTJ*, 7:16). Madison was certain that if the rebellion had not collapsed so easily, it would have been made an excuse for raising a standing army (to Jefferson, November 16, 1794, *PJM*, 15:379; to Monroe, December 4, 1794, *ibid.*, 406).

28. More than forty of these popular associations emerged throughout the country in the aftermath of the proclamation of the French Republic, and most of them were as determined to assert the people's rights at home as to support the Revolution in France. See Eugene Perry Link, *Democratic-Republican Societies, 1790–1800* (New York, 1942). Members of the Mingo Creek, Yough, and Washington County societies in western Pennsylvania were involved in the insurrection, but it was also said that the Philadelphia society "could have made a quorum" in the army that marched against it (John C. Miller, *The Federalist Era, 1789–1801* [New York, 1960], 161).

29. The parallel was striking and explicit. Madison's December 4 letter to James Monroe, calling Washington's denunciation "perhaps the greatest error of his political life," described the outcome of the insurrection as "critical . . . for the cause of liberty." The "real authors" of the rebellion "if not in the service, were, in the most effectual manner, doing the business of despotism. You well know the general tendency of insurrections to increase the momentum of power. You will recollect the particular effect of what happened some years ago in Massachusetts. Precisely the same calamity [for the cause of republicanism] was to be dreaded on a larger scale in this case. There were enough, as you may well suppose, ready to give the same turn to the crisis and to propagate the same impressions from it. It happened most auspiciously, however, that with a spirit truly republican, the people everywhere and of every description condemned the resistance to the will of the majority and obeyed with alacrity the call to vindicate the laws." The reference to an "attack on the most sacred principles of our Constitution" is from a letter to Jefferson, November 30, 1794, *PJM*, 15:396.

30. *PJM*, 15:386–87. The people had shown, the draft continued, "that they understand the indissoluble union between true

liberty and regular government; that they feel their duties no less than they are watchful over their rights; that they will be as ready, at all times, to crush licentiousness, as they have been to defeat usurpation: in a word, that they are capable of carrying into execution that noble plan of self government, which they have chosen as the guarantee of their own happiness and the asylum for that of all from every clime who may wish to unite their destiny with ours." For a powerful discussion of the role of popular sovereignty and public opinion in crushing the Whiskey Rebellion and undoing the Democratic clubs, see Stanley Elkins and Erik McKitrick, *The Age of Federalism: The Early American Republic, 1788–1800* (New York, 1993), chap. 10.

31. To James Monroe, *PJM*, 15:406. Jefferson also found it "wonderful indeed that the President should have permitted himself to be the organ of such an attack on the freedom of discussion, the freedom of writing, printing, and publishing" (to Madison, December 28, 1794, *ibid.*, 426–27). Characteristically, both men tried to see Washington as the unwitting dupe of Hamilton and other plotters, but Dumas Malone suggests that this letter marks the point at which Jefferson first began to question Washington's own wisdom (*Jefferson and His Time*, 3:188–91).

32. Speech of November 27, 1794, *PJM*, 15:391.

33. Madison to James Monroe, April 12, 1794, *ibid.*, 407.

34. November 30, 1794, *PJM*, 15:397–98. This episode is also discussed briefly in Ralph Ketcham, *James Madison: A Biography* (New York, 1971), 354–55; Brant, 3:415–19; and Malone, 3:188–91.

35. "Government of the United States," published originally in the *National Gazette* of February 4, 1792, and reprinted in *PJM*, 14:217–19; document 24.

36. *The Federalist* 37.

37. *The Federalist* 10.

38. *The Federalist* 57 and 46.

39. Jefferson to Edward Carrington, January 16, 1787; Peterson, *Thomas Jefferson*, 880–81,

40. "Government of the United States" is quoted in the text above. The other quotation is from "Who Are the Best Keepers of the People's Liberties" (December 20, 1792), *PJM*, 14:426. See

also "Consolidation," insisting on a consolidation of the people's sentiments but not of their governmental system (December 3, 1791; document 25); "Public Opinion," arguing that a large country particularly requires "a general intercourse of sentiments" to preserve its liberties, as encouraged by "a circulation of newspapers through the entire body of the people" (December 19, 1791; document 26); "Government," which insists that "every good citizen" be "a centinel over the rights of the people" (December 31, 1791); and "Charters": "Liberty and order will never be *perfectly* safe until a trespass on the constitutional provisions for either shall be felt with the same keenness that resents an invasion of the dearest rights; until every citizen shall be an ARGUS to espy and an ÆGEON to avenge the unhallowed deed" (January 18, 1792). Relevant passages are in *PJM*, 14:138–39, 178, 179, 192, 218.

41. James Morton Smith, *Freedom's Fetters: The Alien and Sedition Laws and American Civil Liberties* (Ithaca, N.Y., 1956); John C. Miller, *Crisis in Freedom: The Alien and Sedition Acts* (Boston, 1951).

42. Adrienne Koch and Harry Ammon, "The Virginia and Kentucky Resolutions: An Episode in Jefferson's and Madison's Defense of Civil Liberties," *William and Mary Quarterly*, 3rd ser., 5 (1948), 145–76; documents 28 and 29.

43. *PJM*, 17:307–50; quotations at 336–37, 343.

44. Madison to Jefferson, October 17, 1788. On the uses of a bill of rights, see chapter one.

45. Indeed, the model of popular involvement that most completely captured Jefferson's imagination was the New England township and its meetings, which he urged Virginians to imitate by establishing a system of "ward republics." See documents 30 and 31.

46. Here and in the next two paragraphs I summarize the central argument of "Some Second Thoughts on Virtue and the Course of Revolutionary Thinking," which explores the treatment of this concept in the writings of J. G. A. Pocock and Gordon S. Wood.

47. "Observations on Jefferson's Draft of a Constitution for Virginia," *PJM*, 11:286.

48. *The Political Works of James Harrington*, ed. J. G. A. Pocock (Cambridge, Eng., 1977), 172.

49. "Interests and Disinterestedness in the Making of the Constitution" in *Beyond Confederation*, 69–109; and, more broadly, *The Radicalism of the American Revolution* (New York, 1992).

50. Wood is one of many current authors who suggest that Madison and other Federalists of 1787 pinned their hopes for a corrective for the ills of faction mostly on the large election districts of the federal republic, which would make it difficult for men of narrow, selfish, interested views to win a seat in Congress; and Madison did believe that this would be a consequence of an "extension of the sphere." But Madison did not expect the federal representatives to act as "impartial umpires" over the contending interests of the large republic. "A landed interest, a manufacturing interest, a mercantile interest, a monied interest, with many lesser interests, grow up of necessity in civilized nations," says *The Federalist* 10, "and divide them into different classes, actuated by different sentiments and views. The regulation of these various and interfering interests forms the principal task of modern legislation, and involves the spirit of party and faction in the necessary and ordinary operations of government. . . . What are many of the most important acts of legislation but so many judicial determinations, not indeed concerning the rights of single persons, but concerning the rights of large bodies of citizens; and what are the different classes of legislators but advocates and parties to the causes which they determine?" For an excellent discussion of the "disinterested umpire" reading of the tenth *Federalist*, see Alan Gibson, "Impartial Representation and the Extended Republic: Towards a Comprehensive and Balanced Reading of the Tenth *Federalist* Paper," *History of Political Thought*, 12 (1991): 263–304.

51. *PJM*, 12:133. As draftsman of the president's address, Madison was himself responsible for use of such language there. See *ibid.*, 123.

52. *Ibid.*, 70.

53. *Ibid.*, 85–87.

54. *Ibid.*, 119.

55. The legislative history of the Impost and Tonnage Acts in

in Linda Grant De Pauw *et al.*, eds, *The Documentary History of the First Federal Congress* (Washington, D.C., 1972–), 5:940–83; 6:1947–56. A good, brief history is Curtis Nettles, *The Emergence of a National Economy* (New York, 1962), 109–11.

56. *PJM*, 12:373–76. Madison's separation from the other Federalists of 1788 is examined in greater detail in chapter 10 of Banning, *The Sacred Fire of Liberty*.

57. "Helvidius," no. 4 (September 14, 1793), *PJM*, 15:106–7.

58. Madison to Jefferson, March 15, 1800, *ibid.*, 16:373.

59. Madison's essay on "Public Opinion," included as document 26, is an important source.

60. Madison, "A Candid State of Parties," September 22, 1792, *PJM*, 14:370–72; document 27.

61. Madison, "Who Are the Best Keepers of the People's Liberties?" December 20, 1792, *ibid.*, 426–27.

62. Madison to William Eustis, May 22, 1823, in *WJM*, 9:135–36.

63. "Great innovations should not be forced on slender majorities" (Jefferson to Thaddeus Kosciusko, May 2, 1808). I owe this citation to Kaminski.

64. "Autobiography," *Jefferson: Writings*, 12.

65. *Ibid.*, 13–18.

66. *The Federalist* 27.

67. Speech of September 17, *Records of the Federal Convention*, 2:643.

68. *The Federalist* 37.

69. Madison's late-life battles with immoderates of every stripe is a major theme of McCoy's *Last of the Fathers*.

70. Most studies attribute the Massachusetts strategy to leading Federalists in the convention (Rufus King and Theophilus Parsons), and many suggest that Hancock was induced to sponsor the amendments by promises of the vice presidency of the new regime. My account follows Michael Allen Gillespie, "Massachusetts: Creating Consensus," in *Ratifying the Constitution*, 138–67, which constructs a compelling case that the plan of recommendatory amendments emerged from the men around Hancock, resulted from the old revolutionaries' "belief in a politics of consensus," and "rested on a comprehensive conception of the

appropriate character of a good regime" (161). The basic point, however, would seem sound whatever we conclude about the preparation of the plan. The proceedings can be followed in Elliot, *Debates in the Several Conventions*, 2: 1–183. Quotations or paraphrases are at 122–23, 125–26, and 153.

71. Elliot, *Debates*, 2:102.

72. *Ibid.*, 103–4. Compare Thatcher, p. 147.

73. *Ibid.*, 133.

74. *Ibid.*, 169.

75. *Ibid.*, 164.

76. *Ibid.*, 175.

77. John R. Howe, Jr., "Republican Thought and the Political Violence of the 1790s," *American Quarterly* 19 (1967), 147–65.

78. Gary J. Kornblith, "'Cementing the Mechanic Interest': Origins of the Providence Association of Mechanics and Manufacturers," *Journal of the Early Republic* 8 (1988), 355–87; quotations at 381, 378.

79. Jefferson's First Inaugural Address, March 4, 1801, *Jefferson: Writings*, 492–93; document 32.

80. For Jefferson's shortcomings, see Leonard Levy, *Jefferson and Civil Liberties: The Darker Side*, rev. ed. (New York, 1973). The policy failures, culminating in the near-disaster of the War of 1812 and Madison's historical reputation as at best a mediocre president, are emphasized in Forrest McDonald, *The Presidency of Thomas Jefferson* (Lawrence, Kans., 1976); Robert W. Tucker and David C. Hendrickson, *Empire of Liberty: The Statecraft of Thomas Jefferson* (New York, 1990); and (more sympathetically) J. C. A. Stagg, *Mr. Madison's War: Politics, Diplomacy, and Warfare in the Early American Republic, 1783–1830* (Princeton, 1983). But see also the marvelous discussion of the meaning of Madison's character and disposition to the people of his time in McCoy, *The Last of the Fathers*, chap. 1: "The Character of the Good Statesman," together with Ralph Ketcham, "James Madison: The Unimperial President," *Virginia Quarterly Review* 54 (1978), 116–36.

81. Jefferson to Madison, Febuary 17, 1826, *Jefferson: Writings*, 1515.

82. Toasts for an American Dinner, July 4, 1798, *PJM*, 17:161.

DOCUMENTS

CHAPTER THREE
Public Spirit

Introductory Documents

FIRST PRINCIPLES

IN THE SPRING OF 1776, ABOUT A YEAR into the war, sentiment throughout the colonies turned powerfully toward independence. On May 15, Congress passed a resolution calling on those colonies which had not done so by this time to sever their connections with Great Britain and create new governments depending wholly on consent. In Virginia, a convention was already working to prepare a new state constitution. Also on May 15, its members authorized its delegates in Congress to propose a resolution that the colonies were now "and of right ought to be, free and independent states."

The Virginia constitution, adopted on June 29, would soon become a model for the great majority of newly independent states, ten of which wrote new organic laws before the year had passed. The Virginia Declaration of Rights, a separate document adopted on June 12 and printed as document 1, was equally as influential. Following the Old Dominion's lead, most states approved a similar pronouncement or wove a bill of rights into the body of their constitutions. Thomas Jefferson reviewed the document before he wrote the Declaration of Independence. Lafayette and other Frenchmen used it when they wrote the Declaration of the Rights of Man. In preparing the first amendments to the U.S. Constitution, James Madison relied more heavily on Virginia's recommendations, themselves modelled on the Virginia Declaration, than on any other source.

The Virginia Declaration, together with the new state constitution, was written mostly by George Mason, a neighbor of George Washington and, later, one of three important men who worked throughout the summer at the Constitutional Convention, contributed importantly to its deliberations, but refused to sign the finished plan. Suggestively, however, young James Madison was present at the 1776 convention as a delegate from Orange County. Only twenty-five and much too inexperienced to make a greater contribution, Madison was nonetheless responsible for a portentous change of wording in Article 16 of the completed Declaration. Mason's draft insisted on "the fullest toleration" for the dictates of religious conscience. Madison's amendment altered this to recognize an equal *right*, not just to hold, but also to express and freely "exercise" religious views. The change of language placed the rights of conscience on a ground that no society had ever written into law and marked its sponsor as a youth from whom extraordinary things could be expected. It also proved a portent of the lifelong effort by the founder, often working closely with his future friend, to make America the great exemplar of a total freedom of opinion, absolute equality for various denominations (or for people who belonged to none), and the complete withdrawal of the state from its traditional involvement in this sphere.

Virginia's revolutionary struggle over church and state produced some of the most revealing sources for an understanding of the fundamental principles with which the

two Virginia founders commonly began. When Jefferson returned from service in the Second Continental Congress—
his final draft of the Declaration of Independence, with the
changes made by Congress, is printed as document 2—he
hurled himself into this battle, which he called the hardest
of his life. With Madison's assistance, he worked for revoca-
tion of a panoply of statutes punishing religious dissent, providing tax support for the established clergy, and licensing
or regulating both dissenting preachers and the Anglican
parishes and clergy. These and other efforts met with only
limited success, but Jefferson was also able to secure appointment of a small committee to prepare a broad republican
revision of all of Virginia's laws.

Among the many bills that Jefferson himself prepared
for the committee of revisors was the famous Statute for
Establishing Religious Freedom, reproduced as document
3. One of only three accomplishments that Jefferson would
order to be mentioned on his tombstone, the bill was introduced in the Virginia General Assembly in 1779 as number
82 of the revisors' code. It languished there as Jefferson
moved on to serve as governor and U.S. minister to France.
Then, in 1784, Patrick Henry introduced a rival measure to
provide state aid (non-preferentially) to teachers of the
Christian religion. Madison, who had returned to the assembly with a national reputation earned in the Confederation Congress, managed to persuade the legislators to delay
a final vote on the assessment bill until the people could express their views. Between assembly sessions, at the urging
of his friends, he wrote his great Memorial Against Religious Assessments, printed as document 4. Circulated as a
popular petition, the Memorial was signed by 1700 Virginians. Thousands more signed different protests prompted
by Henry's bill. When the legislature reconvened in 1785,
no one tried to resurrect the general assessment, and Madison took full advantage of the swing of popular opinion.

Though there was insufficient time or patience to enact the whole of the revisors' code, he pulled his friend's great bill from the mass of pending propositions and defeated every effort to substantially amend it. The Statute for Religious Freedom was approved on June 19, 1786. With Madison's Memorial, it stands today among the most impressive and most eloquent enunciations of the two Virginians' lifelong effort, in the words of Madison, to extinguish forever "the ambitious hope of making laws for the human mind."

1. The Virginia Declaration of Rights June 12, 1776

A DECLARATION *of* RIGHTS *made by the representatives of the good people of* Virginia, *assembled in full and free Convention; which rights do pertain to them, and their posterity, as the basis and foundation of government.*

1. That all men are by nature equally free and independent, and have certain inherent rights, of which, when they enter into a state of society, they cannot, by any compact, deprive or divest their posterity; namely, the enjoyment of life and liberty, with the means of acquiring and possessing property, and pursuing and obtaining happiness and safety.

2. That all power is vested in, and consequently derived from, the people; that magistrates are their trustees and servants, and at all times amenable to them.

3. That government is, or ought to be, instituted for the common benefit, protection, and security, of the people, nation, or community, of all the various modes and forms of government that is best, which is capable of producing the greatest degree of happiness and safety, and is most effectually secured against the danger of mal-administration; and that whenever any government shall be found inadequate or contrary to these purposes, a majority of the community hath an indubitable, unalienable, and indefeasible right, to reform, alter, or abolish it, in such manner as shall be judged most conducive to the public weal.

4. That no man, or set of men, are entitled to exclusive or separate emoluments or privileges from the community, but in consideration of publick services; which, not being descendible, neither ought the offices of magistrate, legislator, or judge, to be hereditary.

5. That the legislative and executive powers of the state should be separate and distinct from the judiciary; and that the members of the two first may be restrained from oppression, by feeling and participating the burthens of the people, they should at fixed periods, be reduced to a private station, return into that body from which they were originally taken, and the vacancies be supplied

by frequent, certain, and regular elections, in which all, or any part of the former members, to be again eligible, or ineligible, as the laws shall direct.

6. That elections of members to serve as representatives of the people, in assembly, ought to be free; and that all men, having sufficient evidence of permanent common interest with, and attachment to, the community, have the right of suffrage, and cannot be taxed or deprived of their property for publick uses without their own consent, or that of their representatives so elected, nor bound by any law to which they have not, in like manner, assented, for the publick good.

7. That all power of suspending laws, or the execution of laws, by any authority without consent of the representatives of the people, is injurious to their rights, and ought not to be exercised.

8. That in all capital or criminal prosecutions a man hath a right to demand the cause and nature of his accusation, to be confronted with the accusers and witnesses, to call for evidence in his favour, and to a speedy trial by an impartial jury of his vicinage, without whose unanimous consent he cannot be found guilty, nor can he be compelled to give evidence against himself; that no man be deprived of his liberty except by the law of the land, or the judgment of his peers.

9. That excessive bail ought not to be required, nor excessive fines imposed, nor cruel and unusual punishments inflicted.

10. That general warrants, whereby any officer or messenger may be commanded to search suspected places without evidence of a fact committed, or to seize any person or persons not named, or whose offence is not particularly described and supported by evidence, are grievous and oppressive, and ought not to be granted.

11. That in controversies respecting property, and in suits between man and man, the ancient trial by jury is preferable to any other, and ought to be held sacred.

12. That the freedom of the press is one of the great bulwarks of liberty, and can never be restrained but by despotick governments.

13. That a well regulated militia, composed of the body of the people, trained to arms, is the proper, natural, and safe defence of a free state; that standing armies, in time of peace, should be

avoided, as dangerous to liberty: and that, in all cases, the military should be under strict subordination to, and governed by, the civil power.

14. That the people have a right to uniform government; and therefore, that no government separate from, or independent of, the government of *Virginia*, ought to be erected or established within the limits thereof.

15. That no free government, or the blessing of liberty, can be preserved to any people but by a firm adherence to justice, moderation, temperance, frugality, and virtue, and by frequent recurrence to fundamental principles.

16. That religion, or the duty which we owe to our CRE-ATOR, and the manner of discharging it, can be directed only by reason and conviction, not by force or violence, and therefore all men are equally entitled to the free exercise of religion, according to the dictates of conscience; and that it is the mutual duty of all to practice Christian forbearance, love, and charity, towards each other.

2. The Declaration of Independence, June–July, 1776*

A DECLARATION BY THE REPRESENTATIVES OF THE UNITED STATES OF AMERICA, IN GENERAL CONGRESS ASSEMBLED

When in the course of human events it becomes necessary for one people to dissolve the political bands which have connected them with another, and to assume among the powers of the earth the separate & equal station to which the laws of nature and of nature's God entitle them, a decent respect to the opinions of mankind requires that they should declare the causes which impel them to the separation.

We hold these truths to be self-evident: that all men are created equal; that they are endowed by their creator with ~~inherent and~~ *certain* inalienable rights; that among these are life, liberty, & the pursuit of happiness: that to secure these rights, governments are instituted among men, deriving their just powers from the consent of the governed; that whenever any form of government becomes destructive of these ends, it is the right of the people to alter or abolish it, & to institute new government, laying it's foundation on such principles, & organizing it's powers in such form, as to them shall seem more likely to effect their safety & happiness. Prudence indeed will dictate that governments long established should not be changed for light & transient causes; and accordingly all experience hath shown that mankind are more disposed to suffer while evils are sufferable, than to right themselves by abolishing forms to which they are accustomed. But when a long train of abuses & usurpations ~~begun at a distinguished period and~~ pursuing invariably the same object, evinces a design to reduce them under absolute despotism, it is their right, it is their duty to throw off such government, & to provide new guards for their future security. Such has been the patient sufferance of these

*The original words from Jefferson's draft are set in roman type. Additions to the draft made by Congress are set in italic; deletions by Congress from Jefferson's draft are set in cancelled type.

colonies; & such is now the necessity which constrains them to ~~expunge~~ *alter* their former systems of government. The history of the present king of Great Britain is a history of ~~unremitting~~ *repeated* injuries & usurpations, ~~among which appears no solitary fact to contradict the uniform tenor of the rest but all have~~ *all having* in direct object the establishment of an absolute tyranny over these states. To prove this let facts be submitted to a candid world ~~for the truth of which we pledge a faith yet unsullied by falsehood~~.

He has refused his assent to laws the most wholesome & necessary for the public good.

He has forbidden his governors to pass laws of immediate & pressing importance, unless suspended in their operation till his assent should be obtained; & when so suspended, he has utterly neglected to attend to them.

He has refused to pass other laws for the accommodation of large districts of people, unless those people would relinquish the right of representation in the legislature, a right inestimable to them, & formidable to tyrants only.

He has called together legislative bodies at places unusual, uncomfortable, and distant from the depository of their public records, for the sole purpose of fatiguing them into compliance with his measures.

He has dissolved representative houses repeatedly ~~& continually~~ for opposing with manly firmness his invasions on the rights of the people.

He has refused for a long time after such dissolutions to cause others to be elected, whereby the legislative powers, incapable of annihilation, have returned to the people at large for their exercise, the state remaining in the meantime exposed to all the dangers of invasion from without & convulsions within.

He has endeavored to prevent the population of these states; for that purpose obstructing the laws for naturalization of foreigners, refusing to pass others to encourage their migrations hither, & raising the conditions of new appropriations of lands.

He has ~~suffered~~ *obstructed* the administration of justice ~~totally to cease in some of these states~~ *by* refusing his assent to laws for establishing judiciary powers.

He has made ~~our~~ judges dependant on his will alone, for the tenure of their offices, & the amount & paiment of their salaries.

He has erected a multitude of new offices ~~by a self assumed power~~ and sent hither swarms of new officers to harass our people and eat out their substance.

He has kept among us in times of peace standing armies ~~and ships of war~~ without the consent of our legislatures.

He has affected to render the military independant of, & superior to the civil power.

He has combined with others to subject us to a jurisdiction foreign to our constitutions & unacknowledged by our laws, giving his assent to their acts of pretended legislation for quartering large bodies of armed troops among us; for protecting them by a mock-trial from punishment for any murders which they should commit on the inhabitants of these states; for cutting off our trade with all parts of the world; for imposing taxes on us without our consent; for depriving us *in many cases* of the benefits of trial by jury; for transporting us beyond seas to be tried for pretended offences; for abolishing the free system of English laws in a neighboring province, establishing therein an arbitrary government, and enlarging it's boundaries, so as to render it at once an example and fit instrument for introducing the same absolute rule into these ~~states~~ *colonies;* for taking away our charters, abolishing our most valuable laws, and altering fundamentally the forms of our governments; for suspending our own legislatures, & declaring themselves invested with power to legislate for us in all cases whatsoever.

He has abdicated government here ~~withdrawing his governors, and declaring us out of his allegiance & protection~~ *by declaring us out of his protection, and waging war against us.*

He has plundered our seas, ravaged our coasts, burnt our towns, & destroyed the lives of our people.

He is at this time transporting large armies of foreign mercenaries to compleat the works of death, desolation & tyranny already begun with circumstances of cruelty and perfidy *scarcely paralleled in the most barbarous ages, & totally* unworthy the head of a civilized nation.

He has constrained our fellow citizens taken captive on the high seas to bear arms against their country, to become the executioners of their friends & brethren, or to fall themselves by their hands.

He has *excited domestic insurrection among us, & has* endeavored to bring on the inhabitants of our frontiers the merciless Indian savages, whose known rule of warfare is an undistinguished destruction of all ages, sexes, & conditions ~~of existence~~.

He has incited treasonable insurrections of our fellow-citizens, with the allurements of forfeiture & confiscation of our property.

~~He has waged cruel war against human nature itself, violating it's most sacred rights of life and liberty in the persons of a distant people who never offended him, captivating & carrying them into slavery in another hemisphere, or to incur miserable death in their transportation thither. This piratical warfare, the opprobrium of INFIDEL powers, is the warfare of the CHRISTIAN king of Great Britain. Determined to keep open a market where MEN should be bought & sold, he has prostituted his negative for suppressing every legislative attempt to prohibit or to restrain this execrable commerce. And that this assemblage of horrors might want no fact of distinguished die, he is now exciting those very people to rise in arms among us, and to purchase that liberty of which he has deprived them, by murdering the people on whom he also obtruded them: thus paying off former crimes committed against the LIBERTIES of one people, with crimes which he urges them to commit against the LIVES of another.~~

In every stage of these oppressions we have petitioned for redress in the most humble terms: our repeated petitions have been answered only by repeated injuries.

A prince whose character is thus marked by every act which may define a tyrant is unfit to be the ruler of a *free* people ~~who mean to be free. Future ages will scarcely believe that the hardiness of one man adventured, within the short compass of twelve years only, to lay a foundation so broad & so undisguised for tyranny over a people fostered & fixed in principles of freedom.~~

Nor have we been wanting in attentions to our British brethren. We have warned them from time to time of attempts by their legislature to extend ~~a~~ *an unwarrantable* jurisdiction over ~~these our states~~ *us*. We have reminded them of the circumstances of our emigration & settlement here, ~~no one of which could warrant so strange a pretension: that these were effected at the expense of our own blood & treasure, unassisted by the wealth or the strength of Great Britain: that in constituting indeed our several forms of government, we had adopted one common king, thereby laying a foundation for perpetual league & amity with them: but that submission to their parliament was no part of our constitution, nor ever in idea, if history may be credited: and~~, we *have* appealed to their native justice and magnanimity ~~as well as to~~ *and we have conjured them by* the ties of our common kindred to disavow these usurpations which ~~were likely to~~ *would inevitably* interrupt our connection and correspondence. They too have been deaf to the voice of justice & of consanguinity, ~~and when occasions have been given them, by the regular course of their laws, of removing from their councils the disturbers of our harmony, they have, by their free election, re-established them in power. At this very time too they are permitting their chief magistrate to send over not only soldiers of our common blood, but Scotch & foreign mercenaries to invade & destroy us. These facts have given the last stab to agonizing affection, and manly spirit bids us to renounce forever these unfeeling brethren. We must endeavor to forget our former love for them, and hold them as we hold the rest of mankind, enemies in war, in peace friends. We might have been a free and a great people together; but a communication of grandeur & of freedom it seems is below their dignity. Be it so, since they will have it. The road to happiness & to glory is open to us too. We will tread it apart from them, and~~ *We must therefore* acquiesce in the necessity which denounces our ~~eternal~~ separation *and hold them as we hold the rest of mankind, enemies in war, in peace friends!*

~~We therefore the representatives of the United States of America in General Congress assembled do in the name & by authority of the good people of these states reject & renounce all allegiance & subjection to the kings of Great Britain & all others who may hereafter claim by, through or under them: we utterly dissolve all political connection which may heretofore have subsisted between us & the people or parliament of Great Britain: & finally we do assert & declare these colonies to be free & independent states, & that as free & independent states, they have full~~

~~power to levy war, conclude peace, contract alliances, establish commerce, & to do all other acts & things which independent states may of right do.~~

~~And for the support of this declaration we mutually pledge to each other our lives, our fortunes, & our sacred honor.~~

We therefore the representatives of the United States of America in General Congress assembled, appealing to the supreme judge of the world for the rectitude of our intentions, do in the name, & by the authority of the good people of these colonies, solemnly publish & declare that these united colonies are & of right ought to be free & independent states; that they are absolved from all allegiance to the British crown, and that all political connection between them & the state of Great Britain is, & ought to be, totally dissolved; & that as free & independent states they have full power to levy war, conclude peace, contract alliances, establish commerce & to do all other acts & things which independant states may of right do.

And for the support of this declaration, with a firm reliance on the protection of divine providence we mutually pledge to each other our lives, our fortunes, & our sacred honor.

3. Thomas Jefferson, A Bill for Establishing Religious Freedom, January 19, 1786

Section I. Well aware that the opinions and belief of men depend not on their own will, but follow involuntarily the evidence proposed to their minds; that Almighty God hath created the mind free, and manifested his supreme will that free it shall remain by making it altogether insusceptible of restraint; that all attempts to influence it by temporal punishments, or burthens, or by civil incapacitations, tend only to beget habits of hypocrisy and meanness, and are a departure from the plan of the holy author of our religion, who being lord both of body and mind, yet chose not to propagate it by coercions on either, as was in his Almighty power to do, but to extend it by its influence on reason alone; that the impious presumption of legislators and rulers, civil as well as ecclesiastical, who, being themselves but fallible and uninspired men, have assumed dominion over the faith of others, setting up their own opinions and modes of thinking as the only true and infallible, and as such endeavoring to impose them on others, hath established and maintained false religions over the greatest part of the world and through all time: That to compel a man to furnish contributions of money for the propagation of opinions which he disbelieves and abhors, is sinful and tyrannical; that even the forcing him to support this or that teacher of his own religious persuasion, is depriving him of the comfortable liberty of giving his contributions to the particular pastor whose morals he would make his pattern, and whose powers he feels most persuasive to righteousness; and is withdrawing from the ministry those temporary rewards, which proceeding from an approbation of their personal conduct, are an additional incitement to earnest and unremitting labours for the instruction of mankind; that our civil rights have no dependance on our religious opinions, any more than our opinions in physics or geometry; that therefore the proscribing any citizen as unworthy the public confidence by laying upon him an incapacity of being called to offices of trust and emolument, unless he profess or renounce this or that religious opinion, is depriving him injuriously of those privileges and advantages to which, in common with his fellow citizens, he has a natural right; that it tends also to corrupt the principles of that very religion it is meant to encourage, by bribing, with a monopoly of worldly honours and emoluments, those who will externally profess and conform to it; that though indeed these are criminal who do not withstand such temptation, yet neither are those innocent who lay the bait in their way; that the opinions of men are not the object of civil government, nor under its jurisdiction; that to suffer the civil magistrate to intrude his powers into the field of opinion and to restrain the profession or propagation of principles on supposition of their ill tendency is a dangerous falacy, which at once destroys all religious liberty, because he being of course judge of that tendency will make his opinions the rule of judgment, and approve or condemn the sentiments of others only as they shall square with or differ from his own; that it is time enough for the rightful purposes of civil government for its officers to interfere when principles break out into overt acts against peace and good order; and finally, that truth is great and will prevail if left to herself; that she is the proper and sufficient antagonist to error, and has nothing to fear from the conflict unless by human interposition disarmed of her natural weapons, free argument and debate; errors ceasing to be dangerous when it is permitted freely to contradict them.

Sect. II. WE the General Assembly of Virginia do enact that no man shall be compelled to frequent or support any religious worship, place, or ministry whatsoever, nor shall be enforced, restrained, molested, or burthened in his body or goods, nor shall otherwise suffer, on account of his religious opinions or belief; but that all men shall be free to profess, and by argument to maintain, their opinions in matters of religion, and that the same shall in no wise diminish, enlarge, or affect their civil capacities.

Sect. III. And though we well know that this Assembly, elected by the people for the ordinary purposes of legislation only, have no power to restrain the acts of succeeding Assemblies, constituted with powers equal to our own, and that therefore to declare this act irrevocable would be of no effect in law; yet we are free to declare, and do declare, that the rights hereby asserted are of the natural rights of mankind, and that if any act shall be hereafter passed to repeal the present or to narrow its operation, such act will be an infringement of natural right.

4. James Madison, A Memorial and Remonstrance Against Religious Assessments, June, 1785

We the subscribers, citizens of [Virginia], having taken into serious consideration, a Bill printed by order of the last Session of General Assembly, entitled "A Bill establishing a provision for Teachers of the Christian Religion," and conceiving that the same if finally armed with the sanctions of a law, will be a dangerous abuse of power, are bound as faithful members of a free State to remonstrate against it, and to declare the reasons by which we are determined. We remonstrate against the said Bill.

1. Because we hold it for a fundamental and undeniable truth, "that Religion or the duty which we owe to our Creator and the manner of discharging it, can be directed only by reason and conviction, not by force or violence." The Religion then of every man must be left to the conviction and conscience of every man; and it is the right of every man to exercise it as these may dictate. This right is in its nature an unalienable right. It is unalienable, because the opinions of men, depending only on the evidence contemplated by their own minds cannot follow the dictates of other men: It is unalienable also, because what is here a right towards men, is a duty towards the Creator. It is the duty of every man to render to the Creator such homage and such only as he believes to be acceptable to him. This duty is precedent, both in order of time and in degree of obligation, to the claims of Civil Society. Before any man can be considered as a member of Civil Society, he must be considered as a subject of the Governour of the Universe: And if a member of Civil Society, who enters into any subordinate Association, must always do it with a reservation of his duty to the General Authority; much more must every man who becomes a member of any particular Civil Society, do it with a saving of his allegiance to the Universal Sovereign. We maintain therefore that in matters of Religion, no mans right is abridged by the institution of Civil Society and that Religion is wholly exempt from its cognizance. True it is, that no other rule exists, by which any question which may divide a Society, can be ultimately

determined, but the will of the majority; but it is also true that the majority may trespass on the rights of the minority.

2. Because if Religion be exempt from the authority of the Society at large, still less can it be subject to that of the Legislative Body. The latter are but the creatures and vicegerents of the former. Their jurisdiction is both derivative and limited: it is limited with regard to the co-ordinate departments, more necessarily is it limited with regard to the constituents. The preservation of a free Government requires not merely, that the metes and bounds which separate each department of power be invariably maintained; but more especially that neither of them be suffered to overleap the great Barrier which defends the rights of the people. The Rulers who are guilty of such an encroachment, exceed the commission from which they derive their authority, and are Tyrants. The People who submit to it are governed by laws made neither by themselves nor by an authority derived from them, and are slaves.

3. Because it is proper to take alarm at the first experiment on our liberties. We hold this prudent jealousy to be the first duty of Citizens, and one of the noblest characteristics of the late Revolution. The free men of America did not wait till usurped power had strengthened itself by exercise, and entangled the question in precedents. They saw all the consequences in the principle, and they avoided the consequences by denying the principle. We revere this lesson too much soon to forget it. Who does not see that the same authority which can establish Christianity, in exclusion of all other Religions, may establish with the same ease any particular sect of Christians, in exclusion of all other Sects? that the same authority which can force a citizen to contribute three pence only of his property for the support of any one establishment, may force him to conform to any other establishment in all cases whatsoever?

4. Because the Bill violates that equality which ought to be the basis of every law, and which is more indispensible, in proportion as the validity or expediency of any law is more liable to be impeached. If "all men are by nature equally free and independent," all men are to be considered as entering into Society on equal conditions; as relinquishing no more, and therefore retain-

ing no less, one than another, of their natural rights. Above all are they to be considered as retaining an "*equal* title to the free exercise of Religion according to the dictates of Conscience." Whilst we assert for ourselves a freedom to embrace, to profess and to observe the Religion which we believe to be of divine origin, we cannot deny an equal freedom to those whose minds have not yet yielded to the evidence which has convinced us. If this freedom be abused, it is an offence against God, not against man: To God, therefore, not to man, must an account of it be rendered. As the Bill violates equality by subjecting some to peculiar burdens, so it violates the same principle, by granting to others peculiar exemptions. Are the Quakers and Menonists the only sects who think a compulsive support of their Religions unnecessary and unwarrantable? Can their piety alone be entrusted with the care of public worship? Ought their Religions to be endowed above all others with extraordinary privileges by which proselytes may be enticed from all others? We think too favorably of the justice and good sense of these denominations to believe that they either cover pre-eminences over their fellow citizens or that they will be seduced by them from the common opposition to the measure.

5. Because the Bill implies either that the Civil Magistrate is a competent Judge of Religious Truth; or that he may employ Religion as an engine of Civil policy. The first is an arrogant pretension falsified by the contradictory opinions of Rulers in all ages, and throughout the world: the second an unhallowed perversion of the means of salvation.

6. Because the establishment proposed by the Bill is not requisite for the support of the Christian Religion. To say that it is, is a contradiction to the Christian Religion itself, for every page of it disavows a dependence on the powers of this world: it is a contradiction to fact; for it is known that this Religion both existed and flourished, not only without the support of human laws, but in spite of every opposition from them, and not only during the period of miraculous aid, but long after it had been left to its own evidence and the ordinary care of Providence. Nay, it is a contradiction in terms; for a Religion not invented by human policy, must have pre-existed and been supported, before it was established by human policy. It is moreover to weaken in those who

profess this Religion a pious confidence in its innate excellence and the patronage of its Author; and to foster in those who still reject it, a suspicion that its friends are too conscious of its fallacies to trust it to its own merits.

7. Because experience witnesseth that ecclesiastical establishments, instead of maintaining the purity and efficacy of Religion, have had a contrary operation. During almost fifteen centuries has the legal establishment of Christianity been on trial. What have been its fruits? More or less in all placed, pride and indolence in the Clergy, ignorance and servility in the laity, in both, superstition, bigotry and persecution. Enquire of the Teachers of Christianity for the ages in which it appeared in its greatest lustre; those of every sect, point to the ages prior to its incorporation with Civil policy. Propose a restoration of this primitive State in which its Teachers depended on the voluntary rewards of their flocks, many of them predict its downfall. On which Side ought their testimony to have greatest weight, when for or when against their interest?

8. Because the establishment in question is not necessary for the support of Civil Government. If it be urged as necessary for the support of Civil Government only as it is a means of supporting Religion, and it be not necessary for the latter purpose, it cannot be necessary for the former. If Religion be not within the cognizance of Civil Government how can its legal establishment be necessary to Civil Government? What influence in fact have ecclesiastical establishments had on Civil Society? In some instances they have been seen to erect a spiritual tyranny on the ruins of the Civil authority; in many instances they have been seen upholding the thrones of political tyranny: in no instance have they been seen the guardians of the liberties of the people. Rulers who wished to subvert the public liberty, may have found an established Clergy convenient auxiliaries. A just Government instituted to secure & perpetuate it needs them not. Such a Government will be best supported by protecting every Citizen in the enjoyment of his Religion with the same equal hand which protects his person and his property; by neither invading the equal rights of any Sect, nor suffering any Sect to invade those of another.

9. Because the proposed establishment is a departure from that

generous policy, which, offering an Asylum to the persecuted and oppressed of every Nation and Religion, promised a lustre to our country, and an accession to the number of its citizens. What a melancholy mark is the Bill of sudden degeneracy? Instead of holding forth an Asylum to the persecuted, it is itself a signal of persecution. It degrades from the equal rank of Citizens all those whose opinions in Religion do not bend to those of the Legislative authority. Distant as it may be in its present form from the Inquisition, it differs from it only in degree. The one is the first step, the other the last in the career of intolerance. The magnanimous sufferer under this cruel scourge in foreign Regions, must view the Bill as a Beacon on our Coast, warning him to seek some other haven, where liberty and philanthropy in their due extent, may offer a more certain repose from his Troubles.

10. Because it will have a like tendency to banish our Citizens. The allurements presented by other situations are every day thinning their number. To superadd a fresh motive to emigration by revoking the liberty which they now enjoy, would be the same species of folly which has dishonoured and depopulated flourishing kingdoms.

11. Because it will destroy that moderation and harmony which the forbearance of our laws to intermeddle with Religion has produced among its several sects. Torrents of blood have been split in the old world, by vain attempts of the secular arm, to extinguish Religious discord, by proscribing all difference in Religious opinion. Time has at length revealed the true remedy. Every relaxation of narrow and rigorous policy, wherever it has been tried, has been found to assuage the disease. The American Theatre has exhibited proofs that equal and compleat liberty, if it does not wholly eradicate it, sufficiently destroys its malignant influence on the health and prosperity of the State. If with the salutary effects of this system under our own eyes, we begin to contract the bounds of Religious freedom, we know no name that will too severely reproach our folly. At least let warning be taken at the first fruits of the threatened innovation. The very appearance of the Bill has transformed "that Christian forbearance, love and charity," which of late mutually prevailed, into animosities and jealousies, which may not soon be appeased. What mischiefs may not be

dreaded, should this enemy to the public quiet be armed with the force of a law?

12. Because the policy of the Bill is adverse to the diffusion of the light of Christianity. The first wish of those who enjoy this precious gift ought to be that it may be imparted to the whole race of mankind. Compare the number of those who have as yet received it with the number still remaining under the dominion of false Religions; and how small is the former! Does the policy of the Bill tend to lessen the disproportion? No; it at once discourages those who are strangers to the light of revelation from coming into the Region of it; and countenances by example the nations who continue in darkness, in shutting out those who might convey it to them. Instead of Levelling as far as possible, every obstacle to the victorious progress of Truth, the Bill with an ignoble and unchristian timidity would circumscribe it with a wall of defence against the encroachments of error.

13. Because attempts to enforce by legal sanctions, acts obnoxious to so great a proportion of Citizens, tend to enervate the laws in general, and to slacken the bands of Society. If it be difficult to execute any law which is not generally deemed necessary or salutary, what may be the case, where it is deemed invalid and dangerous? And what may be the effect of so striking an example of impotency in the Government, on its general authority?

14. Because a measure of such singular magnitude and delicacy ought not to be imposed, without the clearest evidence that it is called for by a majority of citizens, and no satisfactory method is yet proposed by which the voice of the majority in this case may be determined, or its influence secured. "The people of the respective counties are indeed requested to signify their opinion respecting the adoption of the Bill to the next Session of Assembly." But the representation must be made equal, before the voice either of the Representatives or of the Counties will be that of the people. Our hope is that neither of the former will, after due consideration, espouse the dangerous principle of the Bill. Should the event disappoint us, it will still leave us in full confidence, that a fair appeal to the latter will reverse the sentence against our liberties.

15. Because finally, "the equal right of every citizen to the free exercise of his Religion according to the dictates of conscience" is held by the same tenure with all our other rights. If we recur to its origin, it is equally the gift of nature; if we weigh its importance, it cannot be less dear to us; if we consult the "Declaration of those rights which pertain to the good people of Virginia, as the basis and foundation of Government," it is enumerated with equal solemnity, or rather studied emphasis. Either then, we must say, that the Will of the Legislature is the only measure of their authority; and that in the plenitude of this authority, they may sweep away all our fundamental rights; or, that they are bound to leave this particular right untouched and sacred: Either we must say, that they may controul the freedom of the press, may abolish the Trial by Jury, may swallow up the Executive and Judiciary Powers of the State; nay that they may despoil us of our very right of suffrage, and erect themselves into an independent and hereditary Assembly or, we must say, that they have no authority to enact into law the Bill under consideration. We the Subscribers say, that the General Assembly of this Commonwealth have no such authority: And that no effort may be omitted on our part against so dangerous an usurpation, we oppose to it, this remonstrance; earnestly praying, as we are in duty bound, that the Supreme Lawgiver of the Universe, by illuminating those to whom it is addressed, may on the one hand, turn their Councils from every act which would affront his holy prerogative, or violate the trust committed to them: and on the other, guide them into every measure which may be worthy of his blessing, may redound to their own praise, and may establish more firmly the liberties, the prosperity and the happiness of the Commonwealth.

Documents for Chapter One

PARCHMENT BARRIERS AND FUNDAMENTAL RIGHTS

Jefferson and Madison both dated their acquaintance to the fall of 1776, when Jefferson returned from Congress and launched his long campaign for a republican revision of Virginia's laws and institutions. He found a willing ally in the youthful delegate from Orange, though Madison was then too modest and retiring to provide much more than regular support—and even that for just a single session. Defeated in the spring election—he refused, on principle, to ply the voters with their customary treats—Madison had nevertheless sufficiently impressed his legislative colleagues that they soon selected him to be a member of the Council of State. Here, until the legislature picked him as a delegate to Congress in the fall of 1779, he served with Governor Patrick Henry and then, quite briefly, under Jefferson himself as part of what was actually the plural executive of the union's largest state.

Though Madison's acquaintanceship with Jefferson grew deeper during 1779, it did not warm into a lasting friendship until the spring of 1783. While Madison was winning national stature as the hardest-working, most effective member of the Continental Congress, Jefferson completed a distressing second year as governor, withdrew into retirement, and was nearly crushed by the death of his wife. It required appointment as a peace commissioner to draw the penman out of his retreat and on to Philadelphia, where he took up lodgings at the boarding house where Madison had lived for the past three years. Through several weeks of conversation and association, as Jefferson prepared to sail for Europe, travelled down to Baltimore, discovered that a treaty had already been concluded, and travelled back to Philadelphia again, the two Virginians found themselves in close accord on state and federal affairs. By November 1783, when Madison's eligibility to serve in Congress expired, an intimate political and personal alliance had been sealed. Madison returned to the Virginia General Assembly to pursue their mutual agenda. Jefferson replaced him at the seat of Congress, then accepted his appointments, first as one of the commissioners to make commercial treaties with the European powers, then as minister to France.

When asked to name the most important author of the Constitution, college freshmen often name the author of the Declaration, blending and confusing two great charters. Jefferson, of course, was not a member of the Constitutional Convention, did not try to influence its deliberations, and was shocked, at first, by its decision to abandon the Articles of Confederation in favor of a thoroughgoing reconstruction of the federal system. Madison, by contrast, played a leading role at every step surrounding the creation and inauguration of the reconstructed system. He was a member of the Annapolis Convention of 1786, which called for the appointment of a plenary convention. He led the union's largest commonwealth, which led the other states, in organizing a successful meeting. He was principally responsible for the Virginia Plan, which served as the preliminary outline for the Constitution. When the great convention ended, he took a major part in the campaign for popular adoption of the Constitution, joined with Alexander Hamilton to write the most important commentary on the plan, captained its supporters to their triumph in Virginia's state convention, and as legislative leader of the first new Congress, drafted the first amendments. Jefferson's important contribution through these vital years was his determined effort to secure the quick addition of a bill of rights.

The letters printed in this section are mostly from the long-range dialogue between the two Virginians from the close of the great convention to the eve of Madison's introduction of his constitutional amendments. Jefferson's appeals were not the only reason for Madison's decision to prepare the Bill of Rights. Long delays in passing letters back and forth across the ocean usually assured that their exchanges had been dated by the hurry of events. Thus, Jefferson had seen a copy of the Constitution before he got his friend's report on the convention. Most of Jefferson's appeals for constitutional amendments did not arrive in the United States until his friend had made the critical decisions. Only the letter of March 15, 1789, in which the minister to France observed that the addition of a bill of rights would arm the courts with an important check on legislative or executive abuses, can be shown to have exerted a specific influence on its sponsor. Still, Jefferson's persistence on the subject surely helped the younger man to understand the value and necessity of adding libertarian amendments. Their conversations on the Constitution, Shays's Rebellion, and the Bill of Rights are fine examples of the workings of the long collaboration and of two great minds engaged with one another in the process of confronting several of the largest questions of their day.

5. Thomas Jefferson to William Stephens Smith Paris, November 13, 1787*

. . . I do not know whether it is to yourself or Mr. Adams I am to give my thanks for the copy of the new constitution. I beg leave through you to place them where due. It will be yet three weeks before I shall receive them from America. There are very good articles in it: & very bad. I do not know which preponderate. What we have lately read in the history of Holland, in the chapter on the Stadtholder, would have sufficed to set me against a chief magistrate eligible for a long duration, if I had ever been disposed towards one: & what we have always read of the elections of Polish kings should have forever excluded the idea of one continuable for life. Wonderful is the effect of impudent & persevering lying. The British ministry have so long hired their gazetteers to repeat and model into every form lies about our being in anarchy, that the world has at length believed them, the English nation has believed them, the ministers themselves have come to believe them, & what is more wonderful, we have believed them ourselves. Yet where does this anarchy exist? Where did it ever exist, except in the single instance of Massachusetts? And can history produce an instance of rebellion so honourably conducted? I say nothing of it's motives. They were founded in ignorance, not wickedness. God forbid we should ever be 20 years without such a rebellion. The people cannot be all, & always, well informed. The part which is wrong will be discontented in proportion to the importance of the facts they misconceive. If they remain quiet under such misconceptions it is a lethargy, the forerunner of death to the public liberty. We have had 13. states independent 11. years. There has been one rebellion. That comes to one rebellion in a century & a half for each state. What country before ever existed a century & half without a rebellion? & what country can preserve it's liberties if their rulers are not warned from time to time that their people preserve the spirit of resistance? Let them take arms. The remedy

*Smith was the son-in-law and secretary of John Adams, who was serving as U.S. minister to Great Britain.

is to set them right as to facts, pardon & pacify them. What signify a few lives lost in a century or two? The tree of liberty must be refreshed from time to time with the blood of patriots & tyrants. It is it's natural manure. Our Convention has been too much impressed by the insurrection of Massachusetts: and in the spur of the moment they are setting up a kite to keep the hen-yard in order. I hope in God this article will be rectified before the new constitution is accepted.

6. James Madison to Thomas Jefferson
Philadelphia, September 6, 1787*

... The Convention consists now as it has generally done of Eleven States. There has been no intermission of its Sessions since a house was formed; except an interval of about ten days allowed a Committee appointed to detail the general propositions agreed on in the House. The term of its dissolution cannot be more than one or two weeks distant. A Govermt. will probably be submitted to the pe*ople of* the *states* consisting of a [President] *cloathed* with *executive power:* a *Senate chosen* by the *Legislatures:* and another *house chosen* by the *people of* the *states* jointly *possessing* the *legislative power* and a regular *judiciary* establishment. The mode of constituting the *executive* is among the few points not yet finally settled. The S*enate* will consist of two *members* from each *state* and *appointed sexennially:* The other, of *members appointed biennially* by the *people of* the *states* in proportion to their number. The Legislative power will *extend to taxation trade* and sundry other general matters. The powers of Congress will be *distributed* according to their *nature among the several departments.* The States will be *restricted from paper money* and in a *few other instances.* These are *the outlines.* The extent of them may perhaps surprize you. I hazard an opinion nevertheless that the *plan should* it *be adopted* will neither effectually *answer* its *national object* nor prevent the local *mischiefs* which every where *excite disgusts* agst the *state governments.* The grounds of this opinion will be the subject of a future letter. ...

Nothing can exceed the universal anxiety for the event of the Meeting here. Reports and conjectures abound concerning the nature of the plan which is to be proposed. The public however is certainly in the dark with regard to it. The Convention is equally in the dark as to the reception wch. may be given to it on its publication. All the prepossessions are on the right side, but it may well be expected that certain characters will wage war against any reform whatever. My own idea is that the public mind will now or in a very little time receive any thing that promises stability to the

*Encoded words are set in italic.

public Councils & security to private rights, and that no regard
ought to be had to local prejudices or temporary considerations.
If the present moment be lost it is hard to say what may be our
fate.

Our information from Virginia is far from being agreeable. In
many parts of the Country the drouth has been extremely injurious to the Corn. I fear, tho' I have no certain information, that
Orange & Albemarle share in the distress. The people also are
said to be generally discontented. A paper emission is again a topic
among them. So is an instalment of all debts in some places and
the making property a tender in others. The taxes are another
source of discontent. The weight of them is complained of, and
the abuses in collecting them still more so. In several Counties
the prisons & Court Houses & Clerks offices have been wilfully
burnt. In Green Briar the course of Justice has been mutinously
stopped, and associations entered into agst. the payment of taxes.
No other County has yet followed the example. The approaching
meeting of the Assembly will probably allay the discontents on
one side by measures which will excite them on another.

7. James Madison to Thomas Jefferson
New York, October 24, 1787

. . . You will herewith receive the result of the Convention, which continued its Session till the 17th. of September. I take the liberty of making some observations on the subject which will help to make up a letter, if they should answer no other purpose.

It appeared to be the sincere and unanimous wish of the Convention to cherish and preserve the Union of the States. No proposition was made, no suggestion was thrown out, in favor of a partition of the Empire into two or more Confederacies.

It was generally agreed that the objects of the Union could not be secured by any system founded on the principle of a confederation of sovereign States. A *voluntary* observance of the federal law by all the members, could never be hoped for. *A compulsive* one could evidently never be reduced to practice; and if it could, involved equal calamities to the innocent & the guilty, the necessity of a military force both obnoxious & dangerous, and in general, a scene resembling much more a civil war, than the administration of a regular Government.

Hence was embraced the alternative of a Government which instead of operating, on the States, should operate without their intervention on the individuals composing them: and hence the change in the principle and proportion of representation.

This ground-work being laid, the great objects which presented themselves were 1. to unite a proper energy in the Executive and a proper stability in the Legislative departments, with the essential characters of Republican Government. 2. to draw a line of demarkation which would give to the General Government every power requisite for general purposes, and leave to the States every power which might be most beneficially administered by them. 3. to provide for the different interests of different parts of the Union. 4 to adjust the clashing pretensions of the large and small States. Each of these objects was pregnant with difficulties. The whole of them together formed a task more difficult than can be well concieved by those who were not concerned in the execution of it. Adding to these considerations the natural diversity of human opinions on all new and complicated subjects, it is impossible to consider the degree of concord which ultimately prevailed as less than a miracle.

The first of these objects as it respects the Executive, was peculiarly embarrassing. On the question whether it should consist of a single person, or a plurality of co-ordinate members, on the mode of appointment, on the duration in office, on the degree of power, on the re-eligibility, tedious and reiterated discussions took place. The plurality of co-ordinate members had finally but few advocates. Governour Randolph was at the head of them. The modes of appointment proposed were various, as by the people at large—by electors chosen by the people—by the Executives of the States—by the Congress, some preferring a joint ballot of the two Houses—some a separate concurrent ballot allowing to each a negative on the other house—some a nomination of several candidates by one House, out of whom a choice should be made by the other. Several other modifications were started. The expedient at length adopted seemed to give pretty general satisfaction to the members. As to the duration in office, a few would have preferred a tenure during good behaviour—a considerable number would have done so, in case an easy & effectual removal by impeachment could be settled. It was much agitated whether a long term, seven years for example, with a subsequent & perpetual ineligibility, or a short term with a capacity to be re-elected, should be fixed. In favor of the first opinion were urged the danger of a gradual degeneracy of re-elections from time to time, into first a life and then a heriditary tenure, and the favorable effect of an incapacity to be reappointed, on the independent exercise of the Executive authority. On the other side it was contended that the prospect of necessary degradation, would discourage the most dignified characters from aspiring to the office, would take away the principal motive to ye. faithful discharge of its duties—the hope of being rewarded with a reappointment, would stimulate ambition to violent efforts for holding over the constitutional term—and instead of producing an independent administration, and a firmer defence of the constitutional rights of the department, would render the officer more indifferent to the importance of a place which he would soon be obliged to quit for ever, and more ready to yield to the incroachmts. of the Legislature of which he might again be a member.—The questions concerning the degree of power turned chiefly on the appointment to offices, and the controul on the Legislature. An absolute appointment to all offices—to some offices—to no offices, formed the scale of opinions on the first point. On the second, some contended for an absolute negative, as the only possible mean of reducing to practice, the theory of a free Government which forbids a mixture of the Legislative & Executive powers. Others would be content with a revisionary power to be overruled by three fourths of both Houses. It was warmly urged that the judiciary department should be associated in the revision. The idea of some was that a separate revision should be given to the two departments—that if either objected two thirds; if both three fourths, should be necessary to overrule.

In forming the Senate, the great anchor of the Government, the questions as they came within the first object turned mostly on the mode of appointment, and the duration of it. The different modes proposed were, 1. by the House of Representatives 2. by the Executive, 3. by electors chosen by the people for the purpose. 4. by the State Legislatures. On the point of duration, the propositions descended from good-behavior to four years, through the intermediate terms of nine, seven, six, & five years. The election of the other branch was first determined to be triennial, and afterwards reduced to biennial.

The second object, the due partition of power, between the General & local Governments, was perhaps of all, the most nice and difficult. A few contended for an entire abolition of the States; some for indefinite power of Legislation in the Congress, with a negative on the laws of the States: some for such a power without a negative; some for a limited power of legislation, with such a negative; the majority finally for a limited power without the negative. The question with regard to the Negative underwent repeated discussions, and was finally rejected by a bare majority. As I formerly intimated to you my opinion in favor of this ingredient, I will take this occasion of explaining myself on the subject. Such a check on the States appears to me necessary 1. to prevent encroachments on the General authority. 2. to prevent instability and injustice in the legislation of the States.

1. Without such a check in the whole over the parts, our system involves the evil of imperia in imperio. If a compleat supremacy some where is not necessary in every Society, a controuling power at least is so, by which the general authority may be defended against encroachments of the subordinate authorities, and by which the latter may be restrained from encroachments on each other. If the supremacy of the British Parliament is not necessary as has been contended, for the harmony of that Empire; it is evident I think that without the royal negative or some equivalent controul, the unity of the system would be destroyed. The want of some such provision seems to have been mortal to the antient Confederacies, and to be the disease of the modern. Of the Lycian Confederacy little is known. That of the Amphyctions is well known to have been rendered of little use whilst it lasted, and in the end to have been destroyed by the predominance of the local over the federal authority. The same observation may be made, on the authority of Polybius, with regard to the Achæan League. The Helvetic System scarcely amounts to a Confederacy, and is distinguished by too many peculiarities to be a ground of comparison. The case of the United Netherlands is in point. The authority of a Statholder, the influence of a Standing army, the common interest in the conquered possessions, the pressure of surrounding danger, the guarantee of foreign powers, are not sufficient to secure the authority and interests of the generality, agst. the antifederal tendency of the provincial sovereignties. The German Empire is another example. A Heriditary chief with vast independent resources of wealth and power, a federal Diet, with ample parchment authority, a regular Judiciary establishment, the influence of the neighbourhood of great & formidable Nations, have been found unable either to maintain the subordination of the members, or to prevent their mutual contests & encroachments. Still more to the purpose is our own experience both during the war and since the peace. Encroachments of the States on the general authority, sacrifices of national to local interests, interferences of the measures of different States, form a great part of the history of our political system.—It may be said that the new Constitution is founded on different principles; and will have a different operation. I admit the difference to be material. It presents the aspect

rather of a feudal system of republics, if such a phrase may be used; than of a Confederacy of independent States. And what has been the progress and event of the feudal Constitutions? In all of them a continual struggle between the head and the inferior members, until a final victory has been gained in some instances by one, in others, by the other of them. In one respect indeed there is a remarkable variance between the two cases. In the feudal system the sovereign, though limited, was independent; and having no particular sympathy of interests with the great Barons, his ambition had as full play as theirs in the mutual projects of usurpation. In the American Constitution the general authority will be derived entirely from the subordinate authorities. The Senate will represent the States in their political capacity; the other House will represent the people of the States in their individual capacity. The former will be accountable to the Constituents at moderate, the latter at short periods. The President also derives his appointment from the States, and is periodically accountable to them. This dependence of the General, on the local authorities, seems effectually to guard the latter against any dangerous encroachments of the former; Whilst the latter, within their respective limits, will be continually sensible of the abridgment of their power, and be stimulated by ambition to resume the surrendered portion of it. We find the representatives of Counties and corporations in the Legislatures of the States, much more disposed to sacrifice the aggregate interest, and even authority, to the local views of their Constituents, than the latter to the former. I mean not by these remarks to insinuate that an esprit de corps will not exist in the national Government or that opportunities may not occur, of extending its jurisdiction in some points. I mean only that the danger of encroachments is much greater from the other side, and that the impossibility of dividing powers of legislation, in such a manner, as to be free from different constructions by different interests, or even from ambiguity in the judgment of the impartial, requires some such expedient as I contend for. Many illustrations might be given of this impossibility. How long has it taken to fix, and how imperfectly is yet fixed the legislative power of corporations, though that power is subordinate in the most compleat manner? The line of distinction between the power of regulating trade and that of drawing revenue from it, which was once considered as the barrier of our liberties, was found on fair discussion, to be absolutely undefinable. No distinction seems to be more obvious than that between spiritual and temporal matters. Yet wherever they have been made objects of Legislation, they have clashed and contended with each other, till one or the other has gained the supremacy. Even the boundaries between the Executive, Legislative & Judiciary powers, though in general so strongly marked in themselves, consist in many instances of mere shades of difference. It may be said that the Judicial authority under our new system will keep the States within their proper limits, and supply the place of a negative on their laws. The answer is, that it is more convenient to prevent the passage of a law, than to declare it void after it is passed; that this will be particularly the case, where the law aggrieves individuals, who may be unable to support an appeal agst. a State to the supreme Judiciary; that a State which would violate the Legislative rights of the Union, would not be very ready to obey a Judicial decree in support of them, and that a recurrence to force, which in the event of disobedience would be necessary, is an evil which the new Constitution meant to exclude as far as possible.

2. A constitutional negative on the laws of the States seems equally necessary to secure individuals agst. encroachments on their rights. The mutability of the laws of the States is found to be a serious evil. The injustice of them has been so frequent and so flagrant as to alarm the most stedfast friends of Republicanism. I am persuaded I do not err in saying that the evils issuing from these sources contributed more to that uneasiness which produced the Convention, and prepared the public mind for a general reform, than those which accrued to our national character and interest from the inadequacy of the Confederation to its immediate objects. A reform therefore which does not make provision for private rights, must be materially defective. The restraints agst. paper emissions, and violations of contracts are not sufficient. Supposing them to be effectual as far as they go, they are short of the mark. Injustice may be effected by such an infinitude of legislative expedients, that where the disposition exists it can only be controuled by some provision which reaches all cases whatsoever.

The partial provision made, supposes the disposition which will evade it. It may be asked how private rights will be more secure under the Guardianship of the General Government than under the State Governments, since they are both founded on the republican principle which refers the ultimate decision to the will of the majority, and are distinguished rather by the extent within which they will operate, than by any material difference in their structure. A full discussion of this question would, if I mistake not, unfold the true principles of Republican Government, and prove in contradiction to the concurrent opinions of theoretical writers, that this form of Government, in order to effect its purposes, must operate not within a small but an extensive sphere. I will state some of the ideas which have occurred to me on this subject. Those who contend for a simple Democracy, or a pure republic, actuated by the sense of the majority, and operating within narrow limits, assume or suppose a case which is altogether fictitious. They found their reasoning on the idea, that the people composing the Society, enjoy not only an equality of political rights; but that they have all precisely the same interests, and the same feelings in every respect. Were this in reality the case, their reasoning would be conclusive. The interest of the majority would be that of the minority also; the decisions could only turn on mere opinion concerning the good of the whole, of which the major voice would be the safest criterion; and within a small sphere, this voice could be most easily collected, and the public affairs most accurately managed. We know however that no Society ever did or can consist of so homogeneous a mass of Citizens. In the savage State indeed, an approach is made towards it; but in that State little or no Government is necessary. In all civilized Societies, distinctions are various and unavoidable. A distinction of property results from that very protection which a free Government gives to unequal faculties of acquiring it. There will be rich and poor; creditors and debtors; a landed interest, a monied interest, a mercantile interest, a manufacturing interest. These classes may again be subdivided according to the different productions of different situations & soils, & according to different branches of commerce, and of manufactures. In addition to these natural distinctions, artificial ones will be founded, on accidental differences in political, religious or other opinions, or an attachment to the persons of leading individuals. However erroneous or ridiculous these grounds of dissention and faction, may appear to the enlightened Statesman, or the benevolent philosopher, the bulk of mankind who are neither Statesmen nor Philosophers, will continue to view them in a different light. It remains then to be enquired whether a majority having any common interest, or feeling any common passion, will find sufficient motives to restrain them from oppressing the minority. An individual is never allowed to be a judge or even a witness in his own cause. If two individuals are under the biass of interest or enmity agst. a third, the rights of the latter could never be safely referred to the majority of the three. Will two thousand individuals be less apt to oppress one thousand, or two hundred thousand, one hundred thousand? Three motives only can restrain in such cases. 1. a prudent regard to private or partial good, as essentially involved in the general and permanent good of the whole. This ought no doubt to be sufficient of itself. Experience however shews that it has little effect on individuals, and perhaps still less on a collection of individuals; and least of all on a majority with the public authority in their hands. If the former are ready to forget that honesty is the best policy; the last do more. They often proceed on the converse of the maxim: that whatever is politic is honest. 2. respect for character. This motive is not found sufficient to restrain individuals from injustice, and loses its efficacy in proportion to the number which is to divide the praise or the blame. Besides as it has reference to public opinion, which is that of the majority, the Standard is fixed by those whose conduct is to be measured by it. 3. Religion. The inefficacy of this restraint on individuals is well known. The conduct of every popular Assembly, acting on oath, the strongest of religious ties, shews that individuals join without remorse in acts agst. which their consciences would revolt, if proposed to them separately in their closets. When Indeed Religion is kindled into enthusiasm, its force like that of other passions is increased by the sympathy of a multitude. But enthusiasm is only a temporary state of Religion, and whilst it lasts will hardly be seen with pleasure at the helm. Even in its coolest state, it has been much oftener a motive to oppression than a restraint from it. If then there must be different interests and parties in Society; and a majority when united by a common interest or passion can not be restrained from oppressing the minority, what remedy can be found in a republican Government, where the majority must ultimately decide, but that of giving such an extent of its sphere, that no common interest or passion will be likely to unite a majority of the whole number in an unjust pursuit. In a large Society, the people are broken into so many interests and parties, that a common sentiment is less likely to be felt, and the requisite concert less likely to be formed, by a majority of the whole. The same security seems requisite for the civil as for the religious rights of individuals. If the same sect form a majority and have the power, other sects will be sure to be depressed. Divide et impera, the reprobated axiom of tyranny, is under certain qualifications, the only policy, by which a republic can be administered on just principles. It must be observed however that this doctrine can only hold within a sphere of a mean extent. As in too small a sphere oppressive combinations may be too easily formed agst. the weaker party; so in too extensive a one, a defensive concert may be rendered too difficult against the oppression of those entrusted with the administration. The great desideratum in Government is, so to modify the sovereignty as that it may be sufficiently neutral between different parts of the Society to controul one part from invading the rights of another, and at the same time sufficiently controuled itself, from setting up an interest adverse to that of the entire Society. In absolute monarchies, the Prince may be tolerably neutral towards different classes of his subjects; but may sacrifice the happiness of all to his personal ambition or avarice. In small republics, the sovereign will is controuled from such a sacrifice of the entire Society, but is not sufficiently neutral towards the parts composing it. In the extended Republic of the United States, the General Government would hold a pretty even balance between the parties of particular States, and be at the same time sufficiently restrained by its dependence on the community, from betraying its general interests.

Begging pardon for this immoderate digression I return to the third object abovementioned, the adjustment of the different interests of different parts of the Continent. Some contended for an unlimited power over trade including exports as well as imports, and over slaves as well as other imports; some for such a power, provided the concurrence of two thirds of both Houses were required; Some for such a qualification of the power, with an exemption of exports and slaves, others for an exemption of exports only. The result is seen in the Constitution. S. Carolina & Georgia were inflexible on the point of the slaves.

The remaining object created more embarrassment, and a greater alarm for the issue of the Convention than all the rest put together. The little States insisted on retaining their equality in both branches, unless a compleat abolition of the State Governments should take place; and made an equality in the Senate a sine qua non. The large States on the other hand urged that as the new Government was to be drawn principally from the people immediately and was to operate directly on them, not on the States; and consequently as the States wd. lose that importance which is now proportioned to the importance of their voluntary compliances with the requisitions of Congress, it was necessary that the representation in both Houses should be in proportion to their size. It ended in the compromise which you will see, but very much to the dissatisfaction of several members from the large States.

It will not escape you that three names only from Virginia are subscribed to the Act. Mr. Wythe did not return after the death of his lady. Docr. MClurg left the Convention some time before the adjournment. The Governour and Col. Mason refused to be parties to it. Mr. Gerry was the only other member who refused. The objections of the Govr. turn principally on the latitude of the general powers, and on the connection established between the President and the Senate. He wished that the plan should be proposed to the States with liberty to them to suggest alterations which should all be referred to another general Convention, to be incorporated into the plan as far as might be judged expedient. He was not inveterate in his opposition, and grounded his refusal to subscribe pretty much on his unwillingness to commit himself, so as not to be at liberty to be governed by further lights on the subject. Col. Mason left Philada. in an exceeding ill humour indeed. A number of little circumstances arising in part from the impatience which prevailed towards the close of the business, conspired to whet his acrimony. He returned to Virginia with a fixed disposition to prevent the adoption of the plan if possible. He considers the want of a Bill of Rights as a fatal objection. His other objections are to the substitution of the Senate in place of an Executive Council & to the powers vested in that body—to the powers of the Judiciary—to the vice President being made President of the Senate—to the smallness of the number of Representatives—to the restriction on the States with regard to ex post facto laws—and most of all probably to the power of regulating trade, by a majority only of each House. He has some other lesser objections. Being now under the necessity of justifying his refusal to sign, he will of course muster every possible one. His conduct has given great umbrage to the County of Fairfax, and particularly to the Town of Alexandria. He is already instructed to promote in the Assembly the calling a Convention, and will probably be either not deputed to the Convention, or be tied up by express instructions. He did not object in general to the powers vested in the National Government, so much as to the modification. In some respects he admitted that some further powers would have improved the system. He acknowledged in particular that a negative on the State laws, and the appointment of the State Executives ought to be ingredients; but supposed that the public mind would not now bear them; and that experience would hereafter produce these amendments.

The final reception which will be given by the people at large to the proposed System can not yet be decided. The Legislature of N. Hampshire was sitting when it reached that State and was well pleased with it. As far as the sense of the people there has been expressed, it is equally favorable. Boston is warm and almost unanimous in embracing it. The impression on the Country is not yet known. No symptoms of disapprobation have appeared. The Legislature of that State is now sitting, through which the sense of the people at large will soon be promulged with tolerable certainty. The paper money faction in Rh. Island is hostile. The other party is zealously attached to it. Its passage through Connecticut is likely to be very smooth and easy. There seems to be less agitation in this State [New York] than any where. The discussion of the subject seems confined to the newspapers. The principal characters are known to be friendly. The Governour's party which has hitherto been the popular & most numerous one, is supposed to be on the opposite side; but considerable reserve is practised, of which he sets the example. N. Jersey takes the affirmative side of course. Meetings of the people are declaring their approbation, and instructing their representatives. Penna. Will be divided. The City of Philada., the Republican party, the Quakers, and most of the Germans espouse the Constitution. Some of the Constitutional leaders, backed by the western Country will oppose. An unlucky ferment on the subject in their Assembly just before its late adjournment has irritated both sides, particularly the opposition, and by redoubling the exertions of that party may render the event doubtful. The voice of Maryland I understand from pretty good authority, is, as far as it has been declared, strongly in favor of the Constitution. Mr. Chase is an enemy, but the Town of Baltimore which he represents, is warmly attached to it, and will shackle him as far as they can. Mr. Paca will probably be, as usual, in the politics of Chase. My information from Virginia is as yet extremely imperfect. I have a letter from Genl. Washington which speaks favorably of the impression within a circle of some extent; and another from Chancellor Pendleton which expresses his full acceptance of the plan, and the popularity of it in his district. I am told also that Innis and Marshall are patrons of it. In the opposite scale are Mr. James Mercer, Mr. R. H. Lee, Docr. Lee and their connections of course, Mr. M. Page according to Report, and most of the Judges & Bar of the general Court. The part which Mr. Henry will take is unknown here. Much will depend on it. I had taken it for granted from a variety of circumstances that he wd. be in the opposition, and still think that will be the case. There are reports however which favor a contrary supposition. From the States South of Virginia nothing has been heard. As the deputation from S. Carolina consisted of some of its weightiest characters, who have returned unanimously zealous in favor of the Constitution, it is probable that State will readily embrace it. It is not less probable, that N. Carolina will follow the example unless that of Virginia should counterbalance it. Upon the whole, although, the public mind will not be fully known, nor finally settled for a considerable time, appearances at present augur a more prompt, and general adoption of the Plan than could have been well expected.

8. Thomas Jefferson to James Madison
Paris, December 20, 1787

. . . The season admitting only of operations in the Cabinet, and these being in a great measure secret, I have little to fill a letter. I will therefore make up the deficiency by adding a few words on the Constitution proposed by our Convention. I like much the general idea of framing a government which should go on of itself peaceably, without needing continual recurrence to the state legislatures. I like the organization of the government into Legislative, Judiciary & Executive. I like the power given the Legislature to levy taxes, and for that reason solely approve of the greater house being chosen by the people directly. for tho' I think a house chosen by them will be very illy qualified to legislate for the Union, for foreign nations &c. yet this evil does not weigh against the good of preserving inviolate the fundamental principle that the people are not to be taxed but by representatives chosen immediately by themselves. I am captivated by the compromise of the opposite claims of the great & little states, of the latter to equal, and the former to proportional influence. I am much pleased too with the substitution of the method of voting by persons, instead of that of voting by states: and I like the negative given to the Executive with a third of either house, though I should have liked it better had the Judiciary been associated for that purpose, or invested with a similar and separate power. there are other good things of less moment. I will now add what I do not like. First the omission of a bill of rights providing clearly & without the aid of sophisms for freedom of religion, freedom of the press, protection against standing armies, restriction against monopolies, the eternal & unremitting force of the habeas corpus laws, and trials by jury in all matters of fact triable by the laws of the land & not by the law of Nations. To say, as Mr Wilson* does that a bill of rights was not necessary because all is reserved in the case of the

*In his speech of October 6, 1787, James Wilson of Pennsylvania was the first former delegate to the Constitutional Convention publicly to justify the Constitution.

general government which is not given, while in the particular ones all is given which is not reserved, might do for the Audience to whom it was addressed, but is surely a gratis dictum, opposed by strong inferences from the body of the instrument, as well as from the omission of the clause of our present confederation which had declared that in express terms. It was a hard conclusion to say because there has been no uniformity among the states as to the cases triable by jury, because some have been so incautious as to abandon this mode of trial, therefore the more prudent states shall be reduced to the same level of calamity. It would have been much more just & wise to have concluded the other way that as most of the states had judiciously preserved this palladium, those who had wandered should be brought back to it, and to have established general right instead of general wrong. Let me add that a bill of rights is what the people are entitled to against every government on earth, general or particular, & what no just government should refuse, or rest on inference. The second feature I dislike, and greatly dislike, is the abandonment in every instance of the necessity of rotation in office, and most particularly in the case of the President. Experience concurs with reason in concluding that the first magistrate will always be re-elected if the constitution permits it. He is then an officer for life. This once observed it becomes of so much consequence to certain nations to have a friend or a foe at the head of our affairs that they will interfere with money & with arms. A Galloman or an Angloman will be supported by the nation he befriends. If once elected, and at a second or third election outvoted by one or two votes, he will pretend false votes, foul play, hold possession of the reins of government, be supported by the states voting for him, especially if they are the central ones lying in a compact body themselves & separating their opponents: and they will be aided by one nation of Europe, while the majority are aided by another. The election of a President of America some years hence will be much more interesting to certain nations of Europe than ever the election of a king of Poland was. Reflect on all the instances in history antient & modern, of elective monarchies, and say if they do not give foundation for my fears. The Roman emperors, the popes, while they were of any importance, the German emperors till they became hereditary in practice, the kings of Poland, the Deys of the Ottoman dependancies. It may be said that if elections are to be attended with these disorders, the seldomer they are renewed the better. But experience shews that the only way to prevent disorder is to render them uninteresting by frequent changes. An incapacity to be elected a second time would have been the only effectual preventative. The power of removing him every fourth year by the vote of the people is a power which will not be exercised. The king of Poland is removeable every day by the Diet, yet he is never removed.—Smaller objections are the Appeal in fact as well as law, and the binding all persons Legislative Executive & Judiciary by oath to maintain that constitution. I do not pretend to decide what would be the best method of procuring the establishment of the manifold good things in this constitution, and of getting rid of the bad. Whether by adopting it in hopes of future amendment, or, after it has been duly weighed & canvassed by the people, after seeing the parts they generally dislike, & those they generally approve, to say to them "We see now what you wish. send together your deputies again, let them frame a constitution for you omitting what you have condemned, & establishing the powers you approve. Even these will be a great addition to the energy of your government."—At all events I hope you will not be discouraged from other trials, if the present one should fail of it's full effect.— I have thus told you freely what I like & dislike: merely as a matter of curiosity for I know your own judgment has been formed on all these points after having heard every thing which could be urged on them. I own I am not a friend to a very energetic government. It is always oppressive. The late rebellion in Massachusetts has given more alarm than I think it should have done. Calculate that one rebellion in 13 states in the course of 11 years, is but one for each state in a century & a half. No country should be so long without one. Nor will any degree of power in the hands of government prevent insurrections. France, with all it's despotism, and two or three hundred thousand men always in arms has had three insurrections in the three years I have been here in every one of which greater numbers were engaged than in Massachusetts & a great deal more blood was spilt. In Turkey, which Montesquieu supposes more despotic, insurrections are the events of every day. In England, where the hand of power is lighter than here, but heavier than with us they happen every half dozen years. Compare again the ferocious depredations of their insurgents with the order, the moderation & the almost self extinguishment of ours.—After all, it is my principle that the will of the Majority should always prevail. If they approve the proposed Convention [Constitution] in all it's parts, I shall concur in it chearfully, in hopes that they will amend it whenever they shall find it works wrong. I think our governments will remain virtuous for many centuries; as long as they are chiefly agricultural; and this will be as long as there shall be vacant lands in any part of America. When they get piled upon one another in large cities, as in Europe, they will become corrupt as in Europe. Above all things I hope the education of the common people will be attended to; convinced that on their good sense we may rely with the most security for the preservation of a due degree of liberty. I have tired you by this time with my disquisitions & will therefore only add assurances of the sincerity of those sentiments of esteem & attachment with which I am Dear Sir your affectionate friend & servant.

9. Thomas Jefferson to James Madison
Paris, July 31, 1788

... I sincerely rejoice at the acceptance of our new constitution by nine states. It is a good canvas, on which some strokes only want retouching. What these are, I think are sufficiently manifested by the general voice from North to South, which calls for a bill of rights. It seems pretty generally understood that this should go to Juries, Habeas corpus, Standing armies, Printing, Religion & Monopolies. I conceive there may be difficulty in finding general modifications of these suited to the habits of all the states. But if such cannot be found then it is better to establish trials by Jury, the right of Habeas corpus, freedom of the press & freedom of religion in all cases, and to abolish standing armies in time of peace, and Monopolies, in all cases, than not to do it in any. The few cases wherein these things may do evil, cannot be weighed against the multitude wherein the want of them will do evil. In disputes between a foreigner & a native, a trial by jury may be improper. But if this exception cannot be agreed to, the remedy will be to model the jury by giving the medietas linguae in civil as well as criminal cases. Why suspend the Hab. corp. in insurrections & rebellions? The parties who may be arrested may be charged instantly with a well defined crime. Of course the judge will remand them. If the publick safety requires that the government should have a man imprisoned on less probable testimony in those than in other emergencies; let him be taken & tried, retaken & retried, while the necessity continues, only giving him redress against the government for damages. Examine the history of England: see how few of the cases of the suspension of the Habeas corpus law have been worthy of that suspension. They have been either real treasons wherein the parties might as well have been charged at once, or sham-plots where it was shameful they should ever have been suspected. Yet for the few cases wherein the suspension of the hab. corp. has done real good, that operation is now become habitual, & the minds of the nation almost prepared to live under it's constant suspension. A declaration that the federal government will never restrain the presses from printing any thing they please, will not take away the liability of the printers for false facts printed. The declaration that religious faith shall be unpunished, does not give impunity to criminal acts dictated by religious error. The saying there shall be no monopolies lessens the incitements to ingenuity, which is spurred on by the hope of a monopoly for a limited time, as of 14. years; but the benefit even of limited monopolies is too doubtful to be opposed to that of their general suppression. If no check can be found to keep the number of standing troops within safe bounds, while they are tolerated as far as necessary, abandon them altogether, discipline well the militia, & guard the magazines with them. More than magazine-guards will be useless if few, & dangerous if many. No European nation can ever send against us such a regular army as we need fear, & it is hard if our militia are not equal to those of Canada or Florida. My idea then is, that tho' proper exceptions to these general rules are desireable & probably practicable, yet if the exceptions cannot be agreed on, the establishment of the rules in all cases will do ill in very few. I hope therefore a bill of rights will be formed to guard the people against the federal government, as they are already guarded against their state governments in most instances.

The abandoning the principle of necessary rotation in the Senate, has I see been disapproved by many; in the case of the President, by none. I readily therefore suppose my opinion wrong, when opposed by the majority as in the former instance, & the totality as in the latter. In this however I should have done it with more complete satisfaction, had we all judged from the same position.

10. James Madison to Thomas Jefferson New York, October 17, 1788

... The little pamphlet herewith inclosed will given you a collective view of the alterations which have been proposed for the new Constitution.* Various and numerous as they appear they certainly omit many of the true grounds of opposition. The articles relating to Treaties—to paper money, and to contracts, created more enemies than all the errors in the System positive & negative put together. It is true nevertheless that not a few, particularly in Virginia have contended for the proposed alterations from the most honorable & patriotic motives; and that among the advocates for the Constitution, there are some who wish for further guards to public liberty & individual rights. As far as these may consist of a constitutional declaration of the most essential rights, it is probable they will be added; though there are many who think such addition unnecessary, and not a few who think it misplaced in such a Constitution. There is scarce any point on which the party in opposition is so much divided as to its importance and its propriety. My own opinion has always been in favor of a bill of rights; provided it be so framed as not to imply powers not meant to be included in the enumeration. At the same time I have never thought the omission a material defect, nor been anxious to supply it even by subsequent amendment, for any other reason than that it is anxiously desired by others. I have favored it because I supposed it might be of use, and if properly executed could not be of disservice. I have not viewed it in an important light 1. because I conceive that in a certain degree, though not in the extent argued by Mr. Wilson, the rights in question are reserved by the manner in which the federal powers are granted. 2 because there is great reason to fear that a positive declaration of some of the most essential rights could not be obtained in the requisite latitude. I am

*The Ratifications of the New Federal Constitution, Together with the Amendments, Proposed by the Several States (Richmond, 1788). The pamphlet omitted the ratifications of the five states that did not propose amendments—Delaware, Pennsylvania, New Jersey, Georgia, and Connecticut.

sure that the rights of Conscience in particular, if submitted to public definition would be narrowed much more than they are likely ever to be by an assumed power. One of the objections in New England was that the Constitution by prohibiting religious tests opened a door for Jews Turks & infidels. 3. because the limited powers of the federal Government and the jealousy of the subordinate Governments, afford a security which has not existed in the case of the State Governments, and exists in no other. 4 because experience proves the inefficacy for a bill of rights on those occasions when its controul is most needed. Repeated violations of these parchment barriers have been committed by overbearing majorities in every State. In Virginia I have seen the bill of rights violated in every instance where it has been opposed to a popular current. Notwithstanding the explicit provision contained in that instrument for the rights of Conscience it is well known that a religious establishment wd. have taken place in that State, if the legislative majority had found as they expected, a majority of the people in favor of the measure; and I am persuaded that if a majority of the people were now of one sect, the measure would still take place and on narrower ground than was then proposed, notwithstanding the additional obstacle which the law has since created. Wherever the real power in a Government lies, there is the danger of oppression. In our Governments the real power lies in the majority of the Community, and the invasion of private rights is chie*fly t*o be apprehended, not from acts of Government contrary to the sense of its constituents, but from acts in which the Government is the mere instrument of the major number of the constituents. This is a truth of great importance, but not yet sufficiently attended to: and is probably more strongly impressed on my mind by facts, and reflections suggested by them, than on yours which has contemplated abuses of power issuing from a very different quarter. Wherever there is an interest and power to do wrong, wrong will generally be done, and not less readily by a powerful & interested party than by a powerful and interested prince. The difference, so far as it relates to the superiority of republics over monarchies, lies in the less degree of probability that interest may prompt abuses of power in the former than in the latter; and in the security in the former agst. oppression of

151

more than the smaller part of the society, whereas in the former it may be extended in a manner to the whole. The difference so far as it relates to the point in question—the efficacy of a bill of rights in controuling abuses of power—lies in this, that in a monarchy the latent force of the nation is superior to that of the sovereign, and a solemn charter of popular rights must have a great effect, as a standard for trying the validity of public acts, and a signal for rousing & uniting the superior force of the community; whereas in a popular Government, the political and physical power may be considered as vested in the same hands, that is in a majority of the people, and consequently the tyrannical will of the sovereign is not [to] be controuled by the dread of an appeal to any other force within the community. What use then it may be asked can a bill of rights serve in popular Governments? I answer the two following which though less essential than in other Governments, sufficiently recommend the precaution. 1. The political truths declared in that solemn manner acquire by degrees the character of fundamental maxims of free Government, and as they become incorporated with the national sentiment, counteract the impulses of interest and passion. 2. Altho' it be generally true as above stated that the danger of oppression lies in the interested majorities of the people rather than in usurped acts of the Government, yet there may be occasions on which the evil may spring from the latter sources; and on such, a bill of rights will be a good ground for an appeal to the sense of the community. Perhaps too there may be a certain degree of danger, that a succession of artful and ambitious rulers, may by gradual & well-timed advances, finally erect an independent Government on the subversion of liberty. Should this danger exist at all, it is prudent to guard agst. it, especially when the precaution can do no injury. At the same time I must own that I see no tendency in our governments to danger on that side. It has been remarked that there is a tendency in all Governments to an augmentation of power at the expence of liberty. But the remark as usually understood does not appear to me well founded. Power when it has attained a certain degree of energy and independence goes on generally to further degrees. But when below that degree, the direct tendency is to further degrees of relaxation, until the abuses of liberty beget a sudden transition to an undue degree of power. With this explanation the remark may be true; and in the latter sense only is it in my opinion applicable to the Governments in America. It is a melancholy reflection that liberty should be equally exposed to danger whether the Government have too much or too little power, and that the line which divides these extremes should be so inaccurately defined by experience.

Supposing a bill of rights to be proper the articles which ought to compose it, admit of much discussion. I am inclined to think that absolute restrictions in cases that are doubtful, or where emergencies may overrule them, ought to be avoided. The restrictions however strongly marked on paper will never be regarded when opposed to the decided sense of the public; and after repeated violations in extraordinary cases, they will lose even their ordinary efficacy. Should a Rebellion or insurrection alarm the people as well as the Government, and a suspension of the Hab. Corp. be dictated by the alarm, no written prohibitions on earth would prevent the measure. Should an army in time of peace be gradually established in our neighbourhood by Britn: or Spain, declarations on paper would have as little effect in preventing a standing force for the public safety. The best security agst. these evils is to remove the pretext for them. With regard to monopolies they are justly classed among the greatest nusances in Government. But is it clear that as encouragements to literary works and ingenious discoveries, they are not too valuable to be wholly renounced? Would it not suffice to reserve in all cases a right to the Public to abolish the privilege at a price to be specified in the grant of it? Is there not also infinitely less danger of this abuse in our Governments, than in most others? Monopolies are sacrifices of the many to the few. Where the power is in the few it is natural for them to sacrifice the many to their own partialities and corruptions. Where the power, as with us, is in the many not in the few, the danger can not be very great that the few will be thus favored. It is much more to be dreaded that the few will be unnecessarily sacrificed to the many.

11. James Madison to George Eve
New York, January 2, 1789*

Being informed that reports prevail not only that I am opposed to any amendments whatever to the new federal Constitution; but that I have ceased to be a friend to the rights of Conscience; and inferring from a conversation with my brother William, that you are disposed to contradict such reports as far as your knowledge of my sentiments may justify, I am led to trouble you with this communication of them. As a private Citizen it could not be my wish that erroneous opinions should be entertained, with respect to either of those points, particularly, with respect to religious liberty. But having been induced to offer my services to this district as its representative in the federal Legislature, considerations of a public nature make it proper that, with respect to both, my principles and views should be rightly understood.

I freely own that I have never seen in the Constitution as it now stands those serious dangers which have alarmed many respectable Citizens. Accordingly whilst it remained unratified, and it was necessary to unite the States in some one plan, I opposed all previous alterations as calculated to throw the States into dangerous contentions, and to furnish the secret enemies of the Union with an opportunity of promoting its dissolution. Circumstances are now changed: The Constitution is established on the ratifications of eleven States and a very great majority of the people of America; and amendments, if pursued with a proper moderation and in a proper mode, will be not only safe, but may serve the double purpose of satisfying the minds of well meaning opponents, and of providing additional guards in favour of liberty. Under this change of circumstances, it is my sincere opinion that the Constitution ought to be revised, and that the first Congress meeting under it, ought to prepare and recommend to the States for ratification, the most satisfactory provisions for all essential rights, particularly the rights of Conscience in the fullest latitude, the

*Eve was pastor of the Baptist Blue Run church in Madison's Orange County.

freedom of the press, trials by jury, security against general warrants &c. I think it will be proper also to provide expressly in the Constitution, for the periodical increase of the number of Representatives until the amount shall be entirely satisfactory; and to put the judiciary department into such a form as will render vexatious appeals impossible. There are sundry other alterations which are either eligible in themselves, or being at least safe, are recommended by the respect due to such as wish for them.

I have intimated that the amendments ought to be proposed by the first Congress. I prefer this mode to that of a General Convention, 1st. because it is the most expeditious mode. A convention must be delayed, until 2/3 of the State Legislatures shall have applied for one; and afterwards the amendments must be submitted to the States; whereas if the business be undertaken by Congress the amendments may be prepared and submitted in March next. 2dly. because it is the most certain mode. There are not a few States who will absolutely reject the proposal of a Convention, and yet not be averse to amendments in the other mode. Lastly, it is the safest mode. The Congress, who will be appointed to execute as well as to amend the Government, will probably be careful not to destroy or endanger it. A convention, on the other hand, meeting in the present ferment of parties, and containing perhaps insidious characters from different parts of America, would at least spread a general alarm, and be but too likely to turn every thing into confusion and uncertainty. It is to be observed however that the question concerning a General Convention, will not belong to the federal Legislature. If 2/3 of the States apply for one, Congress can not refuse to call it: if not, the other mode of amendments must be pursued. I am Sir with due respect your friend & Obedt. servant.

12. Thomas Jefferson to James Madison
Paris, March 15, 1789

. . . Your thoughts on the subject of the Declaration of rights in the letter of Oct. 17. I have weighed with great satisfaction. Some of them had not occurred to me before, but were acknowledged just in the moment they were presented to my mind. In the arguments in favor of a declaration of rights, you omit one which has great weight with me, the legal check which it puts into the hands of the judiciary. This is a body, which if rendered independent, & kept strictly to their own department merits great confidence for their learning & integrity. In fact what degree of confidence would be too much for a body composed of such men as Wythe, Blair & Pendleton?* . . . I am happy to find that on the whole you are a friend to this amendment. The Declaration of rights is like all other human blessings alloyed with some inconveniences, and not accomplishing fully it's object. But the good in this instance vastly overweighs the evil. I cannot refrain from making short answers to the objections which your letter states to have been raised. 1. That the rights in question are reserved by the manner in which the federal powers are granted. Answer. A constitutive act may certainly be so formed as to need no declaration of rights. The act itself has the force of a declaration as far as it goes: and if it goes to all material points nothing more is wanting. In the draught of a constitution which I had once a thought of proposing in Virginia, & printed afterwards, I endeavored to reach all the great objects of public liberty, and did not mean to add a declaration of rights. Probably the object was imperfectly executed: but the deficiencies would have been supplied by others in the course of discussion. But in a constitutive act which leaves some precious articles unnoticed, and raises implications against others, a declaration of rights becomes necessary by way of supplement. This is the case of our new federal constitution. This instrument forms us into

*George Wythe, John Blair, and Edmund Pendleton (president) were the three judges of the Virginia Court of Chancery.

one state as to certain objects, and gives us a legislative & executive body for these objects. It should therefore guard us against their abuses of power within the field submitted to them. 2. A positive declaration of some essential rights could not be obtained in the requisite latitude. Answer. Half a loaf is better than no bread. If we cannot secure all our rights, let us secure what we can. 3. The limited powers of the federal government & jealousy of the subordinate governments afford a security which exists in no other instance. Answer. The first member of this seems resolvable into the 1st. objection before stated. The jealousy of the subordinate governments is a precious reliance. But observe that those governments are only agents. They must have principles furnished them whereon to found their opposition. The declaration of rights will be the text whereby they will try all the acts of the federal government. In this view it is necessary to the federal government also: as by the same text they may try the opposition of the subordinate governments. 4. Experience proves the inefficacy of a bill of rights. True. But tho it is not absolutely efficacious under all circumstances, it is of great potency always, and rarely inefficacious. A brace the more will often keep up the building which would have fallen with that brace the less. There is a remarkeable difference between the characters of the Inconveniencies which attend a Declaration of rights, & those which attend the want of it. The inconveniences of the Declaration are that it may cramp government in it's useful exertions. But the evil of this is shortlived, moderate, & reparable. The inconveniencies of the want of a Declaration are permanent, afflicting & irreparable: they are in constant progression from bad to worse. The executive in our governments is not the sole, it is scarcely the principal object of my jealousy. The tyranny of the legislatures is the most formidable dread at present, and will be for long years. That of the executive will come in it's turn, but it will be at a remote period. I know there are some among us who would now establish a monarchy. But they are inconsiderable in number and weight of character. The rising race are all republicans. We were educated in royalism: no wonder if some of us retain that idolatry still. Our young people are educated in republicanism. An apostacy from that to royalism is unprecedented & impossible. I am much pleased with the prospect that a declaration of rights will be added: and hope it will be done in that way which will not endanger the whole frame of the government, or any essential part of it.

Documents for Chapter Two

"The Earth Belongs to the Living"

Questions of political economy were at the heart of the dispute which ended in the quick emergence of the nation's first political parties. The argument began—or, more precisely, disagreements suddenly erupted in the ranks of those whose close cooperation had been critical to the creation of the Constitution—when Madison objected to the plan for managing the revolutionary debt. As subsequent developments would show, the new republic's secretary of the treasury, with whom the legislative leader had collaborated so effectively in the campaign for the adoption of the Constitution, intended his financial measures as a starting point and a foundation for a larger program that would speed the nation's economic growth and arm it, over time, with the financial and commercial underpinnings of a modern nation-state. The clearer this became, the more profoundly Madison objected. Though neither man had understood it clearly at the time, the authors of *The Federalist* had drawn together during the preceding decade to secure reforms which they desired for partially conflicting reasons. Hamilton's intentions, in the end, were incompatible with Madison's contrasting vision for the nation. They threatened, over time, to press American society into a mold that most Virginians saw as inconsistent with the health of a republic.

Conflicting concepts of political economy—a term employed by eighteenth-century thinkers to refer not only to specific governmental measures but to all the ways in which a polity and an economy may intermesh—had been developing since early in the 1780s, though even their most eloquent proponents were only partially and intermittently aware of the profundity of differences between them. Deeply influenced by the thinking of the eighteenth-century critics of the British system of administration and finance, Madison and Jefferson believed that relatively equal farmer-owners were the sort of men best suited to sustain a sound republic. With many of the eighteenth-century British critics of the "modern Whig" regime, the two Virginians felt a deep ambivalence about intensive economic change. Themselves commercial farmers, not admirers of a crude, subsistence style of life, they understood the intimate relationship between prosperity and oceanic trade, championed mechanical improvements, and participated in contemporary celebration of the civilizing benefits of commerce. Nevertheless, they feared the social, moral, and political effects of urban overcrowding, growing inequalities of wealth, and the increasing specialization of labor. Most of all, perhaps, they shared the British opposition's deep revulsion from the mysteries of credit, debt, and chartered corporations, together with a fierce distrust of the corrupting links between executives and monied merchant-financiers that had proliferated in the British system. From early in their friendship, Madison and Jefferson worked constantly to open oceanic trade, which linked the country's agricultural producers with the European markets for their goods and European sources of industrial supplies. They trusted that the opening of the

Atlantic and continual expansion to the west would long delay developments they feared and help perpetuate the mostly agricultural societies that would sustain a healthy public life. Hamilton's attempts to imitate the English system of finance and to promote the rapid growth of manufacturing and commerce, accompanied by his resistance to their own proposals to coerce commercial reciprocity from Britain, pushed the two Virginians into opposition.

Query XIX of Jefferson's *Notes on the State of Virginia*, begun in 1781 as a response to questions from the secretary of the French legation and published in 1785 and 1787 (first in French and then in English), is the classic exposition of the Jeffersonian ideal. It is reproduced as document 19 and followed by two essays from the *National Gazette*, documents 20 and 21, in which his younger partner offered similar expressions of these thoughts. The conversation prompted by Jefferson's distress over poverty in France, beginning with his fireside letter to his friend and stretching through the great discussion of the rights of living generations, constitutes the burden of this section.

13. Thomas Jefferson to James Madison
Fountainebleau, October 28, 1785

Seven o'clock, and retired to my fireside, I have determined to enter into conversation with you; this is a village of about 5000 inhabitants, when the court is not here and 20,000 when they are, occupying a valley thro' which runs a brook, and on each side of it a ridge of small mountains most of which are naked rock. The king comes here, in the fall always, to hunt. His court attend him, as do also the foreign diplomatic corps. But as this is not indispensably required, & my finances do not admit the expence of a continued residence here, I propose to come occasionally to attend the king's levees, returning again to Paris, distant 40 miles. This being the first trip, I set out yesterday morning to take a view of the place. For this purpose I shaped my course towards the highest of the mountains in sight, to the top of which was about a league. As soon as I had got clear of the town I fell in with a poor woman walking at the same rate with myself & going the same course. Wishing to know the condition of the labouring poor I entered into conversation with her, which I began by enquiries for the path which would lead me into the mountain; & thence proceeded to enquiries into her vocation, condition & circumstance. She told me she was a day labourer, at 8. sous or 4 d. sterling the day; that she had two children to maintain, & to pay a rent of 30 livres for her house (which would consume the hire of 75 days) that often she could get no emploiment, and of course was without bread. As we had walked together near a mile & she had so far served me as a guide, I gave her, on parting, 24 sous. She burst into tears of a gratitude which I could perceive was unfeigned, because she was unable to utter a word. She had probably never before received so great an aid. This little attendrissement, with the solitude of my walk led me into a train of reflections on that unequal division of property which occasions the numberless instances of wretchedness which I had observed in this country & is to be observed all over Europe. The property of this country is absolutely concentered in a very few hands, having revenues of from half a million of guineas a year downwards. These employ the flower of the country as servants, some of them having as many as 200 domestics, not labouring. They employ also a great number of manufacturers, & tradesmen, & lastly the class of labouring husbandmen. But after all these comes the most numerous of all the classes, that is, the poor who cannot find work. I asked myself what could be the reason that so many should be permitted to beg who are willing to work, in a country where there is a very considerable proportion of uncultivated lands? These lands are kept idle mostly for the sake of game. It should seem then that it must be because of the enormous wealth of the proprietors which places them above attention to the increase of their revenues by permitting these lands to be laboured. I am conscious that an equal division of property is impracticable. But the consequences of this enormous inequality producing so much misery to the bulk of mankind, legislators cannot invent too many devices for subdividing property, only taking care to let their subdivisions go hand in hand with the natural affections of the human mind. The descent of property of every kind therefore to all the children, or to all the brothers & sisters, or other relations in equal degree is a politic measure, and a practicable one. Another means of silently lessening the inequality of property is to exempt all from taxation below a certain point, & to tax the higher portions of property in geometrical progression as they rise. Whenever there is in any country, uncultivated lands and unemployed poor, it is clear that the laws of property have been so far extended as to violate natural right. The earth is given as a common stock for man to labour & live on. If, for the encouragement of industry we allow it to be appropriated, we must take care that other employment be furnished to those excluded from the appropriation. If we do not the fundamental right to labour the earth returns to the unemployed. It is too soon yet in our country to say that every man who can not find employment but who can find uncultivated land, shall be at liberty to cultivate it, paying a moderate rent. But it is not too soon to provide by every possible means that as few as possible shall be without a little portion of land. The small landholders are the most precious part of a state.

14. James Madison to Thomas Jefferson Orange, June 19, 1786

Since my last which was of the 18th. of May I have recd. your very agreeable favor of the 28th. of Octobr. I began to fear it had miscarried. Your reflections on the idle poor of Europe, form a valuable lesson to the Legislators of every Country, and particularly of a new one. I hope you will enable yourself before you return to America to compare with this description of people in France the Condition of the indigent part of other communities in Europe where the like causes of wretchedness exist in a less degree. I have no doubt that the misery of the lower classes will be found to abate wherever the Government assumes a freer aspect, & the laws favor a subdivision of property. Yet I suspect that the difference will not fully account for the comparative comfort of the Mass of people in the United States. Our limited population has probably as large a share in producing this effect as the political advantages which distinguish us. A certain degree of misery seems inseparable from a high degree of populousness. If the lands in Europe which are now dedicated to the amusement of the idle rich, were parcelled out among the idle poor, I readily conceive the happy revolution which would be experienced by a certain proportion of the latter. But still would there not remain a great proportion unrelieved? No problem in political Oeconomy has appeared to me more puzzling than that which relates to the most proper distribution of the inhabitants of a Country fully peopled. Let the lands be shared among them ever so wisely, & let them be supplied with labourers ever so plentifully; as there must be a great surplus of subsistence, there will also remain a great surplus of inhabitants, a greater by far than will be employed in cloathing both themselves & those who feed them, and in administering to both, every other necessary & even comfort of life. What is to be done with this surplus? Hitherto we have seen them distributed into Manufacturers of superfluities, idle proprietors of productive funds, domestics, soldiers, merchants, mariners, and a few other less numerous classes. All these classes notwithstanding have been found insufficient to absorb the redundant members of a populous society; and yet a reduction of most of those classes enters into the very reform which appears so necessary & desireable. From a more equal partition of property, must result a greater simplicity of manners, consequently a less consumption of manufactured superfluities, and a less proportion of idle proprietors & domestics. From a juster Government must result less need of soldiers either for defence agst. dangers from without or disturbances from within. The number of merchants must be inconsiderable under any modification of Society; and that of Mariners will depend more on geographical position, than on the plan of legislation. But I forget that I am writing a letter not a dissertation. . . .

15. Thomas Jefferson to James Madison
Paris, September 6, 1789

I sit down to write to you without knowing by what occasion I shall send my letter. I do it because a subject comes into my head which I would wish to develop a little more than is practicable in the hurry of the moment of making up general dispatches.

The question Whether one generation of men has a right to bind another, seems never to have been started either on this or our side of the water. Yet it is a question of such consequences as not only to merit decision, but place also, among the fundamental principles of every government. The course of reflection in which we are immersed here on the elementary principles of society has presented this question to my mind; & that no such obligation can be so transmitted I think very capable of proof. I set out on this ground, which I suppose to be self-evident, *'that the earth belongs in usufruct to the living'*: that the dead have neither powers nor rights over it. The portion occupied by any individual ceases to be his when himself ceases to be, & reverts to the society. If the society has formed no rules for the appropriation of it's lands in severalty, it will be taken by the first occupants. These will generally be the wife & children of the decedent. If they have formed rules of appropriation, those rules may give it to the wife and children, or to some one of them, or to the legatee of the deceased. So they may give it to his creditor. But the child, the legatee, or creditor takes it, not by any natural right, but by a law of the society of which they are members, & to which they are subject. Then no man can, by *natural right*, oblige the lands he occupied, or the persons who succeed him in that occupation, to the paiment of debts contracted by him. For if he could, he might, during his own life, eat up the usufruct of the lands for several generations to come, & then the lands would belong to the dead, & not to the living, which would be the reverse of our principle.

What is true of every member of the society individually, is true of them all collectively, since the rights of the whole can be no more than the sum of the rights of the individuals. To keep our ideas clear when applying them to a multitude, let us suppose a

whole generation of men to be born on the same day, to attain
mature age on the same day, & to die on the same day, leaving a
succeeding generation in the moment of attaining their mature
age all together. Let the ripe age be supposed of 21. years, & their
period of life 34. years more, that being the average term given by
the bills of mortality to persons who have already attained 21.
years of age. Each successive generation would, in this way, come
on, and go off the stage at a fixed moment, as individuals do now.
Then I say the earth belongs to each of these generations, during
it's course, fully, and in their own right. The 2d. generation receives it clear of the debts & incumbrances of the 1st, the 3d of
the 2d. & so on. For if the 1st could charge it with a debt, then the
earth would belong to the dead & not the living generation. Then
no generation can contract debts greater than may be paid during
the course of it's own existence. At 21. years of age they may bind
themselves & their lands for 34. years to come: at 22. for 33: at
23. for 32. and at 54. for one year only; because these are the
terms of life which remain to them at those respective epochs.
But a material difference must be noted between the succession of
an individual, & that of a whole generation. Individuals are parts
only of a society, subject to the laws of the whole. These laws may
appropriate the portion of land occupied by a decedent to his creditor rather than to any other, or to his child on condition he satis-
fies the creditor. But when a whole generation, that is, the whole
society dies, as in the case we have supposed, and another generation or society succeeds, this forms a whole, and there is no superior who can give their territory to a third society, who may have
lent money to their predecessors beyond their faculties of paying.

What is true of a generation all arriving to self-government
on the same day, & dying all on the same day, is true of those in a
constant course of decay & renewal, with this only difference. A
generation coming in & going out entire, as in the first case, would
have a right in the 1st. year of their self-dominion to contract a
debt for 33. years, in the 10th. for 24. in the 20th. for 14. in the
30th. for 4. whereas generations, changing daily by daily deaths &
births, have one constant term, beginning at the date of their contract, and ending when a majority of those of full age at that date
shall be dead. The length of that term may be estimated from the

tables of mortality, corrected by the circumstances of climate, occupation &c. peculiar to the country of the contractors. Take, for instance, the table of M. de Buffon wherein he states 23,994 deaths, & the ages at which they happened. Suppose a society in which 23,994 persons are born every year, & live to the ages stated in this table. The conditions of that society will be as follows. 1st. It will consist constantly of 617,703. persons of all ages. 2ly. Of those living at any one instant of time, one half will be dead in 24. years 8. months. 3dly. 10,675 will arrive every year at the age of 21. years complete. 4ly. It will constantly have 348,417 persons of all ages above 21. years. 5ly. And the half of those of 21. years & upwards living at any one instant of time will be dead in 18. years 8. months, or say 19. years as the nearest integral number. Then 19. years is the term beyond which neither the representatives of a nation, nor even the whole nation itself assembled, can validly extend a debt.

To render this conclusion palpable by example, suppose that Louis XIV. and XV. had contracted debts in the name of the French nation to the amount of 10,000 millions of livres, & that the whole had been contracted in Genoa. The interest of this sum would be 500. millions, which is said to be the whole rent roll or nett proceeds of the territory of France. Must the present generation of men have retired from the territory in which nature produced them, & ceded it to the Genoese creditors? No. They have the same rights over the soil on which they were produced, as the preceding generations had. They derive these rights not from their predecessors, but from nature. They then and their soil are by nature clear of the debts of their predecessors.

Again suppose Louis XV. & his cotemporary generation had said to the money-lenders of Genoa, give us money that we may eat, drink, & be merry in our day; and on condition you will demand no interest till the end of 19. years you shall then for ever after receive an annual interest of 12 5/8 per cent. The money is lent on these conditions, is divided among the living, eaten, drank, & squandered. Would the present generation be obliged to apply the produce of the earth & of their labour to replace their dissipations? Not at all.

I suppose that the received opinion, that the public debts of one generation devolve on the next, has been suggested by our seeing habitually in private life that he who succeeds to lands is required to pay the debts of his ancestor or testator: without considering that this requisition is municipal only, not moral; flowing from the will of the society, which has found it convenient to appropriate lands, become vacant by the death of their occupant, on the condition of a paiment of his debts: but that between society & society, or generation & generation, there is no municipal obligation, no umpire but the law of nature. We seem not to have perceived that, by the law of nature, one generation is to another as one independant nation to another.

The interest of the national debt of France being in fact but a two thousandth part of it's rent roll, the paiment of it is practicable enough: & so becomes a question merely of honor, or of expediency. But with respect to future debts, would it not be wise & just for that nation to declare, in the constitution they are forming, that neither the legislature, nor the nation itself, can validly contract more debt than they may pay within their own age, or within the term of 19. years? and that all future contracts will be deemed void as to what shall remain unpaid at the end of 19. years from their date? This would put the lenders, & the borrowers also, on their guard. By reducing too the faculty of borrowing too within it's natural limits, it would bridle the spirit of war, to which too free a course has been procured by the inattention of money-lenders to this law of nature, that succeeding generations are not responsible for the preceding.

On similar ground it may be proved that no society can make a perpetual constitution, or even a perpetual law. The earth belongs always to the living generation. They may manage it then, & what proceeds from it, as they please, during their usufruct. They are masters too of their own persons, & consequently may govern them as they please. But persons & property make the sum of the objects of government. The constitution and the laws of their predecessors extinguished then in their natural course, with those who gave them being. This could preserve that being till it ceased to be itself, & no longer. Every constitution then, & every law, naturally expires at the end of 19 years. If it be enforced longer, it is an act of force, & not of right. It may be said that the succeeding generation exercising in fact the power of repeal, this leaves them as free as if the constitution or law had been expressly limited to 19 years only. In the first place, this objection admits the right, in proposing an equivalent. But the power of repeal is not an equivalent. It might be indeed if every form of government were so perfectly contrived that the will of the majority could always be obtained fairly & without impediment. But this is true of no form. The people cannot assemble themselves. Their representation is unequal & vicious. Various checks are opposed to every legislative proposition. Factions get possession of the public councils. Bribery corrupts them. Personal interests lead them astray from the general interests of their constituents: and other impediments arise so as to prove to every practical man that a law of limited duration is much more manageable than one which needs a repeal.

This principle that the earth belongs to the living, & not to the dead, is of very extensive application & consequences, in every country, and most especially in France. It enters into the resolution of the questions Whether the nation may change the descent of lands holden in tail? Whether they may change the appropriation of lands given antiently to the church, to hospitals, colleges, orders of chivalry, & otherwise in perpetuity? Whether they may abolish the charges & privileges attached on lands, including the whole catalogue ecclesiastical & feudal? It goes to hereditary offices, authorities & jurisdictions; to hereditary orders, distinctions & appellations; to perpetual monopolies in commerce, the arts & sciences; with a long train of et ceteras: and it renders the question of reimbursement a question of generosity & not of right. In all these cases, the legislature of the day could authorize such appropriations & establishments for their own time, but no longer; & the present holders, even where they, or their ancestors, have purchased, are in the case of bona fide purchasers of what the seller had no right to convey.

Turn this subject in your mind, my dear Sir, & particularly as to the power of contracting debts; & develope it with that perspicuity & cogent logic so peculiarly yours. Your station in the councils of our country gives you an opportunity of producing it to public consideration, of forcing it into discussion. At first blush it may be rallied, as a theoretical speculation: but examination will prove it to be solid & salutary. It would furnish matter for a fine preamble to our first law for appropriating the public revenue; & it will exclude at the threshold of our government the contagious & ruinous errors of this quarter of the globe, which have armed despots with means, not sanctioned by nature, for binding in chains their fellow men. We have already given in example one effectual check to the Dog of war, by transferring the power of letting him loose from the Executive to the Legislative body, from those who are to spend to those who are to pay. I should be pleased to see this second obstacle held out by us also in the first instance. No nation can make a declaration against the validity of long-con-tracted debts so disinterestedly as we, since we do not owe a shil-ling which may not be paid with ease, principal & interest, within the time of our own lives. Establish the principle also in the new law to be passed for protecting copyrights & new inventions, by securing the exclusive right for 19. instead of 14. years. Besides familiarising us to this term, it will be an instance the more of our taking reason for our guide, instead of English precedent, the habit of which fetters us with all the political heresies of a nation equally remarkeable for it's early excitement from some errors, and long slumbering under others.

I write you no news, because, when an occasion occurs, I shall write a separate letter for that. I am always with great & sincere esteem, dear Sir Your affectionate friend & servt.

16. James Madison to Thomas Jefferson
New York, February 4, 1790

Your favor of the 9th. of Jany. inclosing one of Sepr. last did not
get to hand till a few days ago. The idea which the latter evolves is
a great one, and suggests many interesting reflections to legislators; particularly when contracting and providing for public debts.
Whether it can be received in the extent your reasonings give it,
is a question which I ought to turn more in my thoughts than I
have yet been able to do, before I should be justified in making up
a full opinion on it. My first thoughts though coinciding with many
of yours, lead me to view the doctrine as not in *all* respects compatible with the course of human affairs. I will endeavor to sketch
the grounds of my skepticism.

> As the earth belongs to the living, not to the dead, a liv-
> ing generation can bind itself only: In every society the
> will of the majority binds the whole: According to the laws
> of mortality, a majority of those ripe at any moment for
> exercise of their will do not live beyond nineteen years:
> To that term then is limited the validity of *every* act of the
> Society: Not within that limitation, can any declaration
> of the public will be valid which is not *express*.

This I understand to be the outline of the argument.

The Acts of a political Society may be divided into three
classes.

1. The fundamental Constitution of the Government.
2. Laws involving stipulations which render them irrevocable at the will of the Legislature.
3. Laws involving no such irrevocable quality.

However applicable in Theory the doctrine may be to a Constitution, it seems liable in practice to some very powerful objections. Would not a Government so often revised become too
mutable to retain those prejudices in its favor which antiquity inspires, and which are perhaps a salutary aid to the most rational

Government in the most enlightened age? Would not such a periodical revision engender pernicious factions that might not otherwise come into existence? Would not, in fine, a Government depending for its existence beyond a fixed date, on some positive and authentic intervention of the Society itself, be too subject to the casualty and consequences of an actual interregnum?

In the 2d. class, exceptions at least to the doctrine seem to be requisite both in Theory and practice.

If the earth be the gift of nature to the living their title can extend to the earth in its natural State only. The *improvements* made by the dead form a charge against the living who take the benefit of them. This charge can no otherwise be satisfyed than by executing the will of the dead accompanying the improvements.

Debts may be incurred for purposes which interest the unborn, as well as the living: such are debts for repelling a conquest, the evils of which descend through many generations. Debts may even be incurred principally for the benefit of posterity: such perhaps is the present debt of the U. States, which far exceeds any burdens which the present generation could well apprehend for itself. The term of 19 years might not be sufficient for discharging the debts in either of these cases.

There seems then to be a foundation in the nature of things, in the relation which one generation bears to another, for the *descent* of obligations from one to another. Equity requires it. Mutual good is promoted by it. All that is indispensable in adjusting the account between the dead & the living is to see that the debits against the latter do not exceed the advances made by the former. Few of the incumbrances entailed on Nations would bear a liquidation even on this principle.

The objections to the doctrine as applied to the 3d. class of acts may perhaps be merely practical. But in that view they appear to be of great force.

Unless such laws should be kept in force by new acts regularly anticipating the end of the term, all the rights depending on positive laws, that is, most of the rights of property would become absolutely defunct; and the most violent struggles be generated between those interested in reviving and those interested in new-modelling the former State of property. Nor would events of this kind be improbable. The obstacles to the passage of laws which render a power to repeal inferior to an opportunity of rejecting, as a security agst. oppression, would here render an opportunity of rejecting, an insecure provision agst. anarchy. Add, that the possibility of an event so hazardous to the rights of property could not fail to depreciate its value; that the approach of the crisis would increase this effect; that the frequent return of periods superseding all the obligations depending on antecedent laws & usages, must be weakening the reverence for those obligations, co-operate with motives to licentiousness already too powerful; and that the uncertainty incident to such a state of things would on one side discourage the steady exertions of industry produced by permanent laws, and on the other, give a disproportionate advantage to the more, over the less, sagacious and interprizing part of the Society.

I find no relief from these consequences, but in the received doctrine that a tacit assent may be given to established Constitutions and laws, and that this assent may be inferred, where no positive dissent appears. It seems less impracticable to remedy, by wise plans of Government, the dangerous operation of this doctrine, than to find a remedy for the difficulties inseparable from the other.

May it not be questioned whether it be possible to exclude wholly the idea of tacit assent, without subverting the foundation of civil Society? On what principle does the voice of the majority bind the minority? It does not result I conceive from the law of nature, but from compact founded on conveniency. A greater proportion might be required by the fundamental constitution of a Society, if it were judged eligible. Prior then to the establishment of this principle, *unanimity* was necessary; and strict Theory at all times presupposes the assent of every member to the establishment of the rule itself. If this assent can not be given tacitly, or be not implied where no positive evidence forbids, persons born in Society would not on attaining ripe age be bound by acts of the Majority; and either a *unanimous* repetition of every law would be necessary on the accession of new members, or an express assent must be obtained from these to the rule by which the voice of the Majority is made the voice of the whole.

If the observations I have hazarded be not misapplied, it follows that a limitation of the validity of national acts to the computed life of a nation, is in some instances not required by Theory, and in others cannot be accomodated to practice. The observations are not meant however to impeach either the utility of the principle in some particular cases; or the general importance of it in the eye of the philosophical Legislator. On the contrary it would give me singular pleasure to see it first announced in the proceedings of the U. States, and always kept in their view, as a salutary curb on the living generation from imposing unjust or unnecessary burdens on their successors. But this is a pleasure which I have little hope of enjoying. The spirit of philosophical legislation has never reached some parts of the Union, and is by no means the fashion here, either within or without Congress. The evils suffered & feared from weakness in Government, and licentiousness in the people, have turned the attention more towards the means of strengthening the former, than of narrowing its extent in the minds of the latter. Besides this, it is so much easier to espy the little difficulties immediately incident to every great plan, than to comprehend its general and remote benefits, that our hemisphere must be still more enlightened before many of the sublime truths which are seen thro' the medium of Philosophy, become visible to the naked eye of the ordinary Politician.

I have nothing to add at present but that I remain always and most affectly. Yours.

17. Thomas Jefferson to John Wayles Eppes
Monticello, June 24, 1813*

This letter will be on politics only. For although I do not often permit myself to think on that subject, it sometimes obtrudes itself, and suggests ideas which I am tempted to pursue. Some of these relating to the business of finance, I will hazard to you, as being at the head of that committee, but intended for yourself individually, or such as you trust, but certainly not for a mixed committee.

It is a wise rule and should be fundamental in a government disposed to cherish its credit, and at the same time to restrain the use of it within the limits of its faculties, never to borrow a dollar without laying a tax in the same instant for paying the interest annually, and the principal within a given term; and to consider that tax as pledged to the creditors on the public faith. On such a pledge as this, sacredly observed, a government may always command, on a *reasonable interest*, all the lendable money of their citizens, while the necessity of an equivalent tax is a salutary warning to them and their constituents against oppressions, bankruptcy, and its inevitable consequence, revolution. But the term of redemption must be moderate, and at any rate within the limits of their rightful powers. But what limits, it will be asked, does this prescribe to their powers? What is to hinder them from creating a perpetual debt? The laws of nature, I answer. The earth belongs to the living, not to the dead. The will and the power of man expire with his life, by nature's law. Some societies give it an artificial continuance, for the encouragement of industry; some refuse it, as our aboriginal neighbors, whom we call barbarians. The generations of men may be considered as bodies or corporations. Each generation has the usufruct of the earth during the period of its continuance. When it ceases to exist, the usufruct passes on to the succeeding generation, free and unincumbered, and so on, successively, from one generation to another forever. We may consider each generation as a distinct nation, with a right, by the will

*Eppes was Jefferson's son-in-law.

of its majority, to bind themselves, but none to bind the succeeding generation, more than the inhabitants of another country. Or the case may be likened to the ordinary one of a tenant for life, who may hypothecate the land for his debts, during the continuance of his usufruct; but at his death, the reversioner (who is also for life only) receives it exonerated from all burthen. The period of a generation, or the term of its life, is determined by the laws of mortality, which, varying a little only in different climates, offer a general average, to be found by observation. I turn, for instance, to Buffon's tables, of twenty-three thousand nine hundred and ninety-four deaths, and the ages at which they happened, and I find that of the numbers of all ages living at one moment, half will be dead in twenty-four years and eight months. But (leaving out minors, who have not the power of self-government) of the adults (of twenty-one years of age) living at one moment, a majority of whom act for the society, one half will be dead in eighteen years and eight months. At nineteen years then from the date of a contract, the majority of the contractors are dead, and their contract with them. Let this general theory be applied to a particular case. Suppose the annual births of the State of New York to be twenty-three thousand nine hundred and ninety-four, the whole number of its inhabitants, according to Buffon, will be six hundred and seventeen thousand seven hundred and three, of all ages. Of these there would constantly be two hundred and sixty-nine thousand two hundred and eighty-six minors, and three hundred and forty-eight thousand four hundred and seventeen adults, of which last, one hundred and seventy-four thousand two hundred and nine will be a majority. Suppose that majority, on the first day of the year 1794, had borrowed a sum of money equal to the fee-simple value of the State, and to have consumed it in eating, drinking and making merry in their day; or, if you please, in quarrelling and fighting with their unoffending neighbors. Within eighteen years and eight months, one half of the adult citizens were dead. Till then, being the majority, they might rightfully levy the interest of their debt annually on themselves and their fellow-revellers, or fellow-champions. But at that period, say at this moment, a new majority have come into place, in their own right, and not under the rights, the conditions, or laws of their predecessors.

Are they bound to acknowledge the debt, to consider the preceding generation as having had a right to eat up the whole soil of their country, in the course of a life, to alienate it from them, (for it would be an alienation to the creditors,) and would they think themselves either legally or morally bound to give up their country and emigrate to another for subsistence? Every one will say no; that the soil is the gift of God to the living, as much as it had been to the deceased generation; and that the laws of nature impose no obligation on them to pay this debt. And although, like some other natural rights, this has not yet entered into any declaration of rights, it is no less a law, and ought to be acted on by honest governments. It is, at the same time, a salutary curb on the spirit of war and indebtment, which, since the modern theory of the perpetuation of debt, has drenched the earth with blood, and crushed its inhabitants under burthens ever accumulating. Had this principle been declared in the British bill of rights, England would have been placed under the happy disability of waging eternal war, and of contracting her thousand millions of public debt. In seeking, then, for an ultimate term for the redemption of our debts, let us rally to this principle, and provide for their payment within the term of nineteen years at the farthest. Our government has not, as yet, begun to act on the rule of loans and taxation going hand in hand. Had any loan taken place in my time, I should have strongly urged a redeeming tax. For the loan which has been made since the last session of Congress, we should now set the example of appropriating some particular tax, sufficient to pay the interest annually, and the principal within a fixed term, less than nineteen years. And I hope yourself and your committee will render the immortal service of introducing this practice. Not that it is expected that Congress should formally declare such a principle. They wisely enough avoid deciding on abstract questions. But they may be induced to keep themselves within its limits.

18. Publius, The Federalist 49
New York *Independent Journal*, February 2, 1788

To the People of the State of New-York.

The author of the *Notes on the State of Virginia*, quoted in the last paper, has subjoined to that valuable work, the draught of a constitution which had been prepared in order to be laid before a convention expected to be called in 1783 by the legislature, for the establishment of a constitution for that commonwealth. The plan, like every thing from the same pen, marks a turn of thinking original, comprehensive and accurate; and is the more worthy of attention, as it equally displays a fervent attachment to republican government, and an enlightened view of the dangerous propensities against which it ought to be guarded. One of the precautions which he proposes, and on which he appears ultimately to rely as a palladium to the weaker departments of power, against the invasions of the stronger, is perhaps altogether his own, and as it immediately relates to the subject of our present enquiry, ought not to be overlooked.

His proposition is, "that whenever any two of the three branches of government shall concur in opinion, each by the voices of two thirds of their whole number, that a convention is necessary for altering the constitution or *correcting breaches of it*, a convention shall be called for the purpose."

As the people are the only legitimate fountain of power, and it is from them that the constitutional charter, under which the several branches of government hold their power, is derived; it seems strictly consonant to the republican theory, to recur to the same original authority, not only whenever it may be necessary to enlarge, diminish, or new-model the powers of government; but also whenever any one of the departments may commit encroachments on the chartered authorities of the others. The several departments being perfectly co-ordinate by the terms of their common commission, neither of them, it is evident, can pretend to an exclusive or superior right of settling the boundaries between their respective powers; and how are the encroachments of the stronger to be prevented, or the wrongs of the weaker to be redressed, without an appeal to the people themselves; who, as the grantors of the commission, can alone declare its true meaning and enforce its observance?

There is certainly great force in this reasoning, and it must be allowed to prove, that a constitutional road to the decision of the people, ought to be marked out, and kept open, for certain great and extraordinary occasions. But there appear to be insuperable objections against the proposed recurrence to the people, as a provision in all cases for keeping the several departments of power within their constitutional limits.

In the first place, the provision does not reach the case of a combination of two of the departments against a third. If the legislative authority, which possesses so many means of operating on the motives of the other departments, should be able to gain to its interest either of the others, or even one third of its members, the remaining department could derive no advantage from this remedial provision. I do not dwell however on this objection, because it may be thought to lie rather against the modification of the principle, than against the principle itself.

In the next place, it may be considered as an objection inherent in the principle, that as every appeal to the people would carry an implication of some defect in the government, frequent appeals would in great measure deprive the government of that veneration, which time bestows on every thing, and without which perhaps the wisest and freest governments would not possess the requisite stability. If it be true that all governments rest on opinion, it is no less true that the strength of opinion in each individual, and its practical influence on his conduct, depend much on the number which he supposes to have entertained the same opinion. The reason of man, like man himself is timid and cautious, when left alone; and acquires firmness and confidence, in proportion to the number with which it is associated. When the examples, which fortify opinion, are *antient* as well as *numerous*, they are known to have a double effect. In a nation of philosophers, this consideration ought to be disregarded. A reverence for the laws, would be sufficiently inculcated by the voice of an enlightened reason. But a nation of philosophers is as little to be expected as the philosophical race of kings wished for by Plato.

And in every other nation, the most rational government will not find it a superfluous advantage, to have the prejudices of the community on its side.

The danger of disturbing the public tranquility by interesting too strongly the public passions, is a still more serious objection against a frequent reference of constitutional questions, to the decision of the whole society. Notwithstanding the success which has attended the revisions of our established forms of government, and which does so much honour to the virtue and intelligence of the people of America, it must be confessed, that the experiments are of too ticklish a nature to be unnecessarily multiplied. We are to recollect that all the existing constitutions were formed in the midst of a danger which repressed the passions most unfriendly to order and concord; of an enthusiastic confidence of the people in their patriotic leaders, which stifled the ordinary diversity of opinions on great national questions; of a universal ardor for new and opposite forms, produced by a universal resentment and indignation against the antient government; and whilst no spirit of party, connected with the changes to be made, or the abuses to be reformed, could mingle its leven in the operation. The future situations in which we must expect to be usually placed, do not present any equivalent security against the danger which is apprehended.

But the greatest objection of all is, that the decisions which would probably result from such appeals, would not answer the purpose of maintaining the constitutional equilibrium of the government. We have seen that the tendency of republican governments is to an aggrandizement of the legislative, at the expence of the other departments. The appeals to the people therefore would usually be made by the executive and judiciary departments. But whether made by one side or the other, would each side enjoy equal advantages on the trial? Let us view their different situations. The members of the executive and judiciary departments, are few in number, and can be personally known to a small part only of the people. The latter by the mode of their appointment, as well as, by the nature and permanency of it, are too far removed from the people to share much in their prepossessions. The former are generally the objects of jealousy: And their administration is always liable to be discoloured and rendered unpopular.

The members of the legislative department, on the other hand, are numerous. They are distributed and dwell among the people at large. Their connections of blood, of friendship and of acquaintance, embrace a great proportion of the most influencial part of the society. The nature of their public trust implies a personal influence among the people, and that they are more immediately the confidential guardians of the rights and liberties of the people. With these advantages, it can hardly be supposed that the adverse party would have an equal chance for a favorable issue.

But the legislative party would not only be able to plead their cause most successfully with the people. They would probably be constituted themselves the judges. The same influence which had gained them an election into the legislature, would gain them a seat in the convention. If this should not be the case with all, it would probably be the case with many, and pretty certainly with those leading characters, on whom every thing depends in such bodies. The convention in short would be composed chiefly of men, who had been, who actually were, or who expected to be, members of the department whose conduct was arraigned. They would consequently be parties to the very question to be decided by them.

It might however sometimes happen, that appeals would be made under circumstances less adverse to the executive and judiciary departments. The usurpations of the legislature might be so flagrant and so sudden, as to admit of no specious colouring. A strong party among themselves might take side with the other branches. The executive power might be in the hands of a peculiar favorite of the people. In such a posture of things, the public decision might be less swayed by prepossessions in favor of the legislative party. But still it could never be expected to turn on the true merits of the question. It would inevitably be connected with the spirit of pre-existing parties, or of parties springing out of the question itself. It would be connected with persons of distinguished character and extensive influence in the community. It would be pronounced by the very men who had been agents in, or opponents of the measures, to which the decision would relate. The *passions* therefore not *the reason*, of the public, would sit in judgment. But it is the reason of the public alone that ought to controul and regulate the government. The passions ought to be controuled and regulated by the government.

We found in the last paper that mere declarations in the written constitution, are not sufficient to restrain the several departments within their legal limits. It appears in this, that occasional appeals to the people would be neither a proper nor an effectual provision, for that purpose. How far the provisions of a different nature contained in the plan above quoted, might be adequate, I do not examine. Some of them are unquestionably founded on sound political principles, and all of them are framed with singular ingenuity and precision.

19. Thomas Jefferson, Manufactures
Notes on the State of Virginia, Query XIX

The present state of manufactures, commerce, interior and exterior trade?

We never had an interior trade of any importance. Our exterior commerce has suffered very much from the beginning of the present contest. During this time we have manufactured within our families the most necessary articles of cloathing. Those of cotton will bear some comparison with the same kinds of manufacture in Europe; but those of wool, flax and hemp are very coarse, unsightly, and unpleasant: and such is our attachment to agriculture, and such our preference for foreign manufactures, that be it wise or unwise, our people will certainly return as soon as they can, to the raising raw materials, and exchanging them for finer manufactures than they are able to execute themselves.

The political oeconomists of Europe have established it as a principle that every state should endeavour to manufacture for itself: and this principle, like many others, we transfer to America, without calculating the difference of circumstance which should often produce a difference of result. In Europe the lands are either cultivated, or locked up against the cultivator. Manufacture must therefore be resorted to of necessity not of choice, to support the surplus of their people. But we have an immensity of land courting the industry of the husbandman. Is it best then that all our citizens should be employed in its improvement, or that one half should be called off from that to exercise manufactures and handicraft arts for the other? Those who labour in the earth are the chosen people of God, if ever he had a chosen people, whose breasts he has made his peculiar deposit for substantial and genuine virtue. It is the focus in which he keeps alive that sacred fire, which otherwise might escape from the face of the earth. Corruption of morals in the mass of cultivators is a phaenomenon of which no age nor nation has furnished an example. It is the mark set on those, who not looking up to heaven, to their own soil and industry, as does the husbandman, for their subsistance, depend on it on the casualties and caprice of customers. Dependance begets subservience and venality, suffocates the germ of virtue, and prepares fit tools for the designs of ambition. This, the natural progress and consequence of the arts, has sometimes perhaps been retarded by accidental circumstances: but, generally speaking, the proportion which the aggregate of the other classes of citizens bears in any state to that of its husbandmen, is the proportion of its unsound to its healthy parts, and is a good-enough barometer whereby to measure its degree of corruption. While we have land to labour then, let us never wish to see our citizens occupied at a work-bench, or twirling a distaff. Carpenters, masons, smiths, are wanting in husbandry: but, for the general operations of manufacture, let our work-shops remain in Europe. It is better to carry provisions and materials to workmen there, than bring them to the provisions and materials, and with them their manners and principles. The loss by the transportation of commodities across the Atlantic will be made up in happiness and permanence of government. The mobs of great cities add just so much to the support of pure government, as sores do to the strength of the human body. It is the manners and spirit of a people which preserve a republic in vigour. A degeneracy in these is a canker which soon eats to the heart of its laws and constitution.

20. James Madison, Republican Distribution of Citizens, *National Gazette*, March 3, 1792

A perfect theory on this subject would be useful, not because it could be reduced to practice by any plan of legislation, or ought to be attempted by violence on the will or property of individuals: but because it would be a monition against empirical experiments by power, and a model to which the free choice of occupations by the people, might gradually approximate the order of society.

The best distribution is that which would most favor *health, virtue, intelligence* and *competency* in the *greatest number* of citizens. It is needless to add to these objects, *liberty* and *safety*. The first is presupposed by them. The last must result from them.

The life of the husbandman is pre-eminently suited to the comfort and happiness of the individual. *Health*, the first of blessings, is an appurtenance of his property and his employment. *Virtue*, the health of the soul, is another part of his patrimony, and no less favored by his situation. *Intelligence* may be cultivated in this as well as in any other walk of life. If the mind be less susceptible of polish in retirement than in a croud, it is more capable of profound and comprehensive efforts. Is it more ignorant of some things? It has a compensation in its ignorance of others. *Competency* is more universally the lot of those who dwell in the country, when liberty is at the same time their lot. The extremes both of want and of waste have other abodes. 'Tis not the country that peoples either the Bridewells or the Bedlams. These mansions of wretchedness are tenanted from the distresses and vices of overgrown cities.

The condition, to which the blessings of life are most denied is that of the sailor. His health is continually assailed and his span shortened by the stormy element to which he belongs. His virtue, at no time aided, is occasionally exposed to every scene that can poison it. His mind, like his body, is imprisoned within the bark that transports him. Though traversing and circumnavigating the globe, he sees nothing but the same vague objects of nature, the same monotonous occurrences in ports and docks; and at home in his vessel, what new ideas can shoot from the unvaried use of the ropes and the rudder, or from the society of comrades as ignorant as himself. In the supply of his wants he often feels a scarcity, seldom more than a bare sustenance; and if his ultimate prospects do not embitter the present moment, it is because he never looks beyond it. How unfortunate, that in the intercourse, by which nations are enlightened and refined, and their means of safety extended, the immediate agents should be distinguished by the hardest condition of humanity.

The great interval between the two extremes, is, with a few exceptions, filled by those who work the materials furnished by the earth in its natural or cultivated state.

It is fortunate in general, and particularly for this country, that so much of the ordinary and most essential consumption, takes place in fabrics which can be prepared in every family, and which constitute indeed the natural ally of agriculture. The former is the work within doors, as the latter is without; and each being done by hands or at times, that can be spared from the other, the most is made of every thing.

The class of citizens who provide at once their own food and their own raiment, may be viewed as the most truly independent and happy. They are more: they are the best basis of public liberty, and the strongest bulwark of public safety. It follows, that the greater the proportion of this class to the whole society, the more free, the more independent, and the more happy must be the society itself.

In appreciating the regular branches of manufacturing and mechanical industry, their tendency must be compared with the principles laid down, and their merits graduated accordingly. Whatever is least favorable to vigor of body, to the faculties of the mind, or to the virtues or the utilities of life, instead of being forced or fostered by public authority, ought to be seen with regret as long as occupations more friendly to human happiness, lie vacant.

The several professions of more elevated pretensions, the merchant, the lawyer, the physician, the philosopher, the divine, form a certain proportion of every civilized society, and readily adjust their numbers to its demands, and its circumstances.

21. James Madison, Fashion
National Gazette, March 20, 1792

An humble address has been lately presented to the Prince of Wales by the BUCKLE MANUFACTURERS of Birmingham, Wassal, Wolverhampton, and their environs, stating that the BUCKLE TRADE gives employment to more than TWENTY THOUSAND persons, numbers of whom, in consequence of the prevailing fashion of SHOESTRINGS & SLIPPERS, are at present without employ, almost destitute of bread, and exposed to the horrors of want at the most inclement season; that to the manufactures of BUCKLES and BUTTONS, Birmingham owes its important figure on the map of England; that it is to no purpose to address FASHION herself, she being void of feeling and deaf to argument, but fortunately accustomed to listen to his voice, and to obey his commands: and finally, IMPLORING his Royal Highness to consider the deplorable condition of their trade, which is in danger of being ruined by the *mutability of fashion*, and to give that direction to the *public taste*, which will insure the lasting gratitude of the petitioners.

Several important reflections are suggested by this address.

I. The most precarious of all occupations which give bread to the industrious, are those depending on mere fashion, which generally changes so suddenly, and often so considerably, as to throw whole bodies of people out of employment.

II. Of all occupations those are the least desirable in a free state, which produce the most servile dependence of one class of citizens on another class. This dependence must increase as the *mutuality* of wants is diminished. Where the wants on one side are the absolute necessaries; and on the other are neither absolute necessaries, nor result from the habitual oeconomy of life, but are the mere caprices of fancy, the evil is in its extreme; or if not,

III. The extremity of the evil must be in the case before us, where the absolute necessaries depend on the caprices of fancy, and the caprice of a single fancy directs the fashion of the community. Here the dependence sinks to the lowest point of servility. We see a proof of it in the *spirit* of the address. *Twenty thousand* persons are to get or go without their bread, as a wanton youth, may fancy to wear his shoes with or without straps, or to fasten his straps with strings or with buckles. Can any despotism be more cruel than a situation, in which the existence of thousands depends on one will, and that will on the most slight and fickle of all motives, a mere whim of the imagination.

IV. What a contrast is here to the independent situation and manly sentiments of American citizens, who live on their own soil, or whose labour is necessary to its cultivation, or who were occupied in supplying wants, which being founded in solid utility, in comfortable accommodation, or in settled habits, produce a reciprocity of dependence, at once ensuring subsistence, and inspiring a dignified sense of social rights.

V. The condition of those who receive employment and bread from the precarious source of fashion and superfluity, is a lesson to nations, as well as to individuals. In proportion as a nation consists of that description of citizens, and depends on external commerce, it is dependent on the consumption and caprice of other nations. If the laws of propriety did not forbid, the manufacturers of Birmingham, Wassal, and Wolverhampton, had as real an interest in supplicating the arbiters of fashion in America, as the patron they have addressed. The dependence in the case of nations is even greater than among individuals of the same nation: for besides the *mutability of fashion* which is the same in both, the *mutability of policy* is another source of danger in the former.

22. James Madison, Universal Peace
National Gazette, January 31, 1792

Among the various reforms which have been offered to the world, the projects for universal peace have done the greatest honor to the hearts, though they seem to have done very little to the heads of their authors. Rousseau, the most distinguished of these philanthropists, has recommended a confederation of sovereigns, under a council of deputies, for the double purpose of arbitrating external controversies among nations, and of guaranteeing their respective governments against internal revolutions. He was aware, neither of the impossibility of executing his pacific plan among governments which feel so many allurements to war, nor, what is more extraordinary, of the tendency of his plan to perpetuate arbitrary power wherever it existed; and, by extinguishing the hope of one day seeing an end of oppression, to cut off the only source of consolation remaining to the oppressed.

A universal and perpetual peace, it is to be feared, is in the catalogue of events, which will never exist but in the imaginations of visionary philosophers, or in the breasts of benevolent enthusiasts. It is still however true, that war contains so much folly, as well as wickedness, that much is to be hoped from the progress of reason; and if any thing is to be hoped, every thing ought to be tried.

Wars may be divided into two classes; one flowing from the mere will of the government, the other according with the will of the society itself.

Those of the first class can no otherwise be prevented than by such a reformation of the government, as may identify its will with the will of the society. The project of Rousseau was, consequently, as preposterous as it was impotent. Instead of beginning with an external application, and even precluding internal remedies, he ought to have commenced with, and chiefly relied on the latter prescription.

He should have said, whilst war is to depend on those whose ambition, whose revenge, whose avidity, or whose caprice may contradict the sentiment of the community, and yet be uncontrouled by it; whilst war is to be declared by those who are to spend the public money, not by those who are to pay it; by those who are to direct the public forces, not by those who are to support them; by those whose power is to be raised, not by those whose chains may be riveted the disease must continue to be *hereditary* like the government of which it is the offspring. As the first step towards a cure, the government itself must be regenerated. Its will must be made subordinate to, or rather the same with, the will of the community.

Had Rousseau lived to see the constitutions of the United States and of France, his judgment might have escaped the censure to which his project has exposed it.

The other class of wars, corresponding with the public will, are less susceptible of remedy. There are antidotes, nevertheless, which may not be without their efficacy. As wars of the first class were to be prevented by subjecting the will of the government to the will of the society, those of the second, can only be controuled by subjecting the will of the society to the reason of the society; by establishing permanent and constitutional maxims of conduct, which may prevail over occasional impressions, and inconsiderate pursuits.

Here our republican philosopher might have proposed as a model to lawgivers, that war should not only be declared by the authority of the people, whose toils and treasures are to support its burdens, instead of the government which is to reap its fruits: but that each generation should be made to bear the burden of its own wars, instead of carrying them on, at the expence of other generations. And to give the fullest energy to his plan, he might have added, that each generation should not only bear its own burdens, but that the taxes composing them, should include a due proportion of such as by their direct operation keep the people awake, along with those, which being wrapped up in other payments, may leave them asleep, to misapplications of their money.

To the objection, if started, that where the benefits of war descend to succeeding generations, the burdens ought also to descend, he might have answered: that the exceptions could not be easily made; that, if attempted, they must be made by one only of the parties interested; that in the alternative of sacrificing excep-

191

tions to general rules, or of converting exceptions into general rules, the former is the lesser evil; that the expense of *necessary* wars, will never exceed the resources of an *entire* generation; that, in fine, the objection vanishes before the *fact*, that in every nation which has drawn on posterity for the support of its wars, *the accumulated interest* of its perpetual debts, has soon become more than *a sufficient principal,* for all its exigencies.

Were a nation to impose such restraints on itself, avarice would be sure to calculate the expences of ambition; in the equipoise of these passions, reason would be free to decide for the public good; and an ample reward would accrue to the state, first, from the avoidance of all its wars of folly, secondly, from the vigor of its unwasted resources for wars of necessity and defence. Were all nations to follow the example, the reward would be doubled to each; and the temple of Janus might be shut, never to be opened more.

Had Rousseau lived to see the rapid progress of reason and reformation, which the present day exhibits, the philanthropy which dictated his project would find a rich enjoyment in the scene before him: And after tracing the past frequency of wars to a will in the government independent of the will of the people; to the practice by each generation of taxing the principal of its debts on future generations; and to the facility with which each generation is seduced into assumptions of the interest, by the deceptive species of taxes which pay it; he would contemplate, in a reform of every government subjecting its will to that of the people, in a subjection of each generation to the payment of its own debts, and in a substitution of a more palpable, in place of an imperceptible mode of paying them, the only hope of UNIVERSAL AND PERPETUAL PEACE.

Documents for Chapter Three

PUBLIC SPIRIT

THE IMAGE OF JAMES MADISON AS Thomas Jefferson's subordinate and aid, although repeatedly discredited by scholars, still retains a stubborn grip on popular imagination. But facts, not theory or interpretations, lie behind the modern scholarly consensus. By 1783, when their acquaintanceship developed into friendship, Madison had won a major reputation of his own. From 1786 through 1789, Madison, not Jefferson, was at the center of the nation's great affairs; and Madison objected to the plan for managing the revolutionary debt before his friend arrived in New York City to assume his place as secretary of state. Through much of 1791, as Jefferson drew heavily on Madison's remarks in Congress for his argument against the national bank, the younger friend was more the leader than the follower in the direction of a governmental opposition to Hamilton's designs. The transformation of that opposition into something like a party was very much the joint endeavor of the two Virginians.

Two developments, like matches to the fuel piled up by the Virginians' quarrel with the funding plan (and Hamilton's resistance to their own attempts to force commercial confrontation with Great Britain), prompted Jefferson and Madison to take their opposition to the public. The first was broad construction of the Constitution, used to justify creation of a national bank, an institution the Virginians feared would seal a dangerous alliance of the national executive with the commercial and financial interests. The second was the open admiration of the British constitution in the writings of John Adams and the undisguised contempt for active popular participation in political affairs that could be heard in higher social circles in the city. Concluding that the economic program and the loose interpretation of the federal charter were alike intended to subvert the Constitution and prepare the way for a revival of aristocrats and kings, the two Virginians urged the revolutionary poet, Philip Freneau, a Princeton classmate of the congressman, to come to Philadelphia to start a national paper. Jefferson provided a position as a part-time clerk in his department. Madison contributed some nineteen essays to the *National Gazette*.

The Jeffersonian Republicans were certainly mistaken in their estimate of the intentions of their foes. Very few Americans—and these did not include the likes of Hamilton or Adams—even wished for a revival of hereditary rights. None of any consequence worked actively for such an end or for reunion with Great Britain. But rather than dismissing Jefferson's or Madison's concerns as paranoiac or outrageous, we might be well advised to recollect that they were living in an age when equal rights were the exception, not the rule—and barely fifteen years since the American renunciation of the king. Where we would speak of despotism or dictatorship, they spoke as naturally of kings. A pro-monarchical revival was within the bounds of a responsible imagination, and the Jeffersonians could cite specific sources for their fear that this was just what certain Federalists desired. Moreover, while the Jeffersonians undoubtedly mistook the ultimate intentions of their foes, they were by no means wrong to think that their opponents wanted to construct a polity and a society which would not have been "republican" by opposition definitions.

The documents presented in this section were selected as an introduction to the two Virginians' views on leadership in a republic, on the role of popular opinion and participation, and on sound construction of the people's Constitution. Madison's brief essays for the *National Gazette* were part of his extended search for ways to guarantee the formulation and expression of popular opinion in a large republic. Jefferson's promotion of the concept of "ward republics" was an unsuccessful effort to implant direct, continuing participation in a system whose creators probably assumed too easily that popular involvement could be taken as a given. The Kentucky and Virginia Resolutions were, at once, a firm (and risky) statement of the compact theory of the Constitution and a logical attempt to use the legislatures of the states as organs for creating and expressing popular opinion. Jefferson's inaugural address delineated the specific policies that he and Madison intended to pursue in order to return the federal government to the original intentions of the people. It was also an expression of their real desire for national conciliation and a great re-grounding of the nation's politics on attitudes more suitable for a republic.

23. Thomas Jefferson to James Madison
Paris, January 30, 1787

My last to you was of the 16th. of Dec. since which I have received yours of Nov. 25. & Dec. 4. which afforded me, as your letters always do, a treat on matters public, individual & oeconomical. I am impatient to learn your sentiments on the late troubles in the Eastern states. So far as I have yet seen, they do not appear to threaten serious consequences. Those states have suffered by the stoppage of the channels of their commerce, which have not yet found other issues. This must render money scarce, and make the people uneasy. This uneasiness has produced acts absolutely unjustifiable: but I hope they will provoke no severities from their governments. A consciousness of those in power that their administration of the public affairs has been honest may perhaps produce too great a degree of indignation: and those characters wherein fear predominates over hope may apprehend too much from these instances of irregularity. They may conclude too hastily that nature has formed man insusceptible of any other government but that of force, a conclusion not founded in truth, nor experience. Societies exist under three forms sufficiently distinguishable. 1. Without government, as among our Indians. 2. Under governments wherein the will of every one has a just influence, as is the case in England in a slight degree and in our states, in a great one. 3. Under governments of force: as is the case in all other monarchies & in most of the other republics. To have an idea of the curse of existence under these last, they must be seen. It is a government of wolves over sheep. It is a problem, not clear in my mind, that the 1st. condition is not the best, but I believe it to be inconsistent with any great degree of population. The second state has a great deal of good in it. The mass of mankind under that enjoys a precious degree of liberty & happiness. It has it's evils too: the principal of which is the turbulence to which it is subject. But weigh this against the oppressions of monarchy, and it becomes nothing. Malo periculosam libertatem quom quietam servitutem. Even this evil is productive of good. It prevents the degeneracy of government, and nourishes a general attention to the public affairs. I hold it that a little rebellion now and then is a good thing, & as necessary in the political world as storms in the physical. Unsuccessful rebellions indeed generally establish the incroachments on the rights of the people which have produced them. An observation of this truth should render honest republican governors so mild in their punishment of rebellions, as not to discourage them too much. It is a medecine necessary for the sound health of government. If these transactions give me no uneasiness, I feel very differently at another piece of intelligence, to wit, the possibility that the navigation of the Missisipi may be abandoned to Spain. I never had any interest Westward of the Alleghaney; & I never will have any. But I have had great opportunities of knowing the character of the people who inhabit that country, and I will venture to say that the act which abandons the navigation of the Missisipi is an act of separation between the Eastern & Western country. It is a relinquishment of five parts out of eight of the territory of the United states, and abandonment of the fairest subject for the paiment of our public debts, & the chaining those debts on our own necks in perpetuum. I have the utmost confidence in the honest intentions of those who concur in this measure; but I lament their want of acquaintance with the character & physical advantages of the people who, right or wrong, will suppose their interests sacrificed on this occasion to the contrary interests of that part of the confederacy in possession of present power. If they declare themselves a separate people, we are incapable of a single effort to retain them. Our citizens can never be induced, either as militia or as soldiers, to go there to cut the throats of their own brothers & sons, or rather to be themselves the subjects instead of the perpetrators of the parricide. Nor would that country quit the cost of being retained against the will of it's inhabitants, could it be done. But it cannot be done. They are able already to rescue the navigation of the Missisipi out of the hands of Spain, & to add New Orleans to their own territory. They will be joined by the inhabitants of Louisiana. This will bring on a war between them & Spain; & that will produce the question with us whether it will not be worth our while to become parties with them in the war, in order to reunite them with us, & thus correct our error? & were I to permit my forebodings to go one step further, I should predict that the inhabitants of the U.S. would force their rulers to take the affirmative of that question. I wish I may be mistaken in all these opinions.

24. James Madison, Government of the United States, *National Gazette*, February 4, 1792

Power being found by universal experience liable to abuses, a distribution of it into separate departments, has become a first principle of free governments. By this contrivance, the portion entrusted to the same hands being less, there is less room to abuse what is granted; and the different hands being interested, each in maintaining its own, there is less opportunity to usurp what is not granted. Hence the merited praise of governments modelled on a partition of their powers into legislative, executive, and judiciary, and a repartition of the legislative into different houses.

The political system of the United States claims still higher praise. The power delegated by the people is first divided between the general government and the state governments; each of which is then subdivided into legislative, executive, and judiciary departments. And as in a single government these departments are to be kept separate and safe, by a defensive armour for each; so, it is to be hoped, do the two governments possess each the means of preventing or correcting unconstitutional encroachments of the other.

Should this improvement on the theory of free government not be marred in the execution, it may prove the best legacy ever left by lawgivers to their country, and the best lesson ever given to the world by its benefactors. If a security against power lies in the division of it into parts mutually controuling each other, the security must increase with the increase of the parts into which the whole can be conveniently formed.

It must not be denied that the task of forming and maintaining a division of power between different governments, is greater than among different departments of the same government; because it may be more easy (though, sufficiently difficult) to separate, by proper definitions, the legislative, executive, and judiciary powers, which are more distinct in their nature, than to discriminate, by precise enumerations, one class of legislative powers from another class, one class of executive from another class, and one class of judiciary from another class; where the powers being of a more kindred nature, their boundaries are more obscure and run more into each other.

If the task be difficult however, it must by no means be abandoned. Those who would pronounce it impossible, offer no alternative to their country but schism, or consolidation; both of them bad, but the latter the worst, since it is the high road to monarchy, than which nothing worse, in the eye of republicans, could result from the anarchy implied in the former.

Those who love their country, its repose, and its republicanism, will therefore study to avoid the alternative, by elucidating and guarding the limits which define the two governments; by inculcating moderation in the exercise of the powers of both, and particularly a mutual abstinence from such as might nurse present jealousies, or engender greater.

In bestowing the eulogies due to the partitions and internal checks of power, it ought not the less to be remembered, that they are neither the sole nor the chief palladium of constitutional liberty. The people who are the authors of this blessing, must also be its guardians. Their eyes must be ever ready to mark, their voice to pronounce, and their arm to repel or repair aggressions on the authority of their constitutions; the highest authority next to their own, because the immediate work of their own, and the most sacred part of their property, as recognising and recording the title to every other.

25. James Madison, Consolidation
National Gazette, December 3, 1791

Much has been said, and not without reason, against a consolidation of the States into one government. The omitting lesser objections, two consequences would probably flow from such a change in our political system, which justify the cautions used against it. *First*, it would be impossible to avoid the dilemma, of either relinquishing the present energy and responsibility of a *single* executive magistrate, for some *plural* substitute, which by dividing so great a trust might lessen the danger of it; or suffering so great an accumulation of powers in the hands of that officer, as might by degrees transform him into a monarch. The incompetency of one Legislature to regulate all the various objects belonging to the local governments, would evidently force a transfer of many of them to the executive department; whilst the encreasing splendour and number of its prerogatives supplied by this source, might prove excitements to ambition too powerful for a sober execution of the elective plan, and consequently strengthen the pretexts for an hereditary designation of the magistrate. *Second*, were the state governments abolished, the same space of country that would produce an undue growth of the executive power, would prevent that controul on the Legislative body, which is essential to a faithful discharge of its trust, neither the voice nor the sense of ten or twenty millions of people, spread through so many latitudes as are comprehended within the United States, could ever be combined or called into effect, if deprived of those local organs, through which both can now be conveyed. In such a state of things, the impossibility of acting together, might be succeeded by the inefficacy of partial expressions of the public mind, and this at length, by a universal silence and insensibility, leaving the whole government to that *self* directed course, which, it must be owned, is the natural propensity of every government.

But if a consolidation of the states into one government be an event so justly to be avoided, it is not less to be desired, on the other hand, that a consolidation should prevail in their interests and affections; and this too, as it fortunately happens, for the very reasons, among others, which lie against a governmental consolidation. For, in the first place, in proportion as uniformity is found to prevail in the interests and sentiments of the several states, will be the practicability of accommodating *Legislative* regulations to them, and thereby of withholding new and dangerous prerogatives from the executive. Again, the greater the mutual confidence and affection of all parts of the Union, the more likely they will be to concur amicably, or to differ with moderation, in the elective designation of the chief magistrate; and by such examples, to guard and adorn the vital principle of our republican constitution. Lastly, the less the supposed difference of interests, and the greater the concord and confidence throughout the great body of the people, the more readily must they sympathize with each other, the more seasonably can they interpose a common manifestation of their sentiments, the more certainly will they take the alarm at usurpation or oppression, and the more effectually will they *consolidate* their defence of the public liberty.

Here then is a proper object presented, both to those who are most jealously attached to the separate authority reserved to the states, and to those who may be more inclined to contemplate the people of America in the light of one nation. Let the former continue to watch against every encroachment, which might lead to a gradual consolidation of the states into one government. Let the latter employ their utmost zeal, by eradicating local prejudices and mistaken rivalships, to consolidate the affairs of the states into one harmonious interest; and let it be the patriotic study of all, to maintain the various authorities established by our complicated system, each in its respective constitutional sphere; and to erect over the whole, one paramount Empire of reason, benevolence and brotherly affection.

26. James Madison, Public Opinion
National Gazette, ca. December 19, 1791

Public opinion sets bounds to every government, and is the real sovereign in every free one.

As there are cases where the public opinion must be obeyed by the government; so there are cases, where not being fixed, it may be influenced by the government. This distinction, if kept in view, would prevent or decide many debates on the respect due from the government to the sentiments of the people.

In proportion as government is influenced by opinion, it must be so, by whatever influences opinion. This decides the question concerning a *Constitutional Declaration of Rights*, which requires an influence on government, by becoming a part of the public opinion.

The larger a country, the less easy for its real opinion to be ascertained, and the less difficult to be counterfeited; when ascertained or presumed, the more respectable it is in the eyes of individuals. This is favorable to the authority of government. For the same reason, the more extensive a country, the more insignificant is each individual in his own eyes. This may be unfavorable to liberty.

Whatever facilitates a general intercourse of sentiments, as good roads, domestic commerce, a free press, and particularly a *circulation of newspapers through the entire body of the people*, and *Representatives going from, and returning among every part of them*, is equivalent to a contraction of territorial limits, and is favorable to liberty, where these may be too extensive.

27. James Madison, A Candid State of Parties
National Gazette, September 22, 1792

As it is the business of the contemplative statesman to trace the history of parties in a free country, so it is the duty of the citizen at all times to understand the actual state of them. Whenever this duty is omitted, an opportunity is given to designing men, by the use of artificial or nominal distinctions, to oppose and balance against each other those who never differed as to the end to be pursued, and may no longer differ as to the means of attaining it. The most interesting state of parties in the United States may be referred to three periods: Those who espoused the cause of independence and those who adhered to the British claims, formed the parties of the first period; if, indeed, the disaffected class were considerable enough to deserve the name of a party. This state of things was superseded by the treaty of peace in 1783. From 1783 to 1787 there were parties in abundance, but being rather local than general, they are not within the present review.

The Federal Constitution, proposed in the latter year, gave birth to a second and most interesting division of the people. Every one remembers it, because every one was involved in it.

Among those who embraced the constitution, the great body were unquestionably friends to republican liberty; tho' there were, no doubt, some who were openly or secretly attached to monarchy and aristocracy; and hoped to make the constitution a cradle for these hereditary establishments.

Among those who opposed the constitution, the great body were certainly well affected to the union and to good government, tho' there might be a few who had a leaning unfavourable to both. This state of parties was terminated by the regular and effectual establishment of the federal government in 1788; out of the administration of which, however, has arisen a third division, which being natural to most political societies, is likely to be of some duration in ours.

One of the divisions consists of those, who from particular interest, from natural temper, or from the habits of life, are more partial to the opulent than to the other classes of society; and having debauched themselves into a persuasion that mankind are incapable of governing themselves, it follows with them, of course, that government can be carried on only by the pageantry of rank, the influence of money and emoluments, and the terror of military force. Men of those sentiments must naturally wish to point the measures of government less to the interest of the many than of a few, and less to the reason of the many than to their weaknesses; hoping perhaps in proportion to the ardor of their zeal, that by giving such a turn to the administration, the government itself may by degrees be narrowed into fewer hands, and approximated to an hereditary form.

The other division consists of those who believing in the doctrine that mankind are capable of governing themselves, and hating hereditary power as an insult to the reason and an outrage to the rights of man, are naturally offended at every public measure that does not appeal to the understanding and to the general interests of the community, or that is not strictly conformable to the principles, and conducive to the preservation of republican government.

This being the real state of parties among us, an experienced and dispassionate observer will be at no loss to decide on the probable conduct of each.

The antirepublican party, as it may be called, being the weaker in point of numbers, will be induced by the most obvious motives to strengthen themselves with the men of influence, particularly of moneyed, which is the most active and insinuating influence. It will be equally their true policy to weaken their opponents by reviving exploded parties, and taking advantage of all prejudices, local, political, and occupational, that may prevent or disturb a general coalition of sentiments.

The Republican party, as it may be termed, conscious that the mass of people in every part of the union, in every state, and of every occupation must at bottom be with them, both in interest and sentiment, will naturally find their account in burying all antecedent questions, in banishing every other distinction than that between enemies and friends to republican government, and in promoting a general harmony among the latter, wherever residing, or however employed.

Whether the republican or the rival party will ultimately establish its ascendance, is a problem which may be contemplated now; but which time alone can solve. On one hand experience shews that in politics as in war, stratagem is often an overmatch for numbers: and among more happy characteristics of our political situation, it is now well understood that there are peculiarities, some temporary, others more durable, which may favour that side in the contest. On the republican side, again, the superiority of numbers is so great, their sentiments are so decided, and the practice of making a common cause, where there is a common sentiment and common interest, in spight of circumstancial and artificial distinctions, is so well understood, that no temperate observer of human affairs will be surprised if the issue in the present instance should be reversed, and the government be administered in the spirit and form approved by the great body of the people.

28. Thomas Jefferson, Draft of the Kentucky Resolutions, October 1798

1. *Resolved,* That the several States composing the United States of America, are not united on the principle of unlimited submission to their General Government; but that, by a compact under the style and title of a Constitution for the United States, and of amendments thereto, they constituted a general Government for special purposes,—delegated to that government certain definite powers, reserving, each State to itself, the residuary mass of right to their own self-government; and that whensoever the General Government assumes undelegated powers, its acts are unauthoritative, void, and of no force; that to this compact each State acceded as a State, and is an integral party, its co-States forming, as to itself, the other party: that the government created by this compact was not made the exclusive or final judge of the extent of the powers delegated to itself; since that would have made its discretion, and not the Constitution, the measure of its powers; but that, as in all other cases of compact among powers having no common judge, each party has an equal right to judge for itself, as well of infractions as of the mode and measure of redress.

2. *Resolved,* That the Constitution of the United States, having delegated to Congress a power to punish treason, counterfeiting the securities and current coin of the United States, piracies, and felonies committed on the high seas, and offences against the law of nations, and no other crimes whatsoever; and it being true as a general principle, and one of the amendments to the Constitution having also declared, that "the powers not delegated to the United States by the Constitution, nor prohibited by it to the States, are reserved to the States respectively, or to the people," therefore the act of Congress, passed on the 14th day of July, 1798, and intituled "An Act in addition to the act intituled An Act for the punishment of certain crimes against the United States," as also the act passed by them on the ___ day of June, 1798, intituled "An Act to punish frauds committed on the bank of the United States," (and all their other acts which assume to create, define, or punish crimes, other than those so enumerated in the Constitu-

tion,) are altogether void, and of no force; and that the power to create, define, and punish such other crimes is reserved, and, of right, appertains solely and exclusively to the respective States, each within its own territory.

3. *Resolved,* That it is true as a general principle, and is also expressly declared by one of the amendments to the Constitution, that "the powers not delegated to the United States by the Constitution, nor prohibited by it to the States, are reserved to the States respectively, or to the people;" and that no power over the freedom of religion, freedom of speech, or freedom of the press being delegated to the United States by the Constitution, nor prohibited by it to the States, all lawful powers respecting the same did of right remain, and were reserved to the States or the people: that thus was manifested their determination to retain to themselves the right of judging how far the licentiousness of speech and of the press may be abridged without lessening their useful freedom, and how far those abuses which cannot be separated from their use should be tolerated, rather than the use be destroyed. And thus also they guarded against all abridgment by the United States of the freedom of religious opinions and exercises, and retained to themselves the right of protecting the same, as this State, by a law passed on the general demand of its citizens, had already protected them from all human restraint or interference. And that in addition to this general principle and express declaration, another and more special provision has been made by one of the amendments to the Constitution, which expressly declares, that "Congress shall make no law respecting an establishment of religion, or prohibiting the free exercise thereof, or abridging the freedom of speech or of the press:" thereby guarding in the same sentence, and under the same words, the freedom of religion, of speech, and of the press: insomuch, that whatever violated either, throws down the sanctuary which covers the others, and that libels, falsehood, and defamation, equally with heresy and false religion, are withheld from the cognizance of federal tribunals. That, therefore, the act of Congress of the United States, passed on the 14th day of July, 1798, intituled "An Act in addition to the act intituled An Act for the punishment of certain crimes against the

United States," which does abridge the freedom of the press, is not law, but is altogether void, and of no force.

4. *Resolved*, That alien friends are under the jurisdiction and protection of the laws of the State wherein they are: that no power over them has been delegated to the United States, nor prohibited to the individual States, distinct from their power over citizens. And it being true as a general principle, and one of the amendments to the Constitution having also declared, that "the powers not delegated to the United States by the Constitution, nor prohibited by it to the States, are reserved to the States respectively, or to the people," the act of the Congress of the United States, passed on the ___ day of July, 1798, intituled "An Act concerning aliens," which assumes powers over alien friends, not delegated by the Constitution, is not law, but is altogether void, and of no force.

5. *Resolved*, That in addition to the general principle, as well as the express declaration, that powers not delegated are reserved, another and more special provision, inserted in the Constitution from abundant caution, has declared that "the migration or importation of such persons as any of the States now existing shall think proper to admit, shall not be prohibited by the Congress prior to the year 1808;" that this commonwealth does admit the migration of alien friends, described as the subject of the said act concerning aliens: that a provision against prohibiting their migration, is a provision against all acts equivalent thereto, or it would be nugatory: that to remove them when migrated, is equivalent to a prohibition of their migration, and is, therefore, contrary to the said provision of the Constitution, and void.

6. *Resolved*, That the imprisonment of a person under the protection of the laws of this commonwealth, on his failure to obey the simple *order* of the President to depart out of the United States, as is undertaken by said act intituled "An Act concerning aliens," is contrary to the Constitution, one amendment to which has provided that "no person shall be deprived of liberty without due process of law;" and that another having provided that "in all criminal prosecutions the accused shall enjoy the right to pubic trial by an impartial jury, to be informed of the nature and cause of the accu-

sation, to be confronted with the witnesses against him, to have compulsory process for obtaining witnesses in his favor, and to have the assistance of counsel for his defence," the same act, undertaking to authorize the President to remove a person out of the United States, who is under the protection of the law, on his own suspicion, without accusation, without jury, without public trial, without confrontation of the witnesses against him, without hearing witnesses in his favor, without defence, without counsel, is contrary to the provision also of the Constitution, is therefore not law, but utterly void, and of no force: that transferring the power of judging any person, who is under the protection of the laws, from the courts to the President of the United States, as is undertaken by the same act concerning aliens, is against the article of the Constitution which provides that "the judicial power of the United States shall be vested in courts, the judges of which shall hold their offices during good behavior;" and that the said act is void for that reason also. And it is further to be noted, that this transfer of judiciary power is to that magistrate of the General Government who already possesses all the Executive, and a negative on all legislative powers.

7. *Resolved*, That the construction applied by the General Government (as is evidenced by sundry of their proceedings) to those parts of the Constitution of the United States which delegate to Congress a power "to lay and collect taxes, duties, imports, and excises, to pay the debts, and provide for the common defence and general welfare of the United States," and "to make all laws which shall be necessary and proper for carrying into execution the powers vested by the Constitution in the government of the United States, or in any department or officer thereof," goes to the destruction of all limits prescribed to their power by the Constitution: that words meant by the instrument to be subsidiary only to the execution of limited powers, ought not to be so construed as themselves to give unlimited powers, nor a part to be so taken as to destroy the whole residue of that instrument: that the proceedings of the General Government under color of these articles, will be a fit and necessary subject of revisal and correction, at a time of greater tranquillity, while those specified in the preceding resolutions call for immediate redress.

8th. *Resolved*, That a committee of conference and correspondence be appointed, who shall have in charge to communicate the preceding resolutions to the legislatures of the several States; to assure them that this commonwealth continues in the same esteem of their friendship and union which it has manifested from that moment at which a common danger first suggested a common union: that it considers union, for specified national purposes, and particularly to those specified in their late federal compact, to be friendly to the peace, happiness and prosperity of all the States: that faithful to that compact, according to the plain intent and meaning in which it was understood and acceded to by the several parties, it is sincerely anxious for its preservation: that it does also believe, that to take from the States all the powers of self-government and transfer them to a general and consolidated government, without regard to the special delegations and reservations solemnly agreed to in that compact, is not for the peace, happiness or prosperity of these States; and that therefore this commonwealth is determined, as it doubts not its co-States are, to submit to undelegated, and consequently unlimited powers in no man or body of men on earth: that in cases of an abuse of the delegated powers, the members of the General Government, being chosen by the people, a change by the people would be the constitutional remedy; but, where powers are assumed which have not been delegated, a nullification of the act is the rightful remedy: that every State has a natural right in cases not within the compact, (casus non foederis,) to nullify of their own authority all assumptions of power by others within their limits: that without this right, they would be under the dominion, absolute and unlimited, of whosoever might exercise this right of judgment for them: that nevertheless, this commonwealth, from motives of regard and respect for its co-States, has wished to communicate with them on the subject: that with them alone it is proper to communicate, they alone being parties to the compact, and solely authorized to judge in the last resort of the powers exercised under it, Congress being not a party, but merely the creature of the compact, and subject as to its assumptions of power to the final judgment of those by whom, and for whose use itself and its powers were all created and modified: that if the acts before specified should stand, these conclusions would flow from them; that the General Government may place any act they think proper on the list of crimes, and punish it themselves whether enumerated or not enumerated by the Constitution as cognizable by them: that they may transfer its cognizance to the President, or any other person, who may himself be the accuser, counsel, judge and jury, whose *suspicions* may be the evidence, his *order* the sentence, his *officer* the executioner, and his breast the sole record of the transaction: that a very numerous and valuable description of the inhabitants of these States being, by this precedent, reduced, as outlaws, to the absolute dominion of one man, and the barrier of the Constitution thus swept away from us all, no rampart now remains against the passions and the powers of a majority in Congress to protect from a like exportation, or other more grievous punishment, the minority of the same body, the legislatures, judges, governors, and counsellors of the States, nor their other peaceable inhabitants, who may venture to reclaim the constitutional rights and liberties of the States and people, or who for other causes, good or bad, may be obnoxious to the views, or marked by the suspicions of the President, or be thought dangerous to his or their election, or other interests, public or personal: that the friendless alien has indeed been selected as the safest subject of a first experiment; but the citizen will soon follow, or rather, has already followed, for already has a sedition act marked him as its prey: that these and successive acts of the same character, unless arrested at the threshold, necessarily drive these States into revolution and blood, and will furnish new calumnies against republican government, and new pretexts for those who wish it to be believed that man cannot be governed but by a rod of iron: that it would be a dangerous delusion were a confidence in the men of our choice to silence our fears for the safety of our rights: that confidence is everywhere the parent of despotism—free government is founded in jealousy, and not in confidence; it is jealousy and not confidence which prescribes limited constitutions, to bind down those whom we are obliged to trust with power: that our Constitution has accordingly fixed the limits to which, and no further, our confidence may go; and let the honest advocate of confidence read the alien and sedition acts, and say if the Constitution has not been wise in fixing limits to the government it created, and whether we should be wise in destroying those limits. Let him say what the government is, if it be not a tyranny, which the men of our choice have conferred on our President, and the President of our choice has assented to, and accepted over the friendly strangers to whom the mild spirit of our country and its laws have pledged hospitality and protection: that the men of our choice have more respected the bare *suspicions* of the President, than the solid right of innocence, the claims of justification, the sacred force of truth, and the forms and substance of law and justice. In questions of power, then, let no more be heard of confidence in man, but bind him down from mischief by the chains of the Constitution. That this commonwealth does therefore call on its co-States for an expression of their sentiments on the acts concerning aliens, and for the punishment of certain crimes herein before specified, plainly declaring whether these acts are or are not authorized by the federal compact. And it doubts not that their sense will be so announced as to prove their attachment unaltered to limited government, whether general or particular. And that the rights and liberties of their co-States will be exposed to no dangers by remaining embarked in a common bottom with their own. That they will concur with this commonwealth in considering the said acts as so palpably against the Constitution as to amount to an undisguised declaration that compact is not meant to be the measure of the powers of the General Government, but that it will proceed in the exercise over these States, of all powers whatsoever: that they will view this as seizing the rights of the States, and consolidating them in the hands of the General Government, with a power assumed to bind the States, not merely as the cases made federal, (casus foederis,) but in all cases whatsoever, by laws made, not with their consent, but by others against their consent: that this would be to surrender the form of government we have chosen, and live under one deriving its powers from its own will, and not from our authority; and that the co-States, recurring to their natural right in cases not made federal, will concur in declaring these acts void, and of no force, and will each take measures of its own for providing that neither these acts, nor any others of the General Government not plainly and intentionally authorized by the Constitution, shall be exercised within their respective territories.

9th. *Resolved*, That the said committee be authorized to communicate by writing or personal conferences, at any times or places whatever, with any person or person who may be appointed by any one or more co-States to correspond or confer with them; and that they lay their proceedings before the next session of Assembly.

29. James Madison, The Virginia Resolutions, December 21, 1798

In the House of Delegates

Resolved, that the General Assembly of Virginia doth unequivocally express a firm resolution to maintain and defend the constitution of the United States, and the Constitution of this state, against every aggression, either foreign or domestic, and that they will support the government of the United States in all measures, warranted by the former.

That this Assembly most solemnly declares a warm attachment to the Union of the States, to maintain which, it pledges all its powers; and that for this end, it is their duty, to watch over and oppose every infraction of those principles, which constitute the only basis of that union, because a faithful observance of them, can alone secure its existence, and the public happiness.

That this Assembly doth explicitly and peremptorily declare, that it views the powers of the federal government, as resulting from the compact to which the states are parties; as limited by the plain sense and intention of the instrument constituting that compact; as no farther valid than they are authorised by the grants enumerated in that compact, and that in case of a deliberate, palpable and dangerous exercise of other powers not granted by the said compact, the states who are parties thereto have the right, and are in duty bound, to interpose for arresting the progress of the evil, and for maintaining within their respective limits, the authorities, rights and liberties appertaining to them.

That the General Assembly doth also express its deep regret that a spirit has in sundry instances, been manifested by the federal government, to enlarge its powers by forced constructions of the constitutional charter which defines them; and that indications have appeared of a design to expound certain general phrases (which having been copied from the very limited grant of powers in the former articles of confederation were the less liable to be misconstrued) so as to destroy the meaning and effect of the particular enumeration, which necessarily explains and limits the general phrases; and so as to consolidate the states by degrees into one sovereignty, the obvious tendency and inevitable consequence of which would be, to transform the present republican system of the United States, into an absolute, or at best a mixed monarchy.

That the General Assembly doth particularly protest against the palpable and alarming infractions of the constitution, in the two late cases of the "alien and sedition acts," passed at the last session of Congress; the first of which exercises a power no where delegated to the federal government; and which by uniting legislative and judicial powers, to those of executive, subverts the general principles of free government, as well as the particular organization and positive provisions of the federal constitution: and the other of which acts, exercises in like manner a power not delegated by the constitution, but on the contrary expressly and positively forbidden by one of the amendments thereto; a power which more than any other ought to produce universal alarm, because it is levelled against that right of freely examining public characters and measures, and of free communication among the people thereon, which has ever been justly deemed, the only effectual guardian of every other right.

That this State having by its convention which ratified the federal constitution, expressly declared, "that among other essential rights, the liberty of conscience and of the press cannot be cancelled, abridged, restrained or modified by any authority of the United States" and from its extreme anxiety to guard these rights from every possible attack of sophistry or ambition, having with other states recommended an amendment for that purpose, which amendment was in due time annexed to the Constitution, it would mark a reproachful inconsistency and criminal degeneracy, if an indifference were now shewn to the most palpable violation of one of the rights thus declared and secured, and to the establishment of a precedent which may be fatal to the other.

That the good people of this Commonwealth having ever felt and continuing to feel the most sincere affection for their brethren of the other states, the truest anxiety for establishing and perpetuating the union of all, and the most scrupulous fidelity to that Constitution which is the pledge of mutual friendship, and the instrument of mutual happiness, the General Assembly doth solemnly appeal to the like dispositions of the other States, in confidence that they will concur with this Commonwealth in declaring, as it does hereby declare, that the acts aforesaid are unconstitutional, and that the necessary and proper measures will be taken by each, for cooperating with this State in maintaining unimpaired the authorities, rights, and liberties, reserved to the States respectively, or to the people.

That the Governor be desired to transmit a copy of the foregoing resolutions to the Executive authority of each of the other States, with a request, that the same may be communicated to the Legislature thereof.

And that a copy be furnished to each of the Senators and Representatives, representing this State in the Congress of the United States.

30. Thomas Jefferson to Samuel Kercheval
Monticello, July 12, 1816

I duly received your favor of June the 13th, with the copy of the letters on the calling a convention, on which you are pleased to ask my opinion. I have not been in the habit of mysterious reserve on any subject, nor of buttoning up my opinions within my own doublet. On the contrary, while in public service especially, I thought the public entitled to frankness, and intimately to know whom they employed. But I am now retired: I resign myself, as a passenger, with confidence to those at present at the helm, and ask but for rest, peace and good will. The question you propose, on equal representation, has become a party one, in which I wish to take no public share. Yet, if it be asked for your own satisfaction only, and not to be quoted before the public, I have no motive to withhold it, and the less from you, as it coincides with your own. At the birth of our republic, I committed that opinion to the world, in the draught of a constitution annexed to the "Notes on Virginia," in which a provision was inserted for a representation permanently equal. The infancy of the subject at that moment, and our inexperience of self-government, occasioned gross departures in that draught from genuine republican canons. In truth, the abuses of monarchy had so much filled all the space of political contemplation, that we imagined everything republican which was not monarchy. We had not yet penetrated to the mother principle, that "governments are republican only in proportion as they embody the will of their people, and execute it." Hence, our first constitutions had really no leading principles in them. But experience and reflection have but more and more confirmed me in the particular importance of the equal representation then proposed. On that point, then, I am entirely in sentiment with your letters; and only lament that a copy-right of your pamphlet prevents their appearance in the newspapers, where alone they would be generally read, and produce general effect. The present vacancy too, of other matter, would give them place in every paper, and bring the question home to every man's conscience.

But inequality of representation in both Houses of our legislature, is not the only republican heresy in this first essay of our revolutionary patriots at forming a constitution. For let it be agreed that a government is republican in proportion as every member composing it has his equal voice in the direction of its concerns (not indeed in person, which would be impracticable beyond the limits of a city, or small township, but) by representatives chosen by himself, and responsible to him at short periods, and let us bring to the test of this canon every branch of our constitution.

In the legislature, the House of Representatives is chosen by less than half the people, and not at all in proportion to those who do choose. The Senate are still more disproportionate, and for long terms of irresponsibility. In the Executive, the Governor is entirely independent of the choice of the people, and of their control; his Council equally so, and at best but a fifth wheel to a wagon. In the Judiciary, the judges of the highest courts are dependent on none but themselves. In England, where judges were named and removable at the will of an hereditary executive, from which branch most misrule was feared, and has flowed, it was a great point gained, by fixing them for life, to make them independent of that executive. But in a government founded on the public will, this principle operates in an opposite direction, and against that will. There, too, they were still removable on a concurrence of the executive and legislative branches. But we have made them independent of the nation itself. They are irremovable, but by their own body, for any depravities of conduct, and even by their own body for the imbecilities of dotage. The justices of the inferior courts are self-chosen, are for life, and perpetuate their own body in succession forever, so that a faction once possessing themselves of the bench of a country, can never be broken up, but hold their country in chains, forever indissoluble. Yet these justices are the real executive as well as judiciary, in all our minor and most ordinary concerns. They tax us at will; fill the office of sheriff, the most important of all the executive officers of the county; name nearly all our military leaders, which leaders, once named, are removable but by themselves. The juries, our judges of all fact, and of law when they choose it, are not selected by the people, nor amenable to them. They are chosen by an officer named by the court and executive. Chosen, did I say? Picked up by the sheriff from the loungings of the court yard, after everything respectable has retired from it. Where then is our republicanism to be found? Not in our constitution certainly, but merely in the spirit of our people. That would oblige even a despot to govern us republicanly. Owing to this spirit, and to nothing in the form of our constitution, all things have gone well. But this fact, so triumphantly misquoted by the enemies of reformation, is not the fruit of our constitution, but has prevailed in spite of it. Our functionaries have done well, because generally honest men. If any were not so, they feared to show it.

But it will be said, it is easier to find faults than to amend them. I do not think their amendment so difficult as is pretended. Only lay down true principles, and adhere to them inflexibly. Do not be frightened into their surrender by the alarms of the timid, or the croakings of wealth against the ascendency of the people. If experience be called for, appeal to that of our fifteen or twenty governments for forty years, and show me where the people have done half the mischief in these forty years, that a single despot would have done in a single year; or show half the riots and rebellions, the crimes and the punishments, which have taken place in any single nation, under kingly government, during the same period. The true foundation of republican government is the equal right of every citizen, in his person and property, and in their management. Try by this, as a tally, every provision of our constitution, and see if it hangs directly on the will of the people. Reduce your legislature to a convenient number for full, but orderly discussion. Let every man who fights or pays, exercise his just and equal right in their election. Submit them to approbation or rejection at short intervals. Let the executive be chosen in the same way, and for the same term, by those whose agent he is to be; and leave no screen of a council behind which to skulk from responsibility. It has been thought that the people are not competent electors of judges *learned in the law*. But I do not know that this is true, and, if doubtful, we should follow principle. In this, as in many other elections, they would be guided by reputation, which would not err oftener, perhaps, than the present mode of appointment. In one State of the Union, at least, it has long been tried, and with the most satisfactory success. The judges of Connecticut have been chosen by the people every six months, for nearly two centuries, and I believe there has hardly ever been an instance of change; so powerful is the curb of incessant responsibility. If prejudice, however, derived from a monarchical institution, is still to prevail against the vital elective principle of our own, and if the existing example among ourselves of periodical election of judges by the people be still mistrusted, let us at least not adopt the evil, and reject the good, of the English precedent; let us retain amovability on the concurrence of the executive and legislative branches, and nomination by the executive alone. Nomination to office is an executive function. To give it to the legislature, as we do, is a violation of the principle of the separation of powers. It swerves the members from correctness, by temptations to intrigue for office themselves, and to a corrupt barter of votes; and destroys responsibility by dividing it among a multitude. By leaving nomination in its proper place, among executive functions, the principle of the distribution of power is preserved, and responsibility weighs with its heaviest force on a single head.

The organization of our county administrations may be thought more difficult. But follow principle, and the knot unties itself. Divide the counties into wards of such size as that every citizen can attend, when called on, and act in person. Ascribe to them the government of their wards in all things relating to themselves exclusively. A justice, chosen by themselves, in each, a constable, a military company, a patrol, a school, the care of their own poor, their own portion of the public roads, the choice of one or more jurors to serve in some court, and the delivery, within their own wards, of their own votes for all elective officers of higher sphere, will relieve the county administration of nearly all its business, will have it better done, and by making every citizen an acting member of the government, and in the offices nearest and most interesting to him, will attach him by his strongest feelings to the independence of his country, and its republican constitution. The justices thus chosen by every ward, would constitute the county court, would do its judiciary business, direct roads and bridges, levy county and poor rates, and administer all the matters of common interest to the whole country. These wards, called townships in New England, are the vital principle of their governments, and have proved themselves the wisest invention ever devised by the wit of man for the perfect exercise of self-government, and for its preservation. We should thus marshal our government into, 1, the general federal republic, for all concerns foreign and federal; 2, that of the State, for what relates to our own citizens exclusively; 3, the county republics, for the duties and concerns of the county; and 4, the ward republics, for the small, and yet numerous and interesting concerns of the neighborhood; and in government, as well as in every other business of life, it is by division and subdivision of duties alone, that all matters, great and small, can be managed to perfection. And the whole is cemented by giving to every citizen, personally, a part in the administration of the public affairs.

The sum of these amendments is, 1. General Suffrage. 2. Equal representation in the legislature. 3. An executive chosen by the people. 4. Judges elective or amovable. 5. Justices, jurors, and sheriffs elective. 6. Ward divisions. And 7. Periodical amendments of the constitution.

I have thrown out these as loose heads of amendment, for consideration and correction; and their object is to secure self-government by the republicanism of our constitution, as well as by the spirit of the people; and to nourish and perpetuate that spirit. I am not among those who fear the people. They, and not the rich, are our dependence for continued freedom. And to preserve their independence, we must not let our rulers load us with perpetual debt. We must make our election between *economy and liberty, or profusion and servitude*. If we run into such debts, as that we must be taxed in our meat and in our drink, in our necessaries and our comforts, in our labors and our amusements, for our callings and our creeds, as the people of England are, our people, like them, must come to labor sixteen hours in the twenty-four, give the earnings of fifteen of these to the government for their debts and daily expenses; and the sixteenth being insufficient to afford us bread, we must live, as they now do, on oatmeal and potatoes; have no time to think, no means of calling the mismanagers to account; but be glad to obtain subsistence by hiring ourselves to rivet their chains on the necks of our fellow-sufferers. Our landholders, too, like theirs, retaining indeed the title and stewardship of estates called theirs, but held really in trust for the treasury, must wander, like theirs, in foreign countries, and be contented with penury, obscurity, exile, and the glory of the nation. This example reads to us the salutary lesson, that private fortunes are destroyed by public as well as by private extravagance. And this is the tendency of all human governments. A departure from principle in one instance becomes a precedent for a second; that second for a third; and so on, till the bulk of the society is reduced to be mere automatons of misery, and to have no sensibilities left but for sinning and suffering. Then begins, indeed, the *bellum omnium in omnia,** which some philosophers observing to be so general in this world, have mistaken it for the natural, instead of the abusive state of man. And the fore horse of this frightful team is pubic debt. Taxation follows that, and in its train wretchedness and oppression.

Some men look at constitutions with sanctimonious reverence, and deem them like the arc of the covenant, too sacred to be touched. They ascribe to the men of the preceding age a wisdom more than human, and suppose what they did to be beyond amendment. I knew that age well; I belonged to it, and labored with it. It deserved well of its country. It was very like the present, but without the experience of the present; and forty years of experience in government is worth a century of book-reading; and this they would say themselves, were they to rise from the dead. I am certainly not an advocate for frequent and untried changes in laws and constitutions. I think moderate imperfections had better be borne with; because, when once known, we accommodate ourselves to them, and find practical means of correcting their ill effects. But I know also, that laws and institutions must go hand in hand with the progress of the human mind. As that becomes more developed, more enlightened, as new discoveries are made, new truths disclosed, and manners and opinions change with the change of circumstances, institutions must advance also, and keep pace with the times. We might as well require a man to wear still the

*A war of all against all.

coat which fitted him when a boy, as civilized society to remain ever under the regimen of their barbarous ancestors. It is this preposterous idea which has lately deluged Europe in blood. Their monarchs, instead of wisely yielding to the gradual change of circumstances, of favoring progressive accommodation to progressive improvement, have clung to old abuses, entrenched themselves behind steady habits, and obliged their subjects to seek through blood and violence rash and ruinous innovations, which, had they been referred to the peaceful deliberations and collected wisdom of the nation, would have been put into acceptable and salutary forms. Let us follow no such examples, nor weakly believe that one generation is not as capable as another of taking care of itself, and of ordering its own affairs. Let us, as our sister States have done, avail ourselves of our reason and experience, to correct the crude essays of our first and unexperienced, although wise, virtuous, and well-meaning councils. And lastly, let us provide in our constitution for its revision at stated periods. What these periods should be, nature herself indicates. By the European tables of mortality, of the adults living at any one moment of time, a majority will be dead in about nineteen years. At the end of that period, then, a new majority is come into place; or, in other words, a new generation. Each generation is as independent as the one preceding, as that was of all which had gone before. It has then, like them, a right to choose for itself the form of government it believes most promotive of its own happiness; consequently, to accommodate to the circumstances in which it finds itself, that received from its predecessors; and it is for the peace and good of mankind, that a solemn opportunity of doing this every nineteen or twenty years, should be provided by the constitution; so that it may be handed on, with periodical repairs, from generation to generation, to the end of time, if anything human can so long endure. It is now forty years since the constitution of Virginia was formed. The same tables inform us, that, within that period, two-thirds of the adults then living are now dead. Have then the remaining third, even if they had the wish, the right to hold in obedience to their will, and to laws heretofore made by them, the other two-thirds, who, with themselves, compose the present mass of adults? If they have not, who has? The dead? But the dead have no rights. They are nothing; and nothing cannot own something. Where there is no substance, there can be no accident. This corporeal globe, and everything upon it, belong to its present corporeal inhabitants, during their generation. They alone have a right to direct what is the concern of themselves alone, and to declare the law of that direction; and this declaration can only be made by their majority. That majority, then, has a right to depute representatives to a convention, and to make the constitution what they think will be the best for themselves. But how [to] collect their voice? This is the real difficulty. If invited by private authority, or county or district meetings, these divisions are so large that few will attend; and their voice will be imperfectly, or falsely pronounced. Here, then, would be one of the advantages of the ward divisions I have proposed. The mayor of every ward, on a question like the present, would call his ward together, take the simple yea or nay of its members, convey these to the county court, who would hand on those of all its wards to the proper general authority; and the voice of the whole people would be thus fairly, fully, and peaceably expressed, discussed, and decided by the common reason of the society. If this avenue be shut to the call of sufferance, it will make itself heard through that of force, and we shall go on, as other nations are doing, in the endless circle of oppression, rebellion, reformation; and oppression, rebellion, reformation, again; and so on forever.

These, Sir, are my opinions of the governments we see among men, and of the principles by which alone we may prevent our own from falling into the same dreadful track. I have given them at greater length than your letter called for. But I cannot say things by halves; and I confide them to your honor, so to use them as to preserve me from the gridiron of the public papers. If you shall approve and enforce them, as you have done that of equal representation, they may do some good. If not, keep them to yourself as the effusions of withered age and useless time. I shall, with not the less truth, assure you of my great respect and consideration.

31.Thomas Jefferson to Joseph C. Cabell
Monticello, February 2, 1816

. . . The way to have good and safe government, is not to trust it all to one, but to divide it among the many, distributing to every one exactly the functions he is competent to. Let the national government be entrusted with the defence of the nation, and its foreign and federal relations; the State governments with the civil rights, laws, police, and administration of what concerns the State generally; the counties with the local concerns of the counties, and each ward direct the interests within itself. It is by dividing and subdividing these republics from the great national one down through all its subordinations, until it ends in the administration of every man's farm by himself; by placing under every one what his own eye may superintend, that all will be done for the best. What has destroyed liberty and the rights of man in every government which has ever existed under the sun? The generalizing and concentrating all cares and powers into one body, no matter whether of the autocrats of Russia or France, or of the aristocrats of a Venetian senate. And I do believe that if the Almighty has not decreed that man shall never be free, (and it is a blasphemy to believe it,) that the secret will be found to be in the making himself the depository of the powers respecting himself, so far as he is competent to them, and delegating only what is beyond his competence by a synthetical process, to higher and higher orders of functionaries, so as to trust fewer and fewer powers in proportion as the trustees become more and more oligarchical. The elementary republics of the wards, the county republics, the State republics, and the republic of the Union, would form a gradation of authorities, standing each on the basis of law, holding every one its delegated share of powers, and constituting truly a system of fundamental balances and checks for the government. Where every man is a sharer in the direction of his ward-republic, or of some of the higher ones, and feels that he is a participator in the government of affairs, not merely at an election one day in the year, but every day; when there shall not be a man in the State who will not be a member of some one of its councils, great or small, he will let the heart be torn out of his body sooner than his power be wrested from him by a Caesar or a Bonaparte. How powerfully did we feel the energy of this organization in the case of embargo? I felt the foundations of the government shaken under my feet by the New England townships. There was not an individual in their States whose body was not thrown with all its momentum into action; and although the whole of the other States were known to be in favor of the measure, yet the organization of this little selfish minority enabled it to overrule the Union. What would the unwieldy counties of the middle, the south, and the west do? Call a county meeting, and the drunken loungers at and about the court houses would have collected, the distances being too great for the good people, and the industrious generally to attend. The character of those who really met would have been the measure of the weight they would have had in the scale of pubic opinion. As Cato, then, concluded every speech with the words, *Carthago delenda est,*" so do I every opinion, with the injunction, "divide the counties into wards." Begin them only for a single purpose; they will soon show for what others they are the best instruments. God bless you, and all our rulers, and give them the wisdom, as I am sure they have the will, to fortify us against the degeneracy of one government, and the concentration of all its powers in the hands of the one, the few, the well-born or the many.

32. Thomas Jefferson, First Inaugural Address March 4, 1801

Friends and Fellow-Citizens,

Called upon to undertake the duties of the first executive office of our country, I avail myself of the presence of that portion of my fellow-citizens which is here assembled to express my grateful thanks for the favor with which they have been pleased to look toward me, to declare a sincere consciousness that the task is above my talents, and that I approach it with those anxious and awful presentiments which the greatness of the charge and the weakness of my powers so justly inspire. A rising nation, spread over a wide and fruitful land, traversing all the seas with the rich productions of their industry, engaged in commerce with nations who feel power and forget right, advancing rapidly to destinies beyond the reach of mortal eye—when I contemplate these transcendent objects, and see the honor, the happiness, and the hopes of this beloved country committed to the issue and the auspices of this day, I shrink from the contemplation, and humble myself before the magnitude of the undertaking. Utterly, indeed, should I despair did not the presence of many whom I here see remind me that in the other high authorities provided by our Constitution I shall find resources of wisdom, of virtue, and of zeal on which to rely under all difficulties. To you, then, gentlemen, who are charged with the sovereign functions of legislation, and to those associated with you, I look with encouragement for that guidance and support which may enable us to steer with safety the vessel in which we are all embarked amidst the conflicting elements of a troubled world.

During the contest of opinion through which we have passed the animation of discussions and of exertions has sometimes worn an aspect which might impose on strangers unused to think freely and to speak and to write what they think; but this being now decided by the voice of the nation, announced according to the rules of the Constitution, all will, of course, arrange themselves under the will of the law, and unite in common efforts for the common good. All, too, will bear in mind this sacred principle, that though the will of the majority is in all cases to prevail, that will to be rightful must be reasonable; that the minority possess their equal rights, which equal law must protect, and to violate would be oppression. Let us, then, fellow-citizens, unite with one heart and one mind. Let us restore to social intercourse that harmony and affection without which liberty and even life itself are but dreary things. And let us reflect that, having banished from our land that religious intolerance under which mankind so long bled and suffered, we have yet gained little if we countenance a political intolerance as despotic, as wicked, and capable of as bitter and bloody persecutions. During the throes and convulsions of the ancient world, during the agonizing spasms of infuriated man, seeking through blood and slaughter his long-lost liberty, it was not wonderful that the agitation of the billows should reach even this distant and peaceful shore; that this should be more felt and feared by some and less by others, and should divide opinions as to measures of safety. But every difference of opinion is not a difference of principle. We have called by different names brethren of the same principle. We are all Republicans, we are all Federalists. If there be any among us who would wish to dissolve this Union or to change its republican form, let them stand undisturbed as monuments of the safety with which error of opinion may be tolerated where reason is left free to combat it. I know, indeed, that some honest men fear that a republican government can not be strong, that this Government is not strong enough; but would the honest patriot, in the full tide of successful experiment, abandon a government which has so far kept us free and firm on the theoretic and visionary fear that this Government, the world's best hope, may by possibility want energy to preserve itself? I trust not. I believe this, on the contrary, the strongest Government on earth. I believe it the only one where every man, at the call of the law, would fly to the standard of the law, and would meet invasions of the public order as his own personal concern. Sometimes it is said that man can not be trusted with the government of himself. Can he, then, be trusted with the government of others? Or have we found angels in the forms of kings to govern him? Let history answer this question.

Let us, then, with courage and confidence pursue our own Federal and Republican principles, our attachment to union and representative government. Kindly separated by nature and a wide ocean from the exterminating havoc of one quarter of the globe; too high-minded to endure the degradations of the others; possessing a chosen country, with room enough for our descendants to the thousandth and thousandth generation, entertaining a due sense of our equal right to the use of our own faculties, to the acquisitions of our own industry, to honor and confidence from our fellow-citizens, resulting not from birth, but from our actions and their sense of them; enlightened by a benign religion, professed, indeed, and practiced in various forms, yet all of them inculcating honesty, truth, temperance, gratitude, and the love of man; acknowledging and adoring an overruling Providence, which by all its dispensations proves that it delights in the happiness of man here and his greater happiness hereafter—with all these blessings, what more is necessary to make us a happy and a prosperous people? Still one thing more, fellow-citizens—a wise and frugal Government, which shall restrain men from injuring one another, shall leave them otherwise free to regulate their own pursuits of industry and improvement, and shall not take from the mouth of labor the bread it has earned. This is the sum of good government, and this is necessary to close the circle of our felicities.

About to enter, fellow-citizens, on the exercise of duties which comprehend everything dear and valuable to you, it is proper you should understand what I deem the essential principles of our Government, and consequently those which ought to shape its Administration. I will compress them within the narrowest compass they will bear, stating the general principle, but not all its limitations. Equal and exact justice to all men, of whatever state or persuasion, religious or political; peace, commerce, and honest friendship with all nations, entangling alliances with none; the support of the State governments in all their rights, as the most competent administrations for our domestic concerns and the surest bulwarks against antirepublican tendencies; the preservation of the General Government in its whole constitutional vigor, as the sheet anchor of our peace at home and safety abroad; a jealous care of the right of election by the people—a mild and safe corrective of abuses which are lopped by the sword of revolution where peaceable remedies are unprovided; absolute acquiescence in the decisions of the majority, the vital principle of republics, from which is no appeal but to force, the vital principle and immediate parent of despotism; a well-disciplined militia, our best reliance in peace and for the first moments of war till regulars may relieve them; the supremacy of the civil over the military authority; economy in the public expense, that labor may be lightly burthened; the honest payment of our debts and sacred preservation of the public faith; encouragement of agriculture, and of commerce as its handmaid; the diffusion of information and arraignment of all abuses at the bar of the public reason; freedom of religion; freedom of the press, and freedom of person under the protection of the habeas corpus, and trial by juries impartially selected. These principles form the bright constellation which has gone before us and guided our steps through an age of revolution and reformation. The wisdom of our sages and blood of our heroes have been devoted to their attainment. They should be the creed of our political faith, the text of civic instruction, the touchstone by which to try the services of those we trust; and should we wander from them in moments of error or of alarm, let us hasten to retrace our steps and to regain the road which alone leads to peace, liberty, and safety.

I repair, then, fellow-citizens, to the post you have assigned me. With experience enough in subordinate offices to have seen the difficulties of this the greatest of all, I have learnt to expect that it will rarely fall to the lot of imperfect man to retire from this station with the reputation and the favor which bring him into it. Without pretensions to that high confidence you reposed in our first and greatest revolutionary character, whose preeminent services had entitled him to the first place in his country's love and destined for him the fairest page in the volume of faithful history, I ask so much confidence only as may give firmness and effect to the legal administration of your affairs, I shall often go wrong through defect of judgment. When right, I shall often be thought wrong by those whose positions will not command a view of the whole ground. I ask your indulgence for my own errors, which will never be intentional, and your support against the errors of others, who may condemn what they would not if seen in all its parts. The approbation implied by your suffrage is a great consolation to me for the past, and my future solicitude will be to retain the good opinion of those who have bestowed it in advance, to conciliate that of others by doing them all the good in my power, and to be instrumental to the happiness and freedom of all.

Relying, then, on the patronage of your good will, I advance with obedience to the work, ready to retire from it whenever you become sensible how much better choice it is in your power to make. And may that Infinite Power which rules the destinies of the universe lead our councils to what is best, and given them a favorable issue for your peace and prosperity.

READING FURTHER

SUPERB BIOGRAPHIES OF THE VIRGINIA FOUNDERS come in every size. From largest to smallest, these include Dumas Malone, *Jefferson and His Time*, 6 vols. (Boston, 1951–1981), Merrill D. Peterson, *Thomas Jefferson and the New Nation, A Biography* (New York, 1970), and Noble E. Cunningham, Jr., *In Pursuit of Reason: The Life of Thomas Jefferson* (Baton Rouge, La., 1987), and Norman K. Risjord, *Thomas Jefferson* (Madison, Wisc., 1994), together with Irving Brant, *James Madison*, 6 vols. (Indianapolis, Ind., 1941–1961), Ralph Ketcham, *James Madison: A Biography* (New York, 1971), and Jack N. Rakove, *James Madison and the Creation of the American Republic* ("Library of American Biography"; Glenview, Ill., 1990). Additional reading might equally well begin with the excellent one-volume editions of their writings: Merrill Peterson's *Thomas Jefferson: Writings* ("Library of America"; New York, 1984); Peterson, *The Portable Thomas Jefferson* (New York, 1975); and Marvin Meyers, ed., *The Mind of the Founder: Sources of the Political Thought of James Madison*, rev. ed. (Hanover, N.H., 1981). W. W. Norton is currently preparing an eagerly awaited, two-volume edition of the Jefferson–Madison correspondence, edited by James Morton Smith.

Adrienne Koch, *Jefferson and Madison: The Great Collaboration* (New York, 1950) is the only book-length study of the friendship, but this is also discussed at length in works such as Richard K. Matthews, *The Radical Politics of Thomas Jefferson: A Revisionist View* (Lawrence, Kans., 1984), Drew R. McCoy, *The Last of the Fathers: James Madison and the Republican Legacy* (Cambridge, 1989), or my own forthcoming study, *The Sacred Fire of Liberty: James Madison and the Founding of the Federal Republic* (Ithaca, N.Y., 1995).

Broader reading on the Revolution and the American Founding should begin with Bernard Bailyn, *The Ideological Origins of the American Revolution* (Cambridge, Mass., 1967) and Gordon S. Wood, *The Creation of the American Republic, 1776–1787* (Chapel Hill, N.C., 1969), the books which initiated the dominant current interpretation of these years. For interpretive developments since 1969, including important challenges to this "republican" interpretation, see *"The Creation of the American Republic, 1776–1787*: A Symposium of Views and Reviews," *William and Mary Quarterly*, 3rd ser., 44 (1987), 549–640; *The Republican Synthesis Revisted: Essays in Honor of George Athan Billias*, ed. Milton M. Klein et al. (Worcester, Mass., 1992); Daniel T. Rodgers, "Republicanism: The Career of a Concept," *Journal of American History* 79 (1992), 11–38; and the sources cited in these texts. The republican interpretation was carried forward into the years after 1789 by Lance Banning, *The Jeffersonian Persuasion: Evolution of a Party Ideology* (Ithaca, N.Y., 1978) and Drew R. McCoy, *The Elusive Republic: Political Economy in Jeffersonian America* (Chapel Hill, N.C., 1980). Its validity for this period has been most influentially challenged by Joyce Appleby, *Capitalism and a New Social Order: The Republican Vision of the 1790s* (New York, 1984) and by the same author's essays, now collected in *Liberalism and Republicanism in the Historical Imagination* (Cambridge, Mass., 1992). The most comprehensive challenge to the republican interpretation is Paul A. Rahe, *Republics Ancient and Modern: Classical Republicanism and the American Revolution* (Chapel Hill, N.C., 1992).

The framing of the Constitution is treated briefly in Banning, "The Constitutional Convention," in Leonard W. Levy and Dennis J. Mahoney, eds., *The Framing and Ratification of the Constitution* (New York, 1987), 112–31. The best of the more comprehensive studies are still Charles Warren, *The Making of the Constitution* (Boston, 1928) and Clinton Rossiter, *1787: The Grand Convention* (New York, 1966). Robert Allen Rutland, *The Ordeal of the Constitution: The Antifederalists and the Ratification Struggle* (Norman, Okla., 1966), long the standard study of the ratification contest, may be supplemented by Michael Allen Gillespie and Michael Lienesch, eds., *Ratifying the Constitution: Ideas and Interests in the Several States* (Lawrence, Kans., 1989) and Patrick T. Conley and John P. Kaminski, eds., *The Constitution and the States: The Role of the Original Thirteen in the Framing and Adoption of the Federal Constitution* (Madison, Wisc.,1988), which contain essays on each of the states.

Major studies of the origins and framing of the Bill of Rights include Robert Allen Rutland, *The Birth of the Bill of Rights* (Chapel Hill, N.C., 1955), Irving Brant, *The Bill of Rights: Its Origins and Meaning* (Indianapolis, Ind., 1965), and Bernard Schwartz, *The Great Rights of Mankind: A History of the American Bill of Rights*, expanded ed. (Madison, Wisc., 1992). Its passage through Congress is ably discussed in Kenneth R. Bowling, "'A Tub to the Whale': The Founding Fathers and the Adoption of the Federal Bill of Rights," *Journal of the Early Republic* 8 (1988), 223–51. That process can also be studied first-hand in Helen E. Veit et al., eds., *Creating the Bill of Rights: The Documentary Record from the First*

Federal Congress (Baltimore, 1991), which includes the critical documents, the record of congressional proceedings and debates, and important correspondence to and from the congressmen involved.

John C. Miller, *The Federalist Era, 1789–1801* (New York, 1960) has served for a generation as an introduction to the first years of the new republic. Two new syntheses appeared while the work in hand was being revised: Stanley Elkins and Eric McKitrick, *The Age of Federalism: The Early American Republic, 1788–1800* (New York, 1993) and, more briefly, James Roger Sharp, *American Politics in the Early Republic: The New Nation in Crisis* (New Haven, Conn., 1993). Finally, readers must not miss the most recent work of the leading current student of the founding era: Gordon S. Wood, *The Radicalism of the American Revolution* (New York, 1992).

INDEX